OFFICE
MADE EASY

Increase Your Productivity

By James Bernstein

Bernstein, James
Office Made Easy
Book 4 in the Computers Made Easy series

For more information on reproducing sections of this book or sales of this book, go to
www.onlinecomputertips.com

10 9 8 7 6 5 4 3 2 1

Contents

Introduction

Microsoft Office has been the de facto office productivity software for many years now, and there doesn't seem to be any end to its domination on home and office computers any time soon. Microsoft has done a great job of gaining the majority of market share for this type of software, just like they have done for operating systems with Windows.

Sure there are other options out there, but if you want to be up to date with your computer skills, and be able to do your job, then you will most likely need to learn how to use Office to some degree. Of course, if you don't use computers for your job, then you still probably have one at home and most likely have some version of Office there. Even if you have a Mac, there is a good chance it has Microsoft Office on it!

The goal of this book is to teach you how to survive using Office at work or at home without making you want to throw your computer out the window. I will go over the common features that all the Office products share, and then focus on each individual product itself so you can obtain a solid understanding of how it works. I will also be covering OneDrive, Office 365, and Office Online, since Microsoft is pushing us to use cloud-based storage and applications

This is not a book on the advanced features of Office, and is not meant for the Office power user, but rather for individuals looking to either start out with Office or improve their Office skills and, hopefully, their productivity. I will try and keep it easy to follow and explain things in an easy to understand manner so it will be easy to follow along. It might be helpful to follow along on your own computer (assuming you have Office installed or a subscription to Office 365).

So, on that note, let's start getting productive!

Chapter 1 – What is Microsoft Office?

Microsoft Office is a collection of Microsoft's productivity software bundled into one package that you can purchase all together. There are different bundles you can buy based on what software you need so you don't get stuck paying for everything and only using some of it. The main components of Office include Word, Excel, Outlook, PowerPoint, Publisher, Access, and OneNote. There are other features to Office that are not as common (such as Skype and OneDrive) based on what version you are using. Here is a quick overview of what each program does, and I will be dedicating a chapter to each of the programs where I will go into more detail.

- **Word** – Word processing program for creating documents such as letters and resumes.

- **Excel** – Spreadsheet application for organizing data and numbers that can then be manipulated as needed.

- **Outlook** – Email and calendar program.

- **PowerPoint** – Presentation software that you can use to make slideshows with animations, graphics, text, music, and so on.

- **Publisher** – Program used to create things like brochures and business cards.

- **Access** – Database software used to store, manipulate, and access information.

- **OneNote** – Note gathering software that can be used to store, categorize, and share information.

History

Office has been around since the beginning of Windows, and there are new versions every few years. Even though Microsoft Word was available for use with MS-DOS (which was before Windows was even out), the first official version of Microsoft Office was released in 1989, and it wasn't even *for* Windows! In fact, the first version of Office was created for the Apple Macintosh computer, and consisted of Word, Excel, and PowerPoint. Then, in 1990, Microsoft released its Office for Windows 1.0, which also had Word, Excel, and PowerPoint.

Here are the other versions of Office and what they have added throughout the years:

- **Office 3.0** – Added the Mail program
- **Office 4.3** – Added Access
- **Office 95** – Added Bookshelf, Binder, and Schedule+ (which were removed in Office 97)
- **Office 97** – Added Outlook, Publisher, and Photo Editor (which was removed in Office 2000)
- **Office 2000** – Added FrontPage and PhotoDraw (which was removed in Office XP)
- **Office XP** – Added SharePoint Team Services (which was removed in Office 2003)
- **Office 2003** – Added InfoPath
- **Office 2007** – Added Groove
- **Office 2010** – Added SharePoint Workspace (to replace Groove) and Lync Messenger
- **Office 2013** – Added OneNote
- **Office 2016** – Added more collaboration features
- **Office 2019** – Released in late 2018 with extra features

When you install Office you have the option to install everything, or you can do a custom installation to only install the components you are going to use. This will help in reserving your hard drive space by not installing unnecessary software. But if you want to add a component later, then all you have to do is run the setup and add the feature you want so you don't have to reinstall the whole thing.

Office Editions

Within the versions of Office (such as Office 2016) there are editions that you can buy based on what software you want to use within Office itself. This comes in handy for people on a budget who can't afford the top of the line Office suite with all the bells and whistles. For comparison, I am going to use the editions available for Office 2016 with standard licensing. There are volume licensing versions that corporations can buy that vary from the versions you will use at home. Keep in mind that there is also Office 365, which is the online\cloud-based version which I will get to later in the book. But for now let's just focus on the desktop version.

- **Office Home & Student for PC and Mac** – Includes Word, Excel, PowerPoint, and OneNote, and can be installed on only one computer.

- **Office Home & Business for PC and Mac** – Includes Word, Excel, PowerPoint, OneNote, and Outlook, and can be installed on only one computer.

- **Office Professional** - Includes Word, Excel, PowerPoint, OneNote, Outlook, Publisher, and Access, and can be installed on only one computer.

Many new computers will come with a 30 or 60 day trial of Office that you can use without limitations. Then, when the trial period is up, you will have to buy it or many or all of the features will stop working. More expensive computers may come with the licensed version of Office installed.

 For most newer versions of Office you can go to the File tab and then click on Accounts to find the version and edition of Office you have, such as Office Professional Plus 2016.

Installing Office

If your computer didn't come with Office installed and you've bought yourself a copy either from a store or as a download from the Microsoft website (or somewhere else, like Amazon) then you will need to install it before you can use it. The process is fairly simple, and I am going to walk you through how to do a custom installation so you can only install the programs you want. The steps may vary a little based on the version of Office you are trying to install. This only applies for the local desktop version of Office and not for the online version (Office 365).

Once you insert the CD or run the setup file you downloaded you should see a screen asking you to accept the license terms. Simply check the *I accept* box and click on *continue*. On the next screen, this is where you want to click on **Customize** so you can decide what programs and options you want to install (figure 1.1).

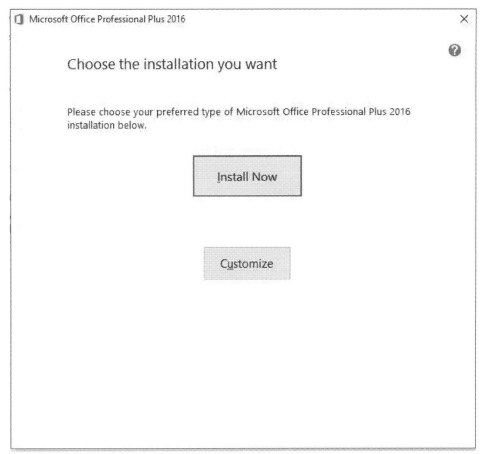

Figure 1.1

On the next screen (figure 1.2) you will be presented with all of the installation options for the available programs and other features that can be installed. You can click on the + next to each one to see what it's going to install. If you don't want to install a particular program, simply click on the down arrow next to that program and choose the *Not Available* option. That will place a red X on that software showing that it won't be installed (like Microsoft OneNote in my example).

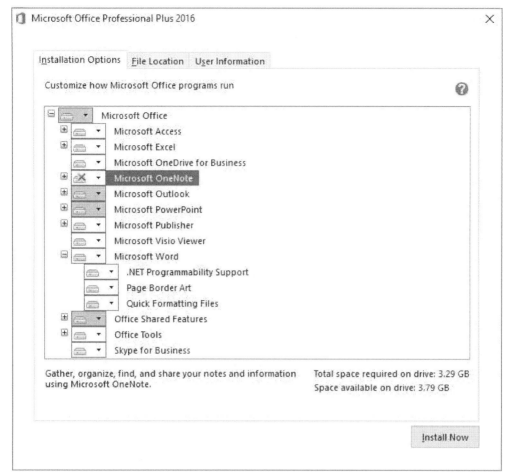

Figure 1.2

You can also go to the File Location tab and change the default installation directory or go to the User Information tab and enter your name and organization to tie it to the software. Once you have made your selections, then click on *Install Now*. The installer will do the rest and let you know when it's done.

Once Office is installed you should be able to find the shortcuts for the various Office software you installed on your Start menu for Windows or your Finder on Macs. You can also create shortcuts on your desktop if you know how to do so. If you want to add or remove an Office feature\program, you can do so by running the setup again and choosing the *modify* option, or from Programs and Features in Windows you can highlight Office and click the *Change* button.

Comparable Software

Now don't go thinking that Microsoft Office is the only game in town, because it's not. It may be the king of the block, but there are other office productivity software programs you can buy and many that are even free! Here is a quick listing of some of your other options:

- **Open Office** – Open Office is an open source office software suite that has many of the same types of programs that Microsoft Office does, such as a word processor, spreadsheet, database, presentation software, etc. It's free to use and can open Microsoft Office files as well. It's been around since 2001, with many improvements since then.

- **LibreOffice** — This is another free office suite that has similar programs to Microsoft Office. Their programs are called Writer (word processor), Calc (spreadsheet), Impress (presentations), Draw (vector graphics and flowcharts), Base (databases), and Math (formula editing). It can also open Microsoft Office files.

- **Softmaker Office** – Softmaker is another similar suite, but this one offers you a ribbon type interface similar to what you get with Microsoft Office. (I will be going over the ribbon in the next chapter.) It works with Windows, Mac, and Linux operating systems. However, this one is not free, and offers a subscription based service that you pay for monthly or yearly as well as a version you can download and install on your computer. There are various editions to choose from as well.

- **WordPerfect Office** – Corel has been around for a long time and makes a variety of products, including their WordPerfect Office suite. It includes such programs as their WordPerfect word processor, Quattro Pro spreadsheet program, Presentations slideshow creator, and WordPerfect Lightning digital notebook (depending on what version you get). They have a Standard and Professional version. Of course, the Professional version costs more, but it does has more features.

- **Google Docs** – Google has their own online version of office software that you can use for free as long as you have a free Google account, which everyone pretty much has by now! The have apps called Docs, Sheets, and Slides which are like Word, Excel, and PowerPoint. They also have an app called Forms for making custom forms. You use Google Docs via a web browser since it's cloud-based (like Office 365).

You can have more than one type of office productivity software installed on your computer, so feel free to try out some of the others to see which one works best for you. Not everyone thinks Microsoft Office is the best!

Chapter 2 – The Office Ribbon

Starting with Office 2007, Microsoft completely changed the user interface for its Office software, making many people very upset because they had to learn how to do everything all over again. If you have only worked with newer versions of Office, then you most likely don't know the difference and assume that the ribbon was always there.

Tabs and Groups

Before we go into tabs and groups, when I say "ribbon" I am referring to the part of the program that has all of your icons and tabs for all of the different things you can do in that particular Office program (figure2.1). Keep in mind that the ribbon for each program (such as Word vs. Excel) will have different options for their tabs.

Figure 2.1

You can see in figure 2.2 that the current ribbon looks a lot different than the toolbar did back in the previous versions of Office (such as 2003 and older).

Figure 2.2

You still have many of the same icons that you had in the olds style toolbar, but on the ribbon they are categorized into different tabs, making things a bit more organized. Within each tab there are category groupings that organize things even further. For example, in figure 2.2 under the *Home* tab there are groupings for Clipboard, Font, Paragraph, Styles, and Editing, and if you click on the arrow icon at the lower right hand corner of the group it will bring up additional options and settings for that group (figure 2.3).

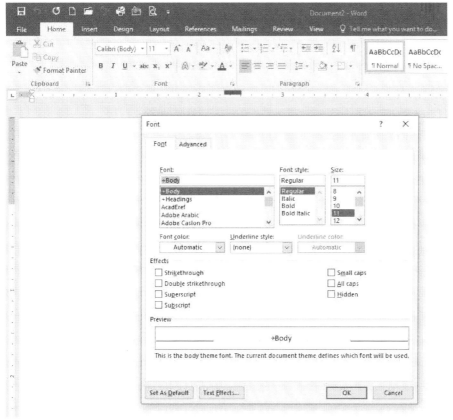

Figure 2.3

When clicking on the arrow button to expand the Font group you can see that we have some additional options related to fonts. Each group will have its own set of commands and settings that relate to that group, and each tab will have its own set of groups. You should take the time to click on each group within each tab to see what types of things you can do from that particular group.

Customizing the Ribbon

The default ribbon settings will work fine for most people, but if you're the type that likes to customize things whenever possible, then you can add your own tabs and groups to the Ribbon. You can also remove some of the default tabs and groups if you desire.

To customize tabs and groups go to the File tab, click on Options and then click on the Customize Ribbon section. As you can see in figure 2.4, on the right side it shows your current tabs and then the current groups within those tabs. As you can see, the Home tab has groups named Clipboard, Font, Paragraph, Styles, and Editing.

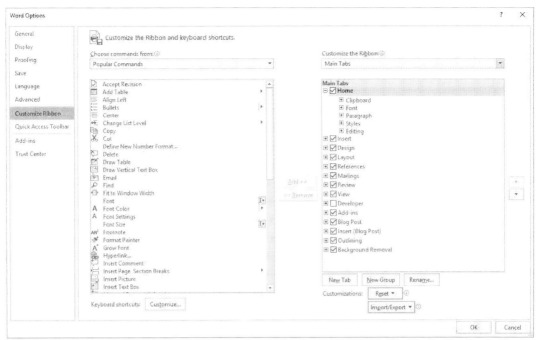

Figure 2.4

To add a new group to an existing tab, click on the tab's name to highlight it and then press the New Group button. Then name your group and insert commands from the left side list into your new group. As you can see in figure 2.5, I made a new group called Custom Group in the Home tab and added the Draw Table and Email commands to that group. Then the results are shown in the ribbon (as you can see in figure 2.6).

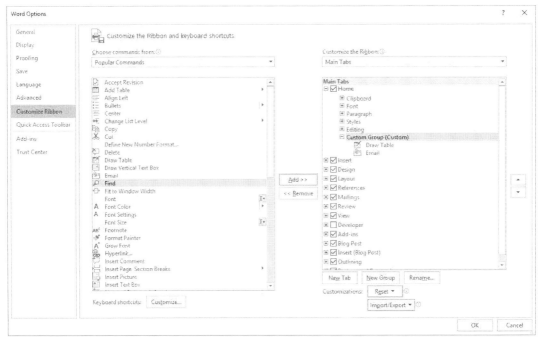

Figure 2.5

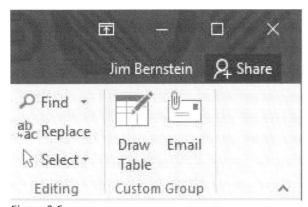

Figure 2.6

You can add and remove commands from a group by clicking on that group to highlight it, then finding the command you want from the left and clicking the Add button to add it to that group. You can also remove commands from the right by highlighting them and clicking the Remove button.

Adding a new tab is a similar process, and all you need to do is click on the tab you want to create a new tab next to, then click the New Tab button. In figure 2.7 you can see that I created a new tab called *My Tab* next to the Insert tab. Then I created a group within this tab called *My Group* and added the Copy and Cut commands to that group.

Customize the Ribbon: ⓘ

Main Tabs	▼

```
Main Tabs
⊞ ☑ Home
⊞ ☑ Insert
⊟ ☑ My Tab (Custom)
        ⊟ My Group (Custom)
              📄  Copy
              ✂  Cut
⊞ ☑ Design
⊞ ☑ Layout
⊞ ☑ References
⊞ ☑ Mailings
⊞ ☑ Review
⊞ ☑ View
⊞ ☐ Developer
⊞ ☑ Add-ins
⊞ ☑ Blog Post
⊞ ☑ Insert (Blog Post)
⊞ ☑ Outlining
⊞ ☑ Background Removal
```

▲

▼

New Tab	New Group	Rename...

Customizations: | Reset ▼ | ⓘ

| Import/Export ▼ | ⓘ

Figure 2.7

Figure 2.8 shows the results of this new tab creation in the Ribbon.

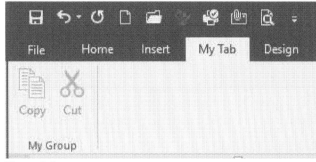

Figure 2.8

Quick Launch Bar

One very useful area of the Ribbon that you will find yourself using all the time is called the Quick Launch Bar. Think of the Quick Launch Bar as the place where you will go to perform the actions that you use the most, such as save, open, and print. If you look back at figure 2.8, you will see a bunch of icons at the top above the tabs. These are your Quick Launch icons and, as you can see, it makes it easy to group all of the icons you use the most in one place.

The icons do not have names, but since they are the ones you will use all the time, you will get to know exactly what each one does. Plus, if you hover the mouse pointer over the icon, it will tell you what it is used for. If you click the little down arrow to the right of the icons it will bring up a list of all the Quick Launch commands that you have available on your Quick Launch Bar (figure 2.9). Then you can check the ones you want displayed on the Quick Launch Bar, or uncheck ones that you don't want to show.

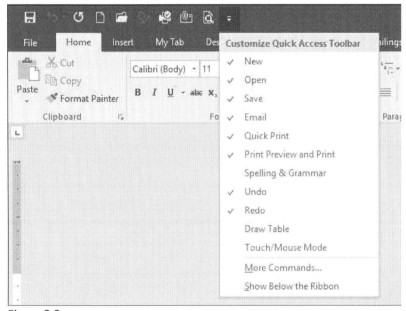

Figure 2.9

If you click on Show Below the Ribbon it will put your Quick Launch icons underneath the ribbon (as shown in figure 2.10).

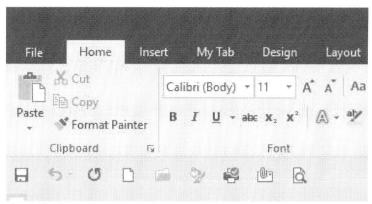

Figure 2.10

Customizing the Quick Launch Bar

Just like with tabs and groups, it's possible to customize the Quick Launch Bar to your liking. When clicking on the down arrow next to the icons (like shown in figure 2.9) there is a choice called More Commands. This will take you to the Quick Access Toolbar customization setting, which you can also get to from the File tab and then Options (figure 2.11).

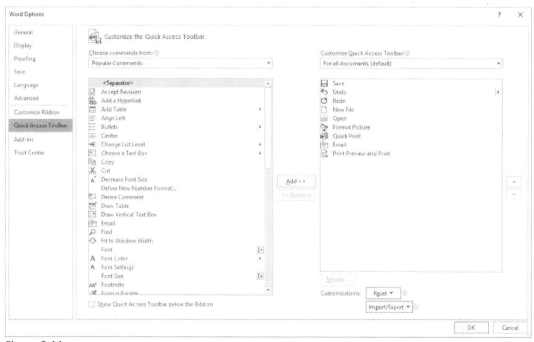

Figure 2.11

From here you can add commands from the right or remove commands from the left. You can also choose if the Quick Launch icons apply to the current document you are working on, or all documents that you create or open.

Another quick way to remove icons from the Quick Launch Bar is to right click them from the bar itself and choose *Remove from Quick Access Toolbar.*

If you have made changes to the Ribbon or Quick Launch Bar and want to revert things back to the Office default, simply go to the options for either one and click the button on the bottom of the window that says Reset (as you can see in figure 2.11). One nice feature is that you can import and export your custom settings to be used on another computer that has Office installed. That way you don't need to configure the other computer from scratch if you have made a lot of changes that you like to use.

Hiding the Ribbon

If, for some reason, you would like some more real estate on your screen and think the Ribbon is in the way, then it's possible to collapse the Ribbon and only have it show when you need it.

To do so you can press Ctrl-F1 on your keyboard when you want to hide the Ribbon, or you can click the small up arrow at the very bottom right of the ribbon to collapse it. Then press Ctrl-F1 to bring it back, or right click any tab and clear the check mark next to *Collapse the Ribbon*. You can also double click any tab to have the ribbon brought back on the screen.

There are also some additional configurations you can set for what shows on the ribbon. If you click on the icon that looks like a box with an arrow in it (figure 2.12) you will be able to set some additional options. You can have Office auto hide the ribbon, show tabs only, or show the tabs with their commands (which is the default).

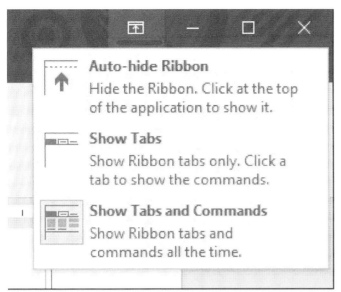

Figure 2.12

Chapter 3 – Office Options

Microsoft Office has many options that you can configure to help streamline your user experience. I talked about two of the main ones in the last chapter when I went over customizing the Ribbon and Quick Launch Bar, but there are many other things you can change if needed, so in this chapter I will go over the option categories and what is included in each one.

One thing you need to keep in mind is that there are different options for different programs, such as Word vs. Excel. I will be using the Word 2016 options for this chapter, but will mention any options for other programs that might be important after going over the options for Word. Also keep in mind that other versions, such as 2010 vs. 2013, might have different settings as well.

You should take a look at your options to see what kind of things you can change for yourself should you need to. You can get to the Office options by clicking on the *File* tab and then on *Options*. One thing to keep in mind is that there may be a slight variance in the common option categories between programs. For example, the General options for Word might be a little different than for Excel, but you will get the idea about what each section does after reading this chapter. I will be using Word with my examples for the common option sections.

General
The General options will have your more generic settings that apply to the program itself rather than specific components. There are four main sections in the General options (figure 3.1).

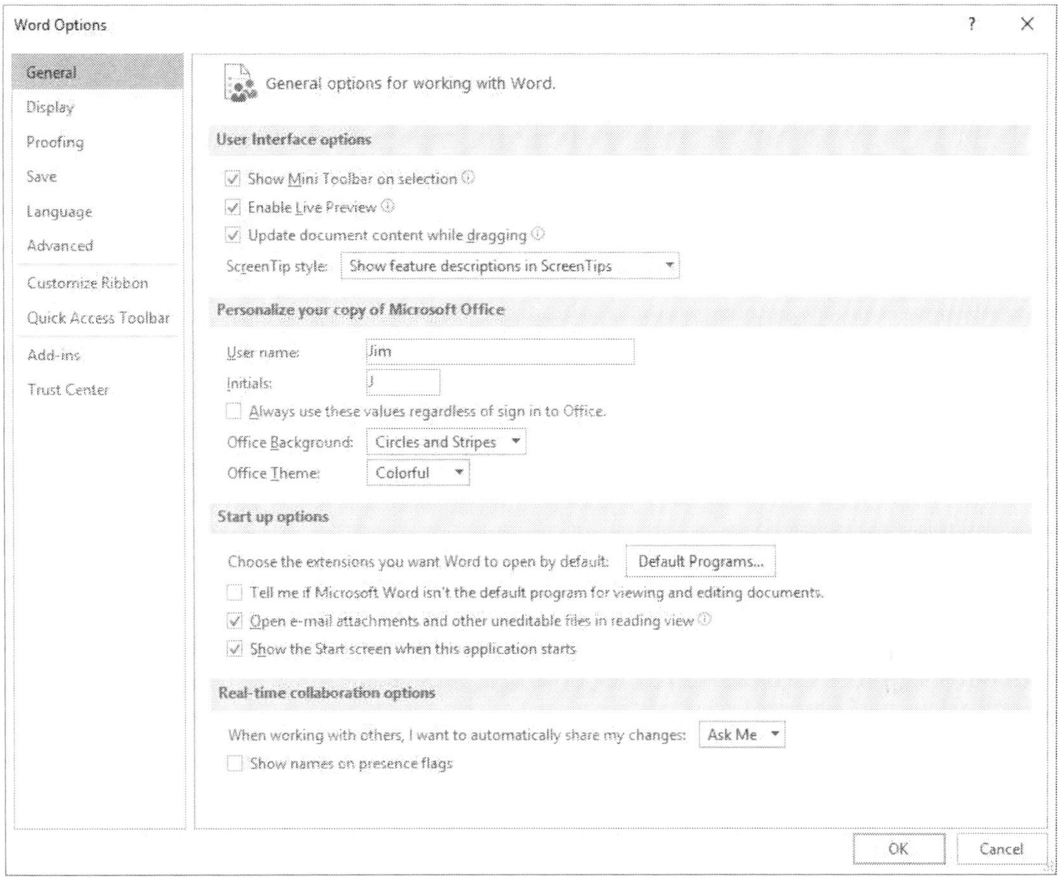

Figure 3.1

User Interface options

- **Show Mini Toolbar on selection**
  When you highlight text on a page you will get a popup toolbar that lets you do things like change the font size or text justification. This is where you turn the feature on or off.

- **Enable Live Preview**
  This will show you how a certain feature will affect your document if you use it when hovering over that feature.

- **Update document content while dragging**
  Shows how the document will look as you do things such as move, resize, or rotate items.

- **ScreenTip style**
  Here you can enable Office to show feature descriptions screen tips, not show feature descriptions in screen tips, or turn off screen tips altogether.

Personalize your copy of Microsoft Office
In this section you can add your user name and initials to your copy of Office, which will show up every time you open the program. You can also change the background design of the particular program in use, as well as its theme.

Start up options
- **Choose the extensions you want Word to open by default**
  File extensions tell Windows what program opens what type of file. So in a file called resume.docx, .docx is the file association for Word, and that tells Windows to open files that have .docx on the end with Word.

- **Tell me if Microsoft Word isn't the default program for viewing and editing documents**
  This box will let you know if your computer is not set to use Word as its default program for opening documents. This also applies to Excel (etc.) if you are in the options section for one of the other Office programs.

- **Open email attachments and other un-editable files in reading view**
  If you have documents that you can't edit (such as email attachments), Word will open them in Reading View, which improves the chances of the document looking correct on the screen.

- **Show the Start screen when this application starts**
  When this box is checked you will see the Start screen when you first open the program. The Start screen shows you things like recent documents and available templates you can use.

Real-Time collaboration options
If you are working with other people on a project and want to share documents, you can use the real-time collaboration feature, which will allow you to see changes to documents as they happen. In this section you can adjust how you share your changes.

Display

The display options will let you configure how documents are displayed on the screen as well as when they are printed. Just because a document looks one way on the screen doesn't necessarily mean it will look that way when printed. There are three main sections for the display options (figure 3.2).

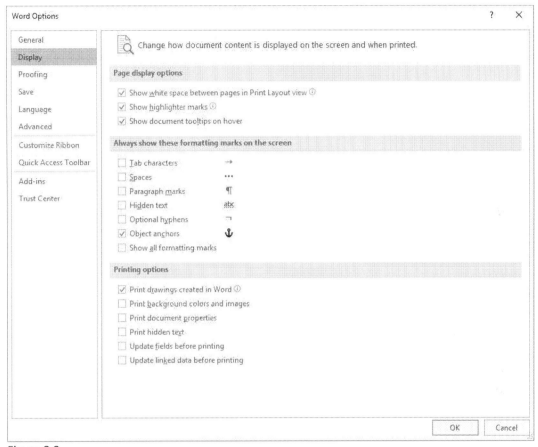

Figure 3.2

Page display options

- **Show white space between pages in Print Layout view**
  This will show the top and bottom margins as well as the header and footer contents.

- **Show highlighter marks**
  Office has a neat feature that lets you use a highlighter pen to highlight text. If this box is checked, the highlighted text will show on the screen and when you print.

- **Show document tooltips on hover**
  As you have probably noticed, there are many icons and buttons in the ribbon that are not labeled, so it can be hard to figure out what they all do. Fortunately, if you have this option enabled, you can hover the mouse over each one and it will pop up a little blurb about what it does.

Always show these formatting marks on the screen

Office programs have special characters that are used to display formatting characteristics (such as tabs and spaces), and sometimes it comes in handy to have these characters displayed on screen to make sure your formatting is set up the way you want it to be. Most of them are turned off by default, since it's not one of those features that are used by the majority of people.

Printing options

Here you can decide what aspects of your document get printed compared to what you see on the screen. For example, if your document has a colored background but you don't want to waste the ink printing the background, then you can uncheck that particular option. If you have any fields or linked data that can be updated you can have that happen before printing so everything is up to date on the printed copy.

Proofing

Office offers many ways to help you get your documents in order before doing things like printing them or sending them out to other people. This way it can catch mistakes that you might not notice, and also make suggestions for things like grammar and punctuation. There are four main sections in the Proofing options (figure 3.3).

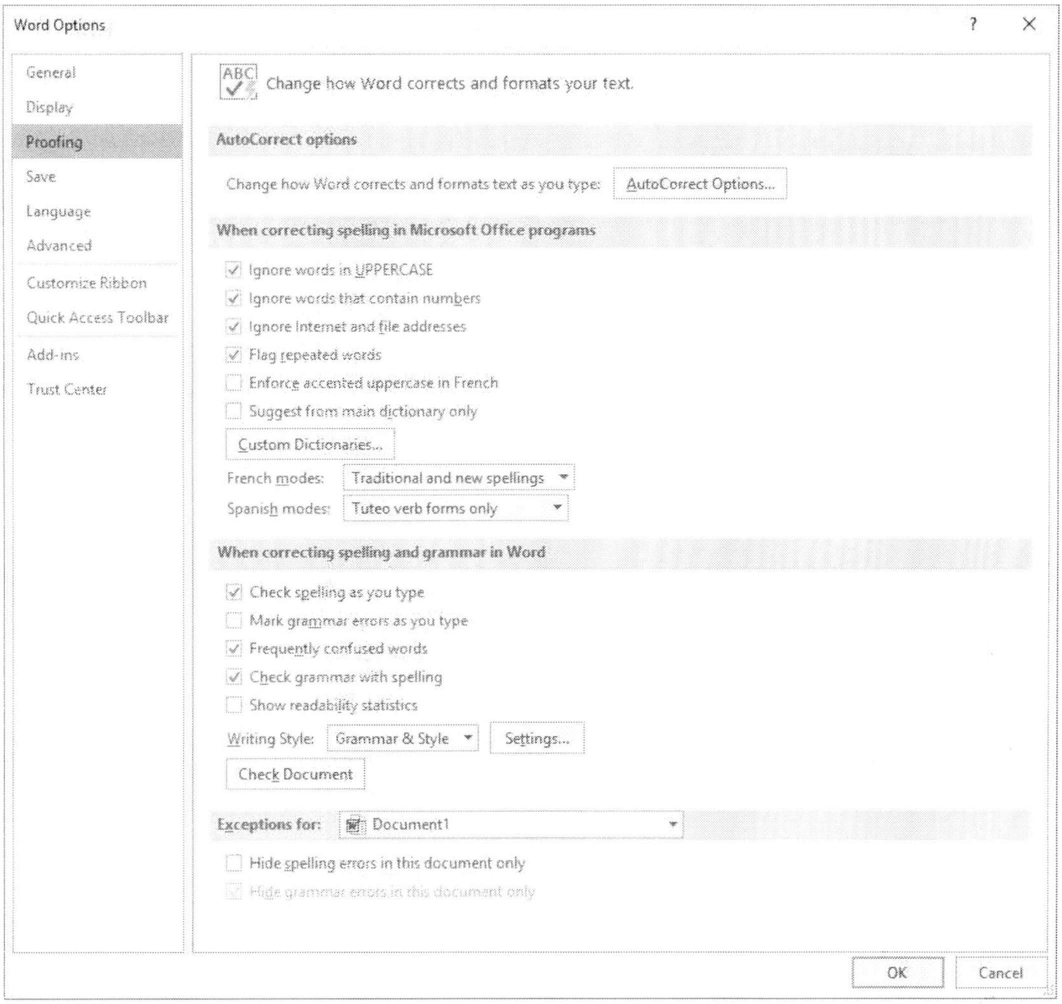

Figure 3.3

AutoCorrect options

Word and other Office programs can automatically correct things like capitalization errors and mathematical mistakes as you type, as well as alert you when you have spelling and grammatical errors. You might have noticed that you will see red underlines under misspelled words and blue underlines under grammatical errors. These features can be turned off if it's something you don't want to be bothered by. If you click on the AutoCorrect Options button (figure 3.4) you can see that you have many options and settings to choose from to customize the way Office "monitors" your typing.

> **Tip**
>
> If you ever run across a time when Word is not marking your spelling and grammar errors go to the *Review* tab and click on *Language* and then click on *Set Proofing Language* and make sure the checkbox for Do not check spelling or grammar is unchecked.

Figure 3.4

When correcting spelling in Microsoft Office programs

If you are the type who feels you know best when it comes to spelling and grammar and don't want Office fixing things that you don't think need to be fixed, then here is where you can disable some of the auto correct features. For example, if you don't want to be alerted when you type a word in all uppercase or have a word that is repeated, then you can check the appropriate boxes here. Clicking on the Custom Dictionaries box will allow you to edit your custom dictionaries, as well as import or create new ones. These custom dictionaries can be used to add words so that Office doesn't think they are mistakes and doesn't flag them as spelling errors. You can also right click a word that it things is wrong and choose *add to dictionary* to have your custom word added on the spot.

When correcting spelling and grammar in Word

This section will vary depending on what program you are in. It is similar to the previous section on correcting spelling mistakes, except it will check for grammatical errors as well. Clicking on *Check Document* will run a spelling and grammar check on the currently opened document.

Exceptions for

In this section you can set exceptions for what documents Office will check spelling and grammar for. So, if you don't want your spelling and grammar checked for a particular document you have open, you can choose it from the dropdown list and have it ignored. You can also choose All New Documents to have it apply to any documents you create in the future.

Save

Of course you know that you can save documents in Microsoft Office as well as most other programs you use on your computer, but with Office you can change many of the settings related to *how* your documents are saved and *where* they are saved. There are three sections for the Save options area (figure 3.5).

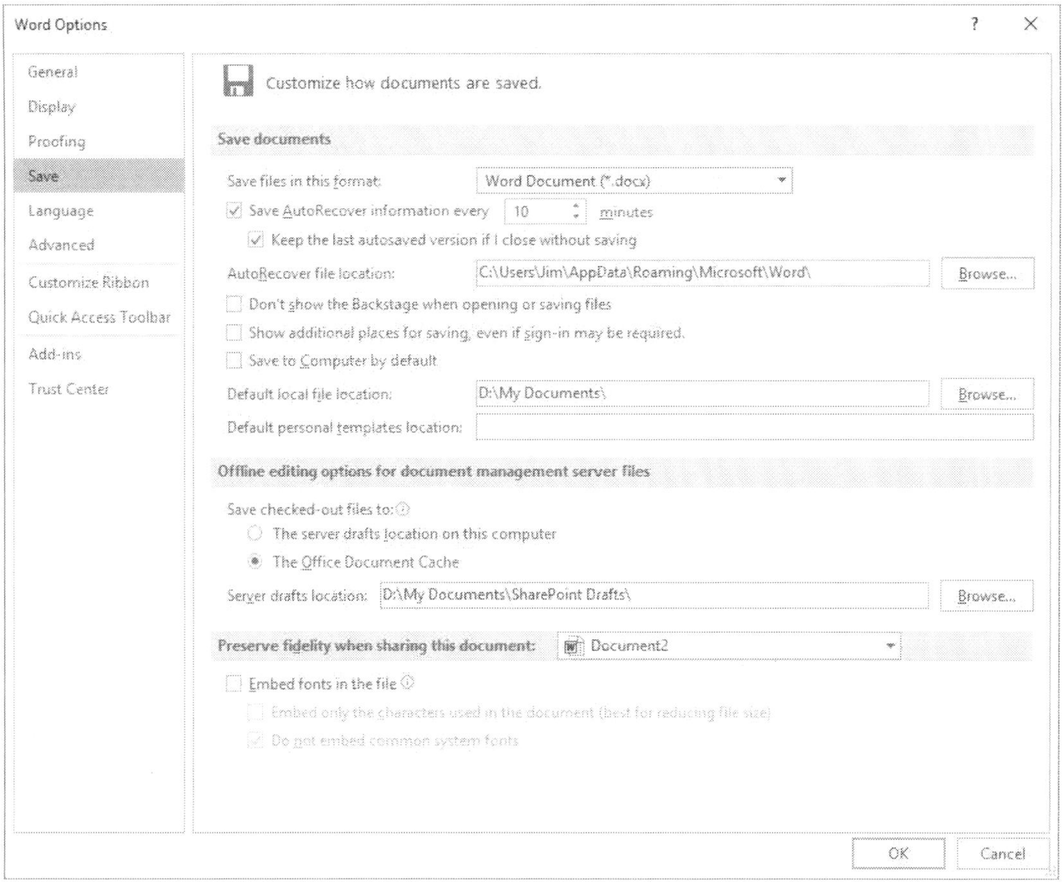

Figure 3.5

Save documents

Here you can tell Office what format to save your documents in, such as the current Office version or earlier versions for backwards compatibility for people who have older versions of Office. You can also save files as templates, webpages, XML documents, and so on.

The AutoRecover feature in Office will let you recover documents if your computer or Office crashes in the middle of working on one and you didn't save your latest changes. The default time between auto saves is 10 minutes, but you can change it to be more or less time. You can also change the default location of these automatically recovered files, but there is not any real reason to do so.

However, the default local file location setting is one that you might find useful to change. If you are not one of those people who like to save their files to the default Windows Documents folder, then you can come in here and enter in the new location where files will be saved. Of course, you will still have the option to manually browse to another location other than the default if needed.

Offline editing option for document management server files
This doesn't apply to home users (and maybe not even to office users) unless you use a document management server to save all your Office files. This feature allows you to share files by checking them in and out as needed.

Preserve fidelity when sharing this document
You may or may not know that in order for fonts to display correctly in a document, you need to have that font installed on your computer. So, if someone sends you a document using a font you don't have installed, then your computer will use a system default font instead to make up for it. The *Preserve fidelity when sharing this document* feature allows you to embed the fonts within the document so that if you open that document on a different computer that doesn't have the font installed, it will still display the way you intended it to. You can apply this setting to any document you have open, or any documents you create in the future.

Language
If you create documents in different languages you might want to consider adding an editing language to your Office program in order to check spelling and grammar (etc.) for those documents. When you go to the language option (figure 3.6) you will be shown what languages you have installed and have the opportunity to add additional languages, as well as set your default language. You can do the same thing for display and help languages.

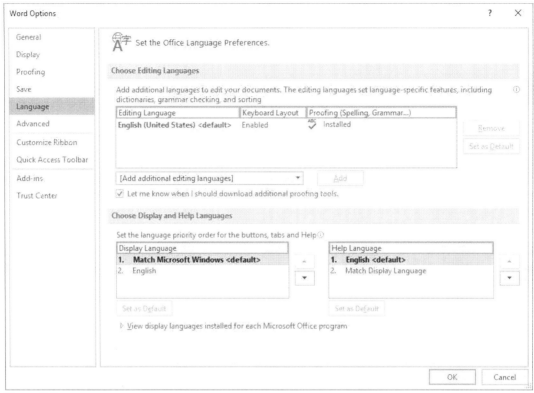

Figure 3.6

Advanced

The Advanced section is where you can change all kinds of settings to really customize how Office works. Since this section is so long, I will only go over the options that I feel are more commonly used, and that you will find more useful.

Chapter 3 – Office Options

Word Options   ?   ✕

General	Advanced options for working with Word.
Display	
Proofing	**Editing options**
Save	☑ Typing replaces selected text
Language	☑ When selecting, automatically select entire word
Advanced	☑ Allow text to be dragged and dropped
Customize Ribbon	☑ Use CTRL + Click to follow hyperlink
Quick Access Toolbar	☐ Automatically create drawing canvas when inserting AutoShapes
Add-ins	☑ Use smart paragraph selection
Trust Center	☑ Use smart cursoring

☐ Use the insert key to control overtype mode
     ☐ Use overtype mode
☐ Prompt to update style
☐ Use Normal style for bulleted or numbered lists
☐ Keep track of formatting
     ☐ Mark formatting inconsistencies
Updating style to match selection: Keep previous numbering and bullets pattern ▾
☑ Enable click and type
     Default paragraph style: Normal ▾
☑ Show AutoComplete suggestions
☐ Do not automatically hyperlink screenshot

Cut, copy, and paste

Pasting within the same document: Keep Source Formatting (Default) ▾
Pasting between documents: Keep Source Formatting (Default) ▾
Pasting between documents when style definitions conflict: Use Destination Styles (Default) ▾
Pasting from other programs: Keep Source Formatting (Default) ▾
Insert/paste pictures as: In line with text ▾
☑ Keep bullets and numbers when pasting text with Keep Text Only option
☐ Use the insert key for paste
☑ Show Paste Options button when content is pasted
☑ Use smart cut and paste   [Settings...]

Image Size and Quality   📄 Document2   ▾
☐ Discard editing data ⓘ
☐ Do not compress images in file ⓘ
Set default target output to: 220 ppi ▾

Chart   📄 Document2   ▾
☑ Properties follow chart data point ⓘ

Show document content
☐ Show background colors and images in Print Layout view
☐ Show text wrapped within the document window
☐ Show picture placeholders ⓘ
☑ Show drawings and text boxes on screen
☐ Show bookmarks
☐ Show text boundaries
☐ Show crop marks
☐ Show field codes instead of their values
Field shading: When selected ▾
☐ Use draft font in Draft and Outline views
     Name   Courier New ▾
     Size   10 ▾
☐ Use fonts that are stored on the printer
[Font Substitution...]
☐ Expand all headings when opening a document ⓘ

[OK]   [Cancel]

Figure 3.7

Editing options
These options determine how the program works when you are making edits to your document. For example, if you check the box for *typing replaces selected text*, it will replace any highlighted text as you type rather than add to it. And when you have hyperlinks to webpages in your document you can have Office use the Ctrl+Click method to open that link. (Usually the defaults in this section work fine for most people.)

Cut, copy, and paste
Here you can change the options for how Office handles cutting, copying, and pasting text. Many times when you paste text from one document to another they are using different fonts and formatting, so it will not match up with the current text and it won't look right. To change this you would want to change the setting for pasting between documents to *keep text only*.

 What I like to do when pasting in text from one document or other thing like a website into my document is to use the *paste special* or *keep text only* option so that it doesn't bring over any formatting from the source document.

The insert/paste pictures setting determines how images are pasted into your document. They can be in line with the text, in front of the text, behind the text, and so on. These settings can be changed per image after you paste it into the document as well.

Image Size and Quality
If you like to have higher resolution graphics in your documents for printing purposes (etc.) then you can change the settings here by checking the *Do not compress images in files* box and setting the default target output to a higher value that suits your needs. For most printing purposes, the default settings are fine.

Show document content
These options will let you make changes as to what is displayed within your document when you view it on your screen. By default, most of the boxes are unchecked to keep things from looking cluttered. As you can see in figure 3.7, you can enable things such as having the background colors and images shown, as well

as bookmarks and picture placeholders. You can experiment with these settings by checking the boxes one at a time and see if it's something you want to keep enabled.

Advanced options continued

Figure 3.8

Display

You might find it helpful to change some of the settings in the Display section rather than use the defaults. The first item will determine how many recent documents Office will display when you go click on open. The default is twenty-five, but you can increase or decrease that number to suit your needs. If you check the box that says *Show this number of unpinned Recent Documents,* then Office will put the most recently opened documents under the File tab so you don't even have to click on Open. Office used to show you your most recently used folders, but it seems they have removed this feature, even though there is still a setting for Recent Folders in the options. You will find with Microsoft products that they tend to move things around and remove useful features to try and get you to do things their way. This is a big issue with Windows 10, but unfortunately we just have to live with it!

Print

Printing is a big part of using Microsoft Office, and there are some settings you can change in the options to make things easier on yourself. One thing I like to do to save time and ink is to print using draft mode. This works great for black and white text that doesn't have to be high quality, and even for some pictures. Using draft mode will use less ink and make your pages print much faster, and the difference in quality is not all that noticeable. If you check the *Use draft quality* box then it will use draft mode to print by default.

The *Print in background* option will allow you to print while still working on your documents. This is the default for most software, but Office gives you the option to disable it if needed.

Print pages in reverse order comes in handy if you need to have your pages in a different order than the default. If you check this box and print them in reverse order, you will not need to re-sort them afterwards.

The *Default tray* option lets you choose which paper tray on your printer is used by default to pull paper from. You can also set it to your manual feeder if you do things like print on cardstock and envelopes primarily.

Advanced options continued

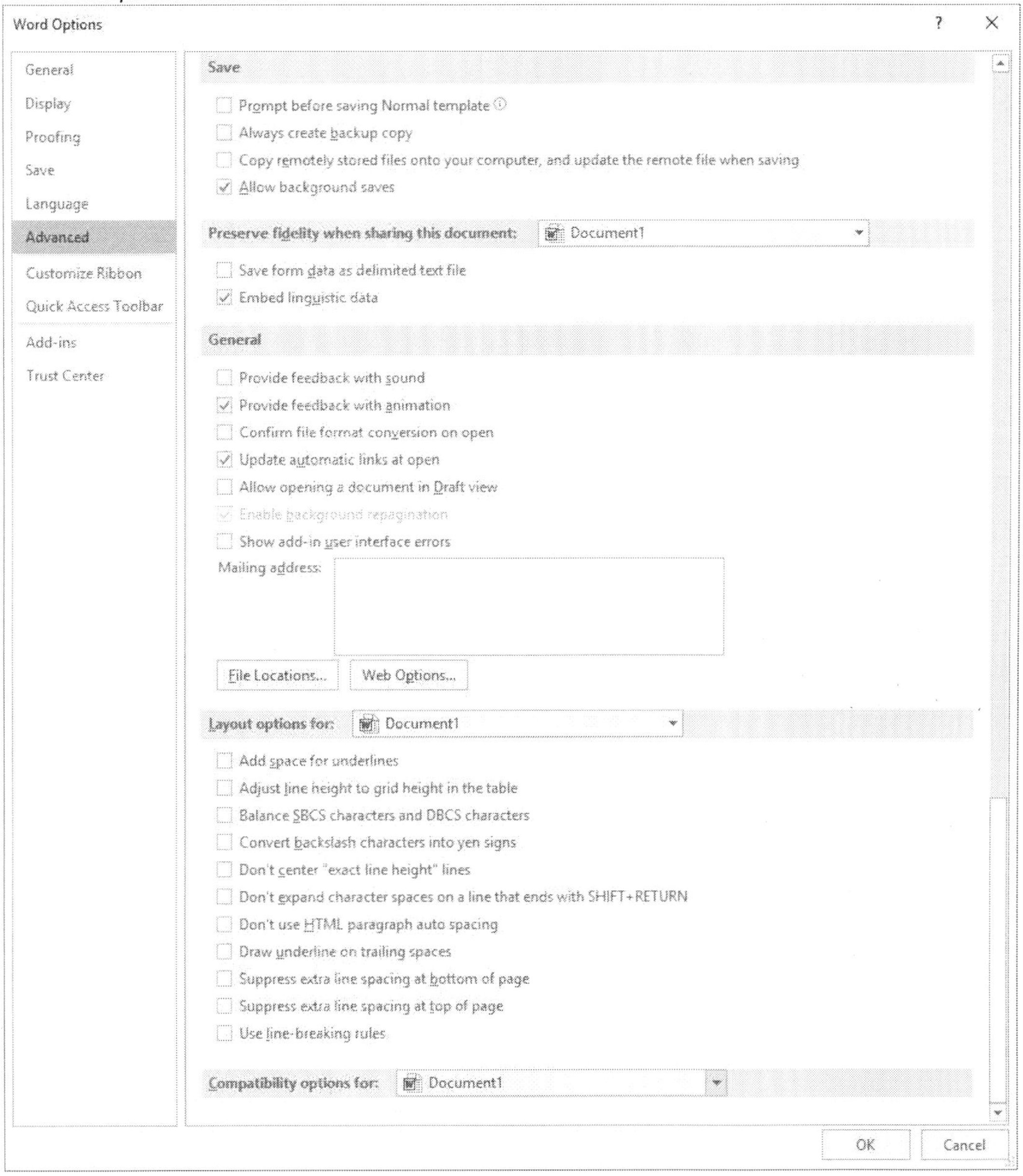

Figure 3.9

Save

The two most important settings in the Save options are the *Always create backup copy* and *Allow background saves* settings.

The *Always create backup copy* option will create a backup of your file every time you save it just in case your main file gets corrupted or deleted on accident. It will only keep one backup of the file, so each time you save the file the previous backup copy will get overwritten.

Allow background saves is use by the AutoRecover feature of Office, and will make periodic saves of your document just in case Office or your computer crashes before you were able to save your changes. Then when you start Office back up, you should be prompted to recover your file from an AutoRecover backup. Keep in mind that your document will only be as current as the last backup save.

Add-ins

Office add-ins allow additional functionality in Office software by integrating other software components into Office itself. Many times when you install certain software it will automatically integrate itself into Office, and sometimes it will ask you if you would like it to.

As you can see in figure 3.10, there is an add-in called Acrobat PDFMaker Office, which allows Office the ability to print to PDF to make PDF files as needed. As you can see, there are also add-ins for OneNote and instant messaging.

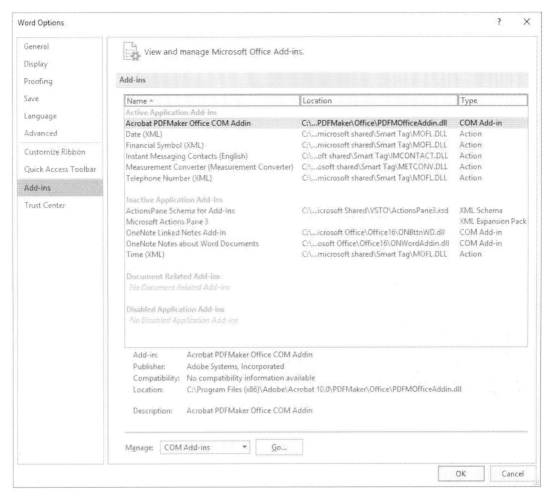

Figure 3.10

There are other add-ins you can manage from the Manage drop down at the bottom of the window. Other add-ins include actions, templates, xml schemas, and disabled items. Most of this is beyond the scope of this book, but if you are having a problem with one of your Office applications freezing up or crashing, you might want to come in here and disable some add-ins you are not using by clicking on the Go button and unchecking the ones you don't want to load when the program starts (figure 3.11).

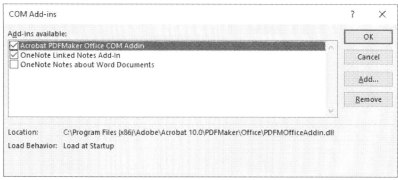

Figure 3.11

Trust Center

I'm just going to briefly go over the Trust Center because you will most likely never have the need to go in there and change any of its settings. When you click on the *Trust Center Settings* button, you will see a screen similar to figure 3.12. This will show you information about things like trusted publishers along with their security certificate information. Trusted Locations will show you what folder locations are to be trusted by Office. You can click through the other settings if you want to see in there, but don't change any of the options if you don't have a reason to.

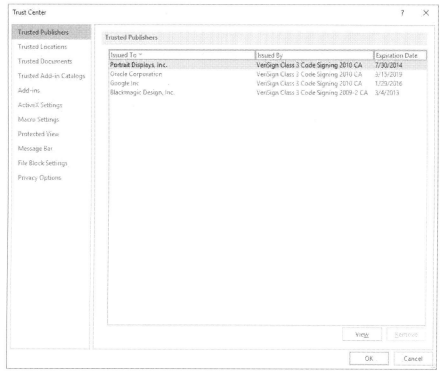

Figure 3.12

Now I will briefly go over some program specific options for programs like Excel, Access, and Outlook. These are settings that you will only find for those particular programs since they don't apply to any other Office program.

Formulas (Excel)

If you are an avid Excel user, then you will most likely have used formulas to do your mathematical calculations for you within your cells. The Formulas options (figure 3.13) contains many settings that you can edit to change how these formulas work. Most users will leave the Workbook Calculation settings on Automatic to let Excel take care of all of the math for you.

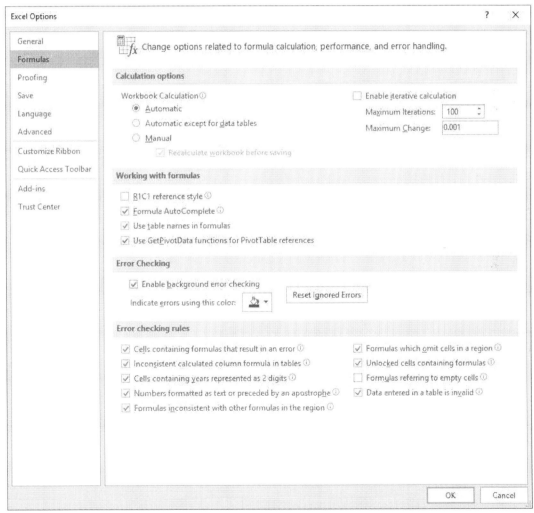

Figure 3.13

What you might want to change are some of the error checking settings just in case there are too many rules getting in the way of your work that you don't need running.

Mail (Outlook)

Microsoft Outlook has a bunch of options that you can change for all sorts of program settings. Outlook has been the most popular email client for many years, and if you use an email client at work, then it is most likely Microsoft Outlook. The Mail options (figure 3.14) in Outlook contain a lot of these settings, and I will go over the key settings next.

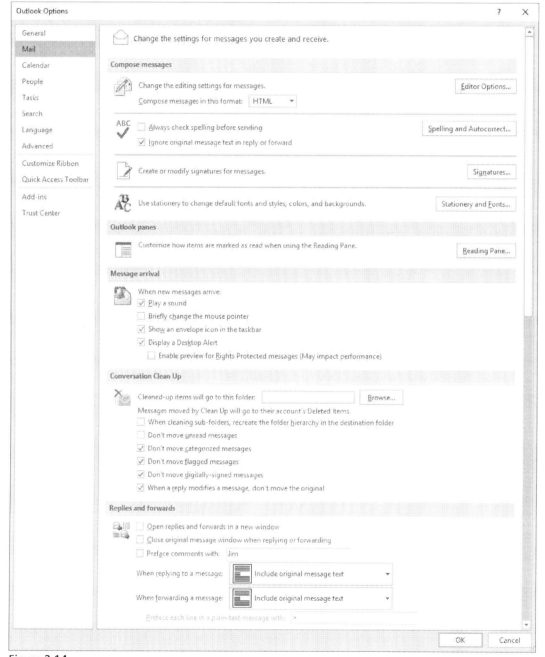

Figure 3.14

Compose Messages

Here is where you can change how you compose email messages, such as using plain text (no formatting), rich text (bold, underline, colored text, etc.) or HTML, which offers you the ability to add images and other custom touches.

Another thing you can do here is change the spell checking options and make Outlook check your spelling before sending out your email. The *Ignore original message text in reply or forward* checkbox will make it so Outlook doesn't bother to spell check the original message that you are replying to or forwarding.

Signatures are commonly used at the end of emails, and can include things such as your name, phone number, email address, fax number, and so on so that when people receive an email from you, they have all the information they need to contact you. You can have Outlook insert a signature in every new email you compose if you like.

Stationary and fonts are used to enhance the look of your emails by adding backgrounds, custom fonts, and custom font colors. There are many themes you can choose from when you click the *Stationary and Fonts* button.

Outlook panes

When you get a new email in your inbox it will show in bold type, indicating that it has not been read. When you read the email then the type changes back to a normal, non-bold view. The Outlook panes section is where you can go to change the conditions that determine how emails are marked as read when using the Reading Pane. The Reading Pane is the window below or next to your email list that shows a preview of the email contents when you click on one.

Message Arrival

You are probably used to hearing notifications on your phone when a new text message or email shows up, and Outlook will do the same thing for a new email. There are several notifications you can receive besides the sound, such as having the mouse pointer change, having an envelope icon down by the clock, and having a notification pop up in the corner of your screen with the email details.

Conversation Cleanup
Using this feature will send redundant messages throughout a conversation to the Deleted Items folder. There are several options to fine tune this feature, including what folder these messages are sent to. Most of the time this feature is turned off.

Replies and Forwards
If you are the type that likes to have all new things open in their own window, then you can enable that for when you are replying to an email or forwarding one. There is also the option to include the original message text when replying and when forwarding emails, that way the recipient has a history of the email conversation to refer to.

Mail options continued

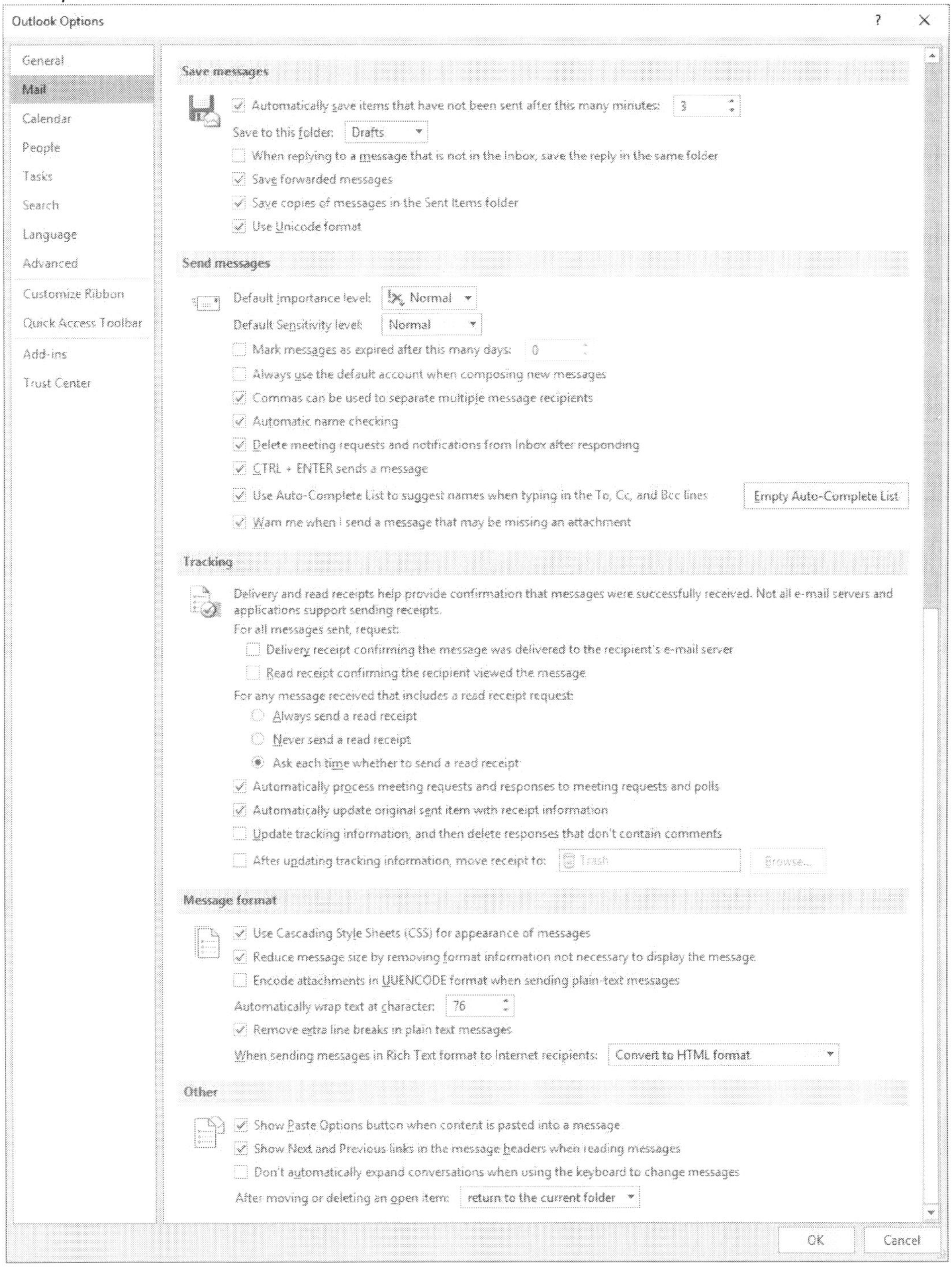

Figure 3.15

Save messages

Here you can tell Outlook how to save your messages and also what messages to save. Some people like to keep copies of their sent and forwarded messages while others don't want to deal with the clutter. Outlook will also automatically save emails that you are working on into the Drafts folder every three minutes, so if you need to go back to one or Outlook or your computer crashes, you will have a saved copy. This interval and the save location can be changed as well.

Send messages
When sending out emails you can tell Outlook how to handle things like marking their importance and sensitivity (privacy) levels so people on the other end will have a better idea of how to respond to them. You can also mark time sensitive messages to expire after a set amount of time so the recipient doesn't act on it after the fact.

Other key settings in the Send options include the usage of commas to separate email addresses when sending an email to multiple recipients so Outlook knows how to distinguish between each one, as well as automatic name checking, which checks names against the Outlook Address Book.

One very useful feature of Outlook is the Auto-Complete List, which is used to automatically suggest email addresses or people as you type in the To, CC, and Bcc boxes. This way you don't have to remember all of a person's email address and can just start typing their name and let Outlook find them for you. If for some reason you want to clear out this list, you can click on the Empty Auto-Complete List button to clear them out (but I don't see why you would ever want to do that). If you want to edit your Auto-Complete list and remove names and addresses you don't need anymore, I suggest using a free program called NK2Edit.

Tracking
If you are on a corporate email system using something like Microsoft Exchange, then you should have the option for tracking emails. When using this, you can do things like receive a message whenever someone reads or receives an email from you so you know that they got it.

Calendar (Outlook)
Microsoft Outlook is not just an email client, but is also used for calendar functionality for personal and corporate use, depending on what type of environment you are working in. For example, in the office you can use the Calendar to schedule meetings and reserve things like projectors and laptops. There are many Calendar options you can change, and I will go over the more commonly used ones (figure 3.16).

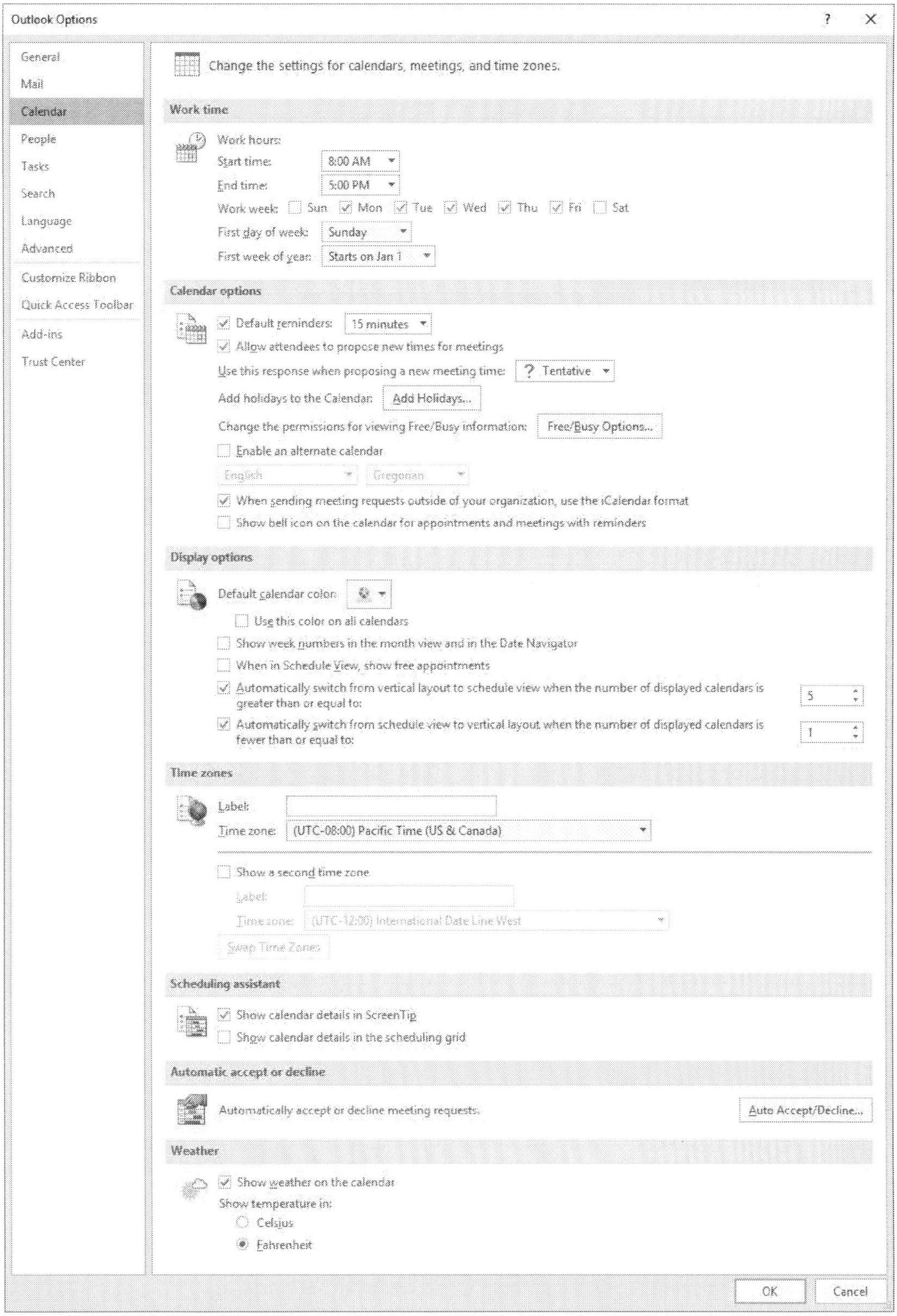

Outlook Options   ?   ✕

General		Change the settings for calendars, meetings, and time zones.

Calendar (selected)

Sidebar items:
- General
- Mail
- Calendar
- People
- Tasks
- Search
- Language
- Advanced
- Customize Ribbon
- Quick Access Toolbar
- Add-ins
- Trust Center

Work time

Work hours:
Start time: 8:00 AM ▼
End time: 5:00 PM ▼
Work week: ☐ Sun ☑ Mon ☑ Tue ☑ Wed ☑ Thu ☑ Fri ☐ Sat
First day of week: Sunday ▼
First week of year: Starts on Jan 1 ▼

Calendar options

☑ Default reminders: 15 minutes ▼
☑ Allow attendees to propose new times for meetings
Use this response when proposing a new meeting time: ? Tentative ▼
Add holidays to the Calendar: Add Holidays...
Change the permissions for viewing Free/Busy information: Free/Busy Options...
☐ Enable an alternate calendar
English ▼   Gregorian ▼
☑ When sending meeting requests outside of your organization, use the iCalendar format
☐ Show bell icon on the calendar for appointments and meetings with reminders

Display options

Default calendar color: ⚙ ▼
☐ Use this color on all calendars
☐ Show week numbers in the month view and in the Date Navigator
☐ When in Schedule View, show free appointments
☑ Automatically switch from vertical layout to schedule view when the number of displayed calendars is greater than or equal to: [5]
☑ Automatically switch from schedule view to vertical layout when the number of displayed calendars is fewer than or equal to: [1]

Time zones

Label: [   ]
Time zone: (UTC-08:00) Pacific Time (US & Canada) ▼

☐ Show a second time zone
Label: [   ]
Time zone: (UTC-12:00) International Date Line West ▼
Swap Time Zones

Scheduling assistant

☑ Show calendar details in ScreenTip
☐ Show calendar details in the scheduling grid

Automatic accept or decline

Automatically accept or decline meeting requests. Auto Accept/Decline...

Weather

☑ Show weather on the calendar
Show temperature in:
○ Celsius
◉ Fahrenheit

OK   Cancel

Figure 3.16
Work time

This setting is mostly used in corporate environments where you have a mail server such as Exchange. When you use this feature, Outlook will mark you as out of the office before your start time and after your end time. This will apply based on the days checked as well.

Calendar options
Here you can change your default reminder times for things like appointments and meetings, as well as your default response when proposing new meeting times (tentative, accept, or decline).

If you click the *Add Holidays* button, Outlook will automatically add all the major holidays to your calendar so you don't have to do it manually.

The Free/Busy options will let you share what days and times that you do not have anything scheduled on your calendar so people can use that information to help schedule meetings that you will be involved in.

Display options
These options let you change your calendar color and also allow you to change the view of your calendar based on the number of displayed calendars. You can have multiple calendars in Outlook, and even open other user's shared calendars and have them all side by side to get a top down view of everything that's going on.

Time zones
Here is where you choose the time zone based on your location. Outlook should pick up this information based on the time zone set on your computer, so you shouldn't have to change this unless you take your computer into a different time zone.

Automatic accept or decline
When someone sends you a meeting request you can have Outlook automatically accept or decline the request based on the options you choose (figure 3.17).

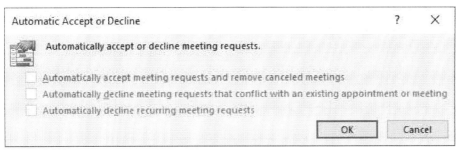

Figure 3.17

People (Outlook)

The People option allows you to tell Outlook how you want it to work with your contacts (figure 3.18).

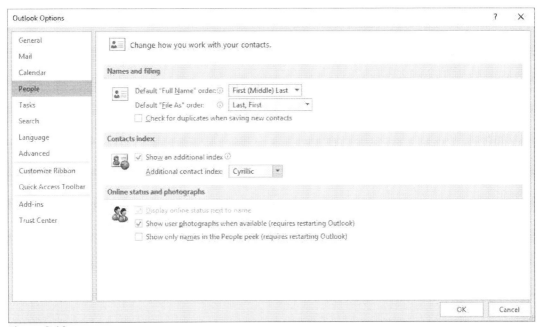

Figure 3.18

Names and filings

Here you can set how you want your contact names to be displayed in regards to first, middle, and last name. The default is first (middle) last, but you can also choose last, first, or first last1 last2. The File As section is used to set the default order for filing new contacts.

Contacts index
Indexes allow programs to quickly find items when searching for them. If you have an additional contacts index for another language, you can add it here.

Online status and photographs
In an office situation with an email server, Outlook can show your status in emails and calendar items. It will read your status from your local computer and let others know if you are available, in a meeting, or away from your computer. You can also add a photograph that will display next to your name if desired.

Tasks (Outlook)
Tasks are items you setup in Outlook to help you track their progress and make sure that they get finished on time (hopefully). You can change the settings from the Tasks options (figure 3.19) to finetune how they work.

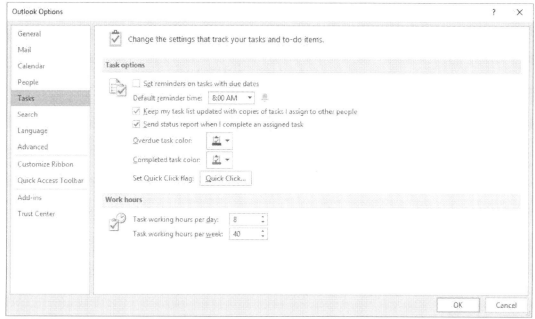

Figure 3.19

Task options
From this section you can set reminders for tasks that will pop up on your screen, alerting you that you have upcoming tasks that need to be completed. You can change the default time of the reminders as well as the overdue and completed task colors to help keep things organized.

Work hours

Here you enter your working hours per day and hours per week to be used when assigning tasks to make sure there are enough hours in the day and in the week to get all of your assigned tasks completed.

Search (Outlook)

Searching is an important feature in Outlook, especially if you are the type who gets tons of email and likes to keep them all. Fine tuning your search options can help speed up the process when you're looking for a particular item and are short on time (figure 3.20).

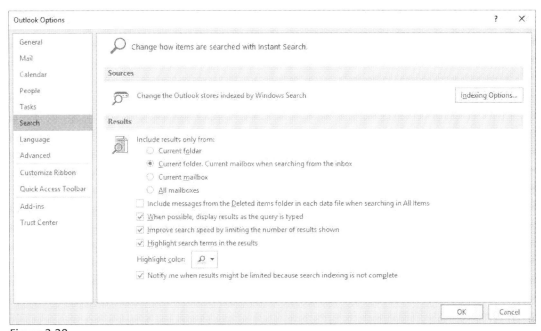

Figure 3.20

Sources

In order to speed up searches in folders and email, you need to set them up to be indexed. This way searches are almost instant compared to taking several minutes (or longer) to complete. Clicking on the *Indexing Options* button will tell Outlook where to index files and email. You can add and remove items from the indexing procedure as you see fit (figure 3.21). Once you add a new location, it will take some time for the initial indexing to complete depending on how much data is in that location.

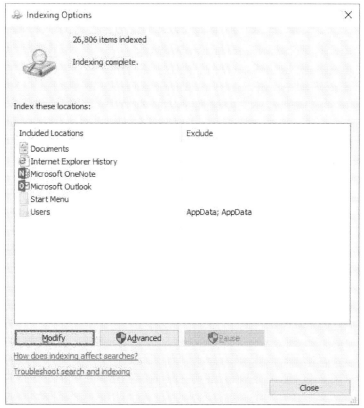

Figure 3.21

Results

When searching in Outlook you can tell it where to look to find the best results possible. The default is to search the current folder in the current mailbox, but if you have multiple mailboxes, you might want to search all of them, and you can change the default behavior here.

You can also have Outlook do things like search your deleted items and highlight search terms in the results, making them easier to sift through. If the indexing process is not complete, then you can have Outlook notify you so you know the search results may not be up to date.

Chapter 4 – Microsoft Word

Now that we have all the boring stuff like the Ribbon and options out of the way, we can begin on the fun stuff, which is learning about the Office programs themselves. The purpose of this book is to get your started on your way to becoming a proficient Office user, not to make you an expert on any one of the Office applications. There are entire books written on each one of the programs that are longer than this entire book, so after you get comfortable with the software, you can look into expanding your knowledge on the specific programs that you use the most.

Word is Microsoft's word processing program, and is used to create things such as letters, resumes, forms, booklets, and many other items. You can add text, tables, images, videos, custom shapes, and so on to make documents that really stand out. In fact, most people only use a fraction of Word's capabilities. Like all Office programs, there are many components to Word, and I will be going over the layout of the program and what you can do within it.

Default Tabs and Groups
You might have noticed that all of the Office programs have similar tabs, but they each have their own set of unique tabs as well. For this chapter I will go over all the tabs in Word, and then for the following chapters I will go over the program specific tabs and their groups so I am not repeating the same information over again. To review, the groups are the sections within the tab that have all the icons that you can use to change the settings. Keep in mind that many also have the arrow on the bottom right of the group that you can click on for even more settings.

As you can see in figure 4.1, there are nine default tabs for Word, with the Home tab being the one that Microsoft starts you out on. Keep in mind that in other versions of Word you might have some variation in the tabs. I am using Office 2016 for my examples.

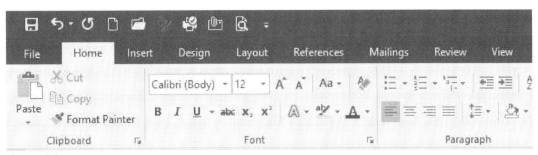

Figure 4.1

File Tab

The File tab is used for things you will do before and after working on your document. As you can see in figure 4.2, you have various options to choose from such as opening, saving, and printing your documents. Most of these options are obvious, but I want to go over a few that might not be.

Figure 4.2

Info – This section will give you specific information about the document you are working on such as its size, number of pages, number of words, last modified date, created data, the author, and so on.

- **Protect Document** – This is where you can do things such as protect your document with a password and restrict editing so nobody can make unauthorized changes.

- **Inspect Document** – Here you can have Word check your document to make sure it's compatible with older versions of Word, or to make sure people with disabilities won't find it hard to read.

- **Manage Document** – If you are using a document server, you will have check in and check out options here. And, if you have any unsaved documents that can be recovered, you can look at them here as well.

Save As – Word allows you to save documents in other formats besides the default Word format. You might have noticed that your Word documents end in .docx, which is the default file extension for Word. If you look at figure 4.3, you can see there are many other formats to choose from, such as a .doc version to be compatible with older versions of Word, PDF file, plain text file, and even as a webpage.

Figure 4.3

Share – If you are the type that's into saving your files "in the cloud" then you have that option in the Share section.

- **Share with People** – To save to the cloud, you will need to have a cloud storage account (such as Microsoft's OneDrive) so you have a place to upload your files. Then, once it's uploaded, you can share with other people so they can view and edit your files from their own computer.

- **Email** – If you have an email client installed on your computer (such as Microsoft Outlook) then you can send your document to your email client and it will open a new email with your document attached.

- **Present Online** – The Office Presentation Service is a free service that allows other people to follow along with your presentation by using a web browser.

- **Post to Blog** – If you have a current blog account you can create a new post using the current document that you have open. However, your blogging site will have to be supported by Microsoft to use this feature. If you don't have a blog account, you can create one from here as well.

Export – This section is similar to the Save As section where you can save your document as a different format, except here you are exporting it rather than saving it.

- **Create PDF/XPS Document** – Many times you will want to create a PDF file of your document to send to other people so they can't edit it. It's also used to reduce the size of the file in case the original has a lot of things (like images) in it which make the file size larger. The XPS document format was created by Microsoft and is similar to a PDF file, but you will need to use a program that can open XPS files in order to view the exported file.

- **Change File Type** – Here you have some common file types you can change your file into just like the Save As option gives you. In fact, there's also a Save As button here allowing you to do the same thing.

Account – The Account section will show you information about your user account such as your name and email address. You can also change the way the software looks in regards to its background and theme. If you have a OneDrive account, it will give you information on that as well. It's also a good place to see if your copy of Office has been activated, and if you need to change the product key for some reason, there's a section for that as well.

Home Tab

The Home tab contains many of the more commonly used settings, and that's why Microsoft has made it the default tab when you open any of their software. If you look back at figure 4.1, you'll see that there are many things you can do from the Home tab. There are five groups within the home tab:

Clipboard – The clipboard is used to hold information about copied text and images to keep them in memory until you are ready to paste them into your document or somewhere else. The clipboard will paste the last copied item unless you expand the Clipboard group by clicking on the little arrow to show other items you have copied. From this section you can paste in different formats, depending on what you are pasting.

Font – Fonts, also known as typestyles, are used to change how the characters look on the screen and when printed. Windows comes with its own default fonts installed and many programs will install additional fonts when you install the actual program, so not every computer will have the same fonts. From the Font section you can do things such as change the font type, color, and size.

Paragraph – Here you can adjust settings to change the text to align to the left or right, be centered, or be justified on both sides. You can also set text indents, line and paragraph spacing, and create borders from this section.

Styles – Styles are used to format paragraphs to fit a certain "style" based on the look you are going for. This way you can have a consistent looking document and an easy way to change the styles for paragraphs that you want to stand out or format differently from the rest. The best way to learn about styles is to type out a couple of paragraphs, highlight them, and then click on the various styles to see how it changes the look of the text.

Editing – If you have a lot of text and want to find a word or phrase to maybe change it or remind yourself if you even typed it at all, you can use the *Find* feature from the Editing group. Simply click on *Find*, type in the information you are searching for, and it will show you all the results in the document. Then you can click on a particular result and it will take you right to it within the document. The *Replace* feature is great to use if you want to replace a certain word with another throughout the whole document. For example, let's say you spelled Jon as John and want to replace all the instances of John with Jon. You can do that with the Replace tool.

Insert Tab

The Insert tab is used to, well, insert things into your documents. There are many things you can insert into your document, and each group within the Insert tab has its own set of options (figure 4.4).

Figure 4.4

Pages – Here you can insert various types of pages into your document.

- **Cover Page** – Word has some default cover pages that you can add to your document to spice it up. All you need to do is edit the text or add pictures to suit your needs.

- **Blank Page** – If you want to insert a new blank page quickly, then just put your cursor where you want the page and click on Blank Page.

- **Page Break** – If you want to insert a page break at a certain point in your document to start a new page, just put your cursor where you want the page and click on Page Break.

Tables – Tables come in handy if you want to create a spreadsheet style table to store information to use in an easy to read format. You can create tables of almost any size and then customize them after they are created. You can either draw your own table, or have one created by entering in the specifications you need (figure 4.5).

Title 1	Title 2	Title 3	Title 4
Data	Data	Data	Data
Data	Data	Data	Data
Data	Data	Data	Data
Data	Data	Data	Data
Data	Data	Data	Data

Figure 4.5

Illustrations – It's a very common practice to insert things like pictures and shapes into your documents, and the Illustration group is one that you will most likely be using a lot.

- **Pictures** - From this group you can insert things like pictures from your hard drive, as well as search for pictures online and have them inserted directly into your document.

- **Shapes** - Shapes are another item that is commonly inserted into documents. Many people like to draw arrows, lines, boxes, and other shapes to highlight important information in their documents.

- **SmartArt** - SmartArt is a way to insert graphics based on certain categories such as hierarchy and pyramids.

- **Charts** - Charts can be used to insert Excel-like information without having to link your document to an Excel file. After you choose your chart type and insert it, you can then edit the values and data for your chart.

- **Screenshot** – If you want to include a screenshot of something you are currently working on, then you can use this tool to take a picture of your screen and then paste it into your document.

Add-ins – This group is not used too often unless you have installed some add-ins to your software. Add-ins will add additional features such as file conversion tools, additional clipart, language translators, training, and more. If you click on the *Store* icon you will be taken to the add-ins store where you can install any add-ins you want to try. Keep in mind that many are free, but there are some that will cost you money to use.

Media – This option allows you to insert a video from an online source (such as YouTube) directly into your document. Then, when others read your document, they will see the video preview and can click on the play button to actually watch the video from your document. They will need to be connected to the Internet to do so, of course.

Links – Office software has the capability to insert various types of links into documents. This comes in handy as a quick way to let your readers access additional information.

- **Hyperlink** – The hyperlink option is used to create a link to things such as a particular website, place within the document, or an email address. Think of it as the same type of link you sometimes get in your emails where you can click on it and it will take you somewhere else.

- **Bookmark** – Bookmarks are used to mark a place that you want to find again easily in the future. After you create a bookmark and click on where you want the bookmark to reside in the document, you can go back to your bookmarks,

- choose the one you want, and it will take you back to that same spot in the document.

- **Cross-reference** - This refers to an item that appears in another location in a document. When you create a cross-reference it will make a link to that cross-referenced item.

Comments – Comments are used to add comments to your document, which will appear off to the right in a special margin. They are usually used when reviewing a document and making a note of such things as errors or changes.

Header & Footer – These are used to display information in documents with multiple pages.

- **Header** – Headers are shown on the top of the page and can contain things such as the document's name or a book's title.

- **Footer** – Footers are on the bottom of the page, and are commonly used for things like references and anything else you want to put there, including information you can put in a header.

- **Page Number** – Word can automatically number your pages for you as you add more, and you can select the style and placement of the page numbers from here.

Text – The Text group has a variety of text related items you can add to your Word document. One of the most commonly used ones is a text box, which lets you add text within a box that you can move around the screen and place on top of images. Other features of the Text group include the ability to embed (insert) other types of documents within your primary document so they can be opened right off the page itself. WordArt has been around for some time, but is still a cool way to add some flash to your documents. All you need to do is click on a WordArt style you like and start typing. Then you can drag your new text box around the screen and place it wherever you want in your document, like shown below.

WordArt Sample

Symbols – These are used when you need to add a specific kind of character to your document such as ©™ π. Equations can be inserted as well if you are the smart type that has a use for that!

Design Tab

The Design tab has some similar features to the other tabs, but let's talk about all the groups within this tab. The main purpose for this tab is to offer various design elements that you can use to change how your documents look to make them stand out (figure 4.6).

Figure 4.6

Themes – Themes allow you to coordinate things like colors, fills, and fonts in your document to give it a more designer look. There are many themes to choose from, and you can also create your own and save it to use on other documents.

Document Formatting – The choices in this area will change based on what theme you choose from the Theme group.

- **Style Set** – Word has a bunch of built-in text styles which are used to make things like quotes, headers, and body text work together so they look like they were made for each other. They can also be saved to use in other documents.

- **Colors** – When you choose a theme it will change the color palette for the document, so you can either use colors designed to work with each other, or even create your own color palette.

- **Fonts** – This is another place to change the font used with your text like we discussed earlier.

- **Paragraph Spacing** – Use paragraph spacing to determine the distance between paragraphs in your document. Some of the choices include compact, relaxed, and double.

- **Effects** – These are sets of lines and fill effects that you can apply to your theme.

- **Set as Default** – Once you get things looking the way you like, you can click the *Set as Default* button to have it apply to all new documents.

Page Background – To really make your documents stand out, you can add features from this group.

- **Watermark** – A watermark is text or sometimes an image that is lightly placed behind your text on the document to indicate things like the document being a draft or confidential. There are defaults you can choose from, or you can create your own custom watermark.

- **Page Color** – This will change the background color of your pages from white to whatever color you choose. This will only change the color on the screen, but not when you print, which is a good thing unless you *like* buying ink! You can turn this on in the Display section of the Word options.

- **Page Borders** – Page borders can be placed around the border of the document and are very customizable. There are many built-in styles to choose from, and you can even use art as a page border (as seen in figure 4.7).

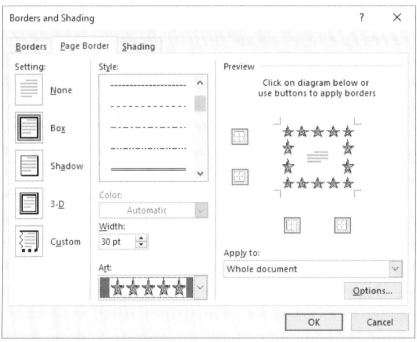

Figure 4.7

Layout Tab

A lot of formatting tasks are done from the Layout tab. As you can see in figure 4.8, there are quite a few things you can do here.

Figure 4.8

Page Setup – This group is one that you will commonly use to change the way your page is initially setup.

- **Margins** – Margins are the amount of white space between the edge of the page and the text on the page. There are built-in margins you can choose from, or you can create your own custom margins. This will apply to the entire document unless you tell Word otherwise.

- **Orientation** – There are two choices for orientation, and they are portrait (which is where the page is up and down the long way) and landscape (which the page is longer from left to right). Most of the time you will use portrait mode.

- **Size** – The default size for Word documents are 8.5x11 (letter), but you can choose from one of the many built-in sizes, or create your own size. This will apply to the entire document unless you tell Word otherwise. Keep in mind when changing the size of your document that if you want to print it, you will have to have that size paper at hand, otherwise it won't print correctly.

- **Breaks** – Here you can apply certain kinds of breaks to the pages, such as a page break, which I mentioned before, or a section break, which lets you apply different formatting to different parts of your document and keeps things separate.

- **Line Numbers** – Line numbers will add sequential numbers to each line. There are other options to choose from here as well, such as having the numbering start back with number 1 on each page rather than continue where it left off on the page before.

- **Hyphenation** – You might have noticed when you type something such as the word "addon" that Word will want it to be typed as "add-on", using a hyphen.

If you choose the automatic hyphenation option, then Word will automatically add hyphens as it sees fit, otherwise it will just suggest that you use one.

Paragraph – This group has settings to manage how your paragraphs are setup in regards to left and right indents and spacing above and below paragraphs. This is something you would use for a specific paragraph, and if you wanted it to apply to all paragraphs, you should do it from the Paragraph and Spacing setting in the Design tab.

Arrange – If you have images in your document, then that's where the settings in the Arrange group come into play. By default, when you insert an image (etc.) into a document, Word places it in line with the text, and that might not be where you want the image to stay.

- **Position** – This allows you to reposition the image so that it's exactly where you want it relative to things like page margins or text columns. The Text Wrapping tab (figure 4.9) comes in handy because you can use it to set the image in front or behind the text, and then just drag and drop it wherever you like on the page.

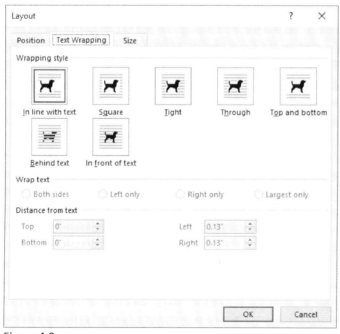

Figure 4.9

- **Wrap Text** – This is similar to the Position option, but readjusts the text to the image rather than the image to the text.

- **Bring Forward and Send Backward** – Sometime you will want to layer images and text on top of each other, and will need either the image to be on top of the text or the text on top of the image. If you click on the item you want to move, then you can either bring it forward or send it to the back in relation to the other items.

- **Selection Pane** – When you have multiple objects you can use the Selection Pane to view them and switch back and forth between them.

- **Align** – This setting will align your objects so they are placed where you want them. You can align them to the right, left, top, bottom, etc., as well as use guidelines to help get everything exactly right.

- **Group** – If you have multiple objects that you want to group together into one object, then you can use the Group setting to do this. For example, let's say you combined some images with a text box, got everything just right, and now want to move or copy the entire thing without accidentally moving things around. When you group the items, they all stay together as one object. (This doesn't work when images are aligned with the text, so keep that in mind.)

- **Rotate** – You can manually rotate images using the mouse, but if you want to fine tune your rotation, you can use this option to enter an exact value of rotation to use.

References Tab

The References tab provides a quick way to enter your document sources, citations, as well as choose styles. You can also set up bibliographies and indexes (as seen in figure 4.10). This is more of an advanced feature of Word so I won't go into too much detail about the settings here.

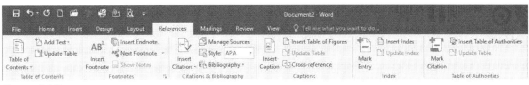
Figure 4.10

Table of Contents – If you are writing something like a book that will have a table of contents, then you can choose from preconfigured tables or create your own custom one. Once you have the TOC done, you can click the *Add Text* button to add new items to whichever level on the TOC you choose.

Footnotes – Footnotes are used to do things such as cite other authors' publications within your documents. Footnotes appear at the bottom of the page and endnotes are used at the end of the document.

Citations and Bibliography – If you need to cite someone else's work within your document or create a bibliography, then this is the place you would come to do so. (A bibliography is a list of books or articles that you used to help you write your own book or article.)

Captions – These are used to add information to an image to help describe or name it. So, as you can see in my book, the captions are named *Figure 4.10* etc. Once you make a caption for an image, you can group the two and then move them wherever you like as one unit.

Index – If you have terminology in your document that you want to index at the end, then you can find that word or phrase in your document, highlight it, and then click on Mark Entry. Word will then keep that entry for use later when creating your index.

Table of Authorities - Table of Authorities are used when creating legal documents where you need to list your references and sources within that document.

Mailings Tab
Word has some nice features that let you print out things like envelopes and labels and allow you to use other files like spreadsheets with names and addresses to create mailers without having to do it all manually. Figure 4.11 shows you the many tools available to create these mailings.

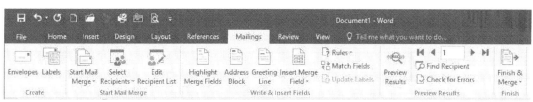

Figure 4.11

Create
In this group you have options to create envelopes and labels by simply entering in the information you want to have printed on them. Then you can choose the size of the envelope or brand and type of label and print them up. As you can see in figure

4.12, the interface is pretty easy to understand, and all you need to do is click on the Options button to pick your size. If you click on the *Add to Document* button, Word will change the layout of your document to fit that size envelope.

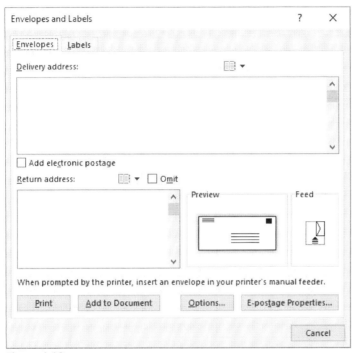

Figure 4.12

Start Mail Merge
Mail Merge is a process where you take a premade listing of names and addresses from something like a spreadsheet and have Word create envelopes, letters, or labels from that list without you having to do them one at a time. For the source of the names and addresses, you can type them in from Word, import a file (like a spreadsheet), or have them pulled from your Outlook contacts.

Write & Insert Fields
This area is where you can format your mailings so they look the way you want and add things such as a greeting line or address block using your imported data. It will remain greyed out until you change the document to Mail Merge main document and link it to a data source for your names and addresses.

Preview Results
After you have everything configured the way you like, then you can click on the *Preview Results* button to see how your mailings will look based on your imported list and how you configured it in the Write & Insert Fields group. If you want to find a specific entry to preview, then click on the *Find Recipient* button.

Finish

Once everything is looking good, simply click on the *Finish & Merge* button to start the mail merge process based on your configuration.

Review Tab

Many people use Word to create documents like papers and books and then send them out for someone else to proofread. Or, you might even send a document to your supervisor for approval and changes before sending it out to a client. This is where the Review tab comes into play (figure 4.13). It lets the reader check the document and make markups to show suggested changes that can be sent back to the creator of the document.

Figure 4.13

Proofing

This group should be pretty obvious as to what it does. You have your spelling and grammar checker, thesaurus, and word count (in case you want to see how many words you have in your document). World also shows the word count at the bottom of the screen, as well the number of pages in your document.

Insights

The Insights feature is kind of interesting because you can highlight a word or phrase, click the Smart Lookup button, and Word will go out on the Internet and find you some information about whatever you have highlighted. For example, I typed in Microsoft Word, highlighted the text, and clicked the Smart Lookup button and here is what I got (figure 4.14).

Figure 4.14

Comments

As the reviewer, you can make comments on certain text that you want the person who you are going to send the document to to read. Click on New Comment to add a new comment, and Word will add a comment section to the right of the page. The Delete button will allow you to delete a comment or all of your comments, and the Previous and Next buttons will scroll through your comments in case you want to review them yourself.

Changes

After you get a document back that has been proofed, you will have the opportunity to accept or reject changes made by the reviewer. You can go through them one at a time, or accept or reject all of them at once.

Compare

After the reviewer makes their changes and you accept or reject their changes, you most likely will have two different versions of the same document. The *Compare* section will allow you to either compare both versions to see the differences, or combine both versions into one document.

Protect

Many times you will have a document that you do not want to have changed by anyone you send it to. The Protect group has two options you can choose from to help with this type of situation. You can either block a certain author from making any changes, or you can restrict editing for everyone and fine tune what you want to be allowed. For example, you can set just formatting restrictions or just editing restrictions.

OneNote

If you have OneNote installed on your computer, then you can open it on one side of your screen so it can automatically link your notes to what you are doing in your Word document.

View Tab

The View tab (figure 4.15) is used to change the way Word looks on the screen to make it easier for you to work on and see how your document is going to look overall.

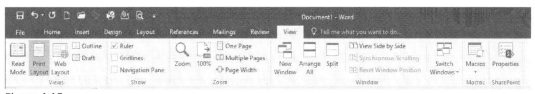
Figure 4.15

Views

Views are used to change how your document looks on the screen. There are five options you can choose from in this group:

- **Read Mode** – This mode is optimized for reading a document on your monitor. It will remove the Ribbon from view to give you the largest reading area possible. It's not obvious how to get out of Read Mode, but if you click on *View* and then *Edit document*, it will take you out of Read Mode and bring the Ribbon back.

- **Print Layout** - This is the default view when opening a document, and is good for seeing what your document will look like when it prints in regards to page breaks.

- **Web Layout** – If you are planning on saving your document as a web page or using it for a web page then the Web Layout view will show you how the formatting will look on a website.

- **Outline** – This view will show the document as an outline and also show the outlining tools.

- **Draft** – Draft mode is used for quick edits and will not show things like images, headers, or footers.

Show

This grouping will allow you to show the ruler at the top of the page as well as gridlines across the body of the page in case you need them to help with alignment of text and images. The Navigation Pane is used to view things like document headings, thumbnail page previews, and search results.

Zoom

If you need to zoom in and out of your document to make things easier to see, you can either click on the Zoom icon and pick a zoom percentage, or click the 100% button to bring the zoom level back to the default. (I like to hold down the Ctrl key on the keyboard and then use the mouse wheel to zoom in and out.)

Other zoom options include the ability to have it fit one page on the screen, show multiple pages side by side on the screen, or have it zoom to exactly the width of the page.

Window

The Window group allows you to change the views when you have more than one document open. You have several view to choose from:

- **New Window** – This will open the existing document in a new window. When you make changes to the document in one window, the other window will update the changes.

- **Arrange All** – This view will arrange all the documents on your screen so you can see all of them. If you have too many documents open at one time, this view doesn't do a lot of good.

- **Split** – This view will split the page in half and allow you to have the top of the page in one pane and the bottom in the other.

- **View Side by Side** – If you have two documents open and you want to work on them both on at the same time, you can have each one take up half the screen so you can see both equally. This is the next best thing to having dual monitors, and works better with larger monitors.

- **Synchronous Scrolling** – When you are using Side by Side mode, you can enable Synchronous Scrolling so that when you scroll up or down on one document, the other will scroll simultaneously.

- **Reset Window Position** – This button will reset the view to how it was before.

- **Switch Windows** – If you have multiple documents open, you can click on this button to switch back and forth between them.

Macros
Macros are used as a time saving tool because they allow you to record a series of steps and then execute those steps by running the macro you created.

SharePoint
If you are opening documents from a SharePoint server in the office, you can use the Properties button in this section to edit SharePoint properties in your Word documents.

Format Tab
One tab that only shows up as needed is called the Format tab (figure 4.16). This tab will appear when you click on objects such as images or shapes that have the ability to be formatted within your document.

Figure 4.16

The groups within this tab will vary depending on what type of object you are trying to format. So, rather than go over every one for each type of object, I will just go over the most commonly used settings.

Some of the things you can do for images include add borders, effects, and styles. You can also change the color of the image and adjust the brightness and contrast if you like. If the image needs to be cropped, then that is easy to do as well.

For shapes, you can change the style, fill, outline, and add effects. It's also possible to add WordArt and text boxes. If you need to align the shape to your text or have it appear behind or in front of text, then there are options for that in the Arrange group. The same goes for pictures.

Creating a Document
Now that you hopefully have a better understanding of what the tools within all the tabs do, let's create a document in Word. When you open Word or click on New from the File tab, it will ask you what type of document you would like to create (figure 4.17). Most of the time you will choose the Blank document option. This will give you a single page document with nothing on it.

Templates
There are many templates you can choose from to get yourself started, if you would like to use one of the preconfigured designs. There are templates for documents such as resumes, brochures, reports, cover letters, flyers, thank you cards, and so on. When you choose one of these templates it will open it in a new file and all you need to do is change the text within that file to suit your needs. You can filter the types of templates by choosing one of the categories at the top, or search for a specific type of template.

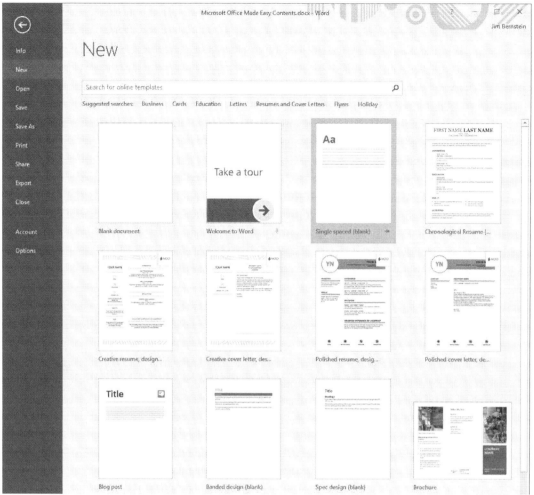

Figure 4.17

Once you have your new document ready then it's time to start adding text and any graphics you would like to include within the document. Let's assume we started with a new blank document.

Entering Text

To add text simply click inside the document. The cursor will then go to the top left of the page. If you want to start down lower on the page, you can press the Enter key a few times. As for the font and size, you can choose it before you start or change it as you're typing. This can be done from the Home tab, which you should be on already. To change the font of any existing text, simply highlight it with the mouse by clicking and dragging from the beginning to the end, or from the end to the beginning. You can also use the keyboard shortcut *Ctrl-a* to highlight all the text in the document. Then, with the text highlighted, change it to whatever font you want and whatever size you want. Then you can start typing away. Word will put the text on the next line automatically as you get to the end of the current line.

Saving

If this document is something you plan on saving to work on later or to email to someone, then it's a good idea to periodically save your work as you go along. Word will do its background saves automatically, but it's always a good idea to do manual saves. The Save option can be found under the File tab, or you can use the keyboard shortcut *Ctrl-s* to save your work. (I always like to add a save icon to the Quick Access Toolbar.)

When you save your document for the first time you will be asked where you would like to save it (figure 4.18). You have several options to choose from. Notice how the image says Save As instead of Save? This is normal.

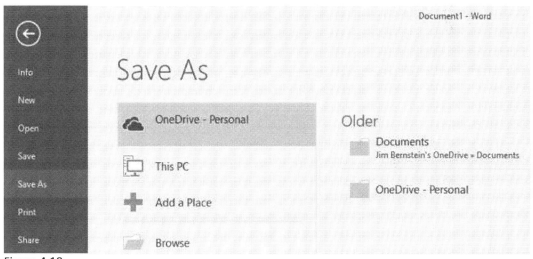

Figure 4.18

Microsoft is pushing people to save to the cloud, so they put OneDrive as the first choice. (I will be talking about OneDrive later on in this book.) Other options include *This PC*, which means your local computer, and *Add a Place*, which will give you other cloud options such as a SharePoint server.

Clicking on *Browse* will allow you to browse the local folders on your computer and choose a location that way. It will also let you choose a name for the file, as well as the type of file you want to save it as. The default is a Word document that will end with .docx. Then, the next time you want to save your document, you just have to click on Save or use the Ctrl-s shortcut and it will save it in the same place with the same name and overwrite your changes from the last save.

If you want to save your document with a different name or in a different folder\location, then you would choose the Save As option from the File tab. This will let you save a copy of the current document while leaving the original as it was from the last save. You can also choose a new file type while doing a Save As. One very important thing to remember is **once you do a Save As, you will be working on the new file and not the old one anymore,** so if you want to go back to the original file, you will need to open it again.

Formatting a Document
Once you get some text into your document, you may find that it doesn't look quite the way you like it, and that is where formatting comes into play. You can change the look and feel of your document in many ways within Word to make things look the way you want them.

Text Formatting
I mentioned changing the font and font size earlier, but you can also do things such as make the text **bold**, *italicized*, or underlined. You can even do things to the text as ~~strike though~~ and $_{subscript}$ and ^{superscript}. If you want to add a little color to your document, then that's possible as well. There are many built-in default colors available, and you can also create your own. Just be careful when creating your own colors because if you want to use that exact color later in a new document, you will need to create it exactly like you did before. Fortunately, this is easy to do if you make a note of the red, blue, and green numbers (figure 4.19), and create the color with the exact same values.

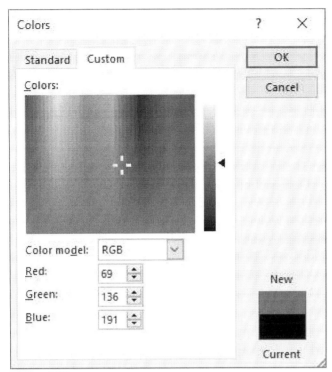

Figure 4.19

Another nice tool you can use when formatting is the highlighter. If you need to highlight something to make it stand out, simply highlight the text and click on the highlighter button to have it highlighted. You can change the color of the highlighter tool as well. The default is yellow.

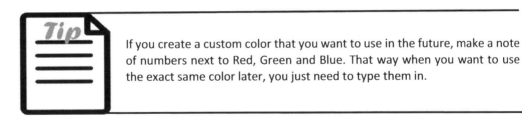

If you create a custom color that you want to use in the future, make a note of numbers next to Red, Green and Blue. That way when you want to use the exact same color later, you just need to type them in.

Creating Lists

Many times you will have a need so create a list within your document, and Word offers many ways for you to do this. Once you have the text you want in the list typed out, you can highlight it and click on the list icons in the Paragraph group on the Home tab. Each one has their defaults, but you can customize things such as what the bullets look like in the bulleted list, and how the numbers are displayed in the numbered list. Here are a couple of examples:

- **First bullet point**
  - Sub point
- **Second bullet point**
  - Sub point
- **Third bullet point**
  - Sub point
  - Sub point

1) **Numbered point 1**
   a. Sub point
2) **Numbered point 2**
   a. Sub point
3) **Numbered point 3**
   a. Sub point
   b. Sub point

Clearing Formatting
Let's say you have formatted your document and realized it doesn't look the way you want it to at all and now you want to clear out all of the formatting changes you've made. To do so, highlight all the text (or use the Ctrl-a keyboard shortcut) and then click on the eraser icon in the Font group on the Home tab. This will remove all the formatting and put things back with the default font, size, and colors. It will also remove the formatting on any lists you have created.

Margins
Margins are important to set because they help determine how your document looks when it is printed. The default margins are set to one inch on the top, bottom, left, and right. You can choose from one of the built-in margin settings, or you can set your own by choosing Custom Margins from the Margins section under the Layout tab (figure 4.20). Once you have this open, simply type in the margins you want for each side. For example, if you want a half inch margin on the type, then enter .5 in the box that says Top. You can have the setting apply to the whole document, or just the selected text. Most of the time you will keep the default of whole document.

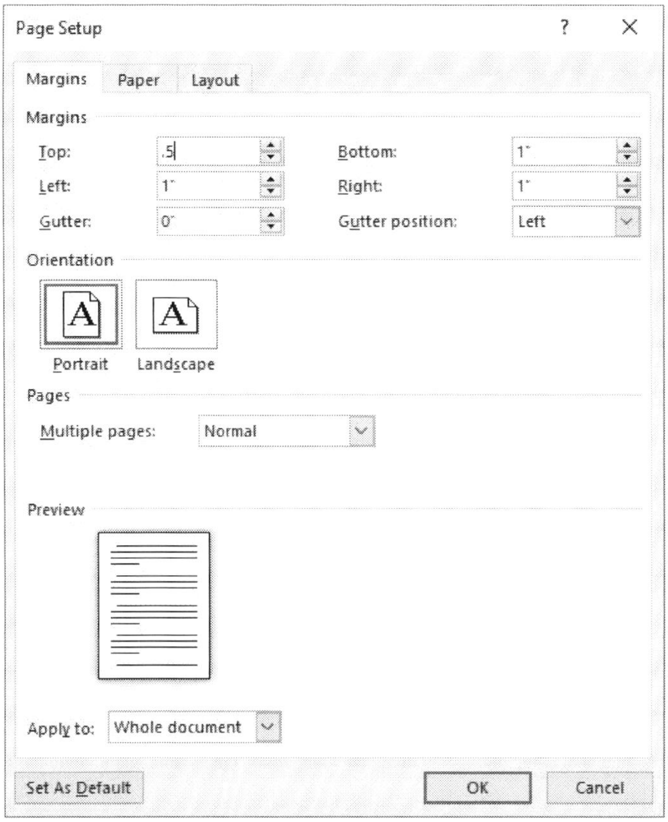

Figure 4.20

Another formatting process you might need to do involves changing the left and right indents. To do so, simply highlight the text you want to change and choose your setting from the Paragraph group under the Layout tab. You might also want to change the line spacing within that paragraph. To do this, go to the small arrow at the bottom right of the Paragraph group and change the line spacing from the Indents and Spacing tab (figure 4.21). I changed it from single to 1.5 lines.

> Here is a sample of a paragraph that has been indented to the right and
>
> has had its line spacing increased so that it is farther apart. Notice how
>
> it looks compared to the other paragraphs in this book?

Figure 4.21

Inserting Links to Websites

One thing many people like to include in their documents are links to websites so that the reader of the document can get additional information on the content within that document, be brought to the writers website, etc.

To insert a link to a website simply put the cursor where you want the link to be on the page, go to the Insert tab, and choose Hyperlink (figure 4.22). From there the *Existing File or Web Page* is selected in the *Link to* section. Then, in the *Address box*, type in the website address, and in the *Text to display* box type in what you want it to say on the page. (If you don't change the *Text to display* information, it will simply show the website address on the page.)

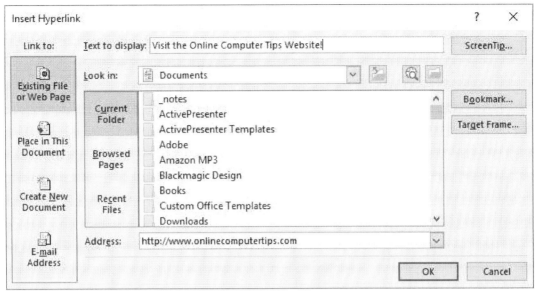

Figure 4.22

Here is the result from what I entered in the Insert Hyperlink box. You will notice how it's underlined and it's also displayed in blue text, which is the default color for hyperlinks.

Visit the Online Computer Tips Website!

To go to that website all the reader would have to do is press Ctrl on their keyboard and then click on the link, which will open up the link in their default web browser.

Adding Borders

Another way to spruce up your document is to add a border around certain text or around the whole page itself. To add a border around a block of text, simply highlight that text, go to the Home tab, then the Paragraph group, and select your border type from the dropdown list or go to Borders and Shading (figure 4.23) and create your own custom border. As you can see, I went with the shadow border with a line that consist of a thick outer line and thin inner line. You can also change the color of your border if you choose. Then you can apply the border to the selected paragraph, or to the entire page.

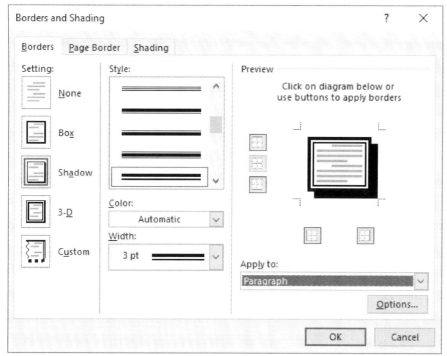

Figure 4.23

Text Wrapping and Images

When adding images to your document, it's important to get it aligned with the text correctly so it looks right on the page. By default, when you insert an image it puts it  in line with the text. Then you can go to the special Format tab that appears when you click on your image and decide how you want the text to align with your image. In my example I chose the square options so the text wraps around the image in a uniform manner. The default is to have the image move with the text, so as you type it will keep the image aligned properly. There are other positions you can choose from as well, and if you want to move the picture independently of the text then you can either choose the *in front of text* or *behind text* setting. One other thing I did in this example was add a text box with some Word Art on top of the image and formatted the text box not to have any fill or any border. (You can add a text box from the Insert tab under the Text group.)

Inserting Shapes

Shapes are another common item to insert into your document to help bring some life to your work or to help clarify key points. To insert a shape, go to the Insert tab and then choose Shapes under the Illustrations group. There are many built-in shapes to choose from (as you can see in figure 4.24), and they are all grouped into categories, making it easy to find what you need.

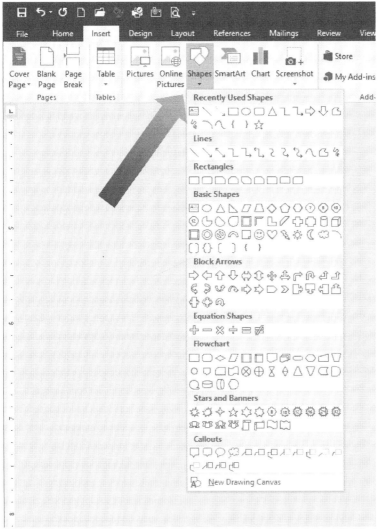

Figure 4.24

As you can see, I inserted an arrow shape and placed it on top of my image. Then I chose a shaded color for the arrow and resized and rotated it to suit my needs by using the special Format tab which appeared after clicking on the arrow I inserted.

There are many other ways to format your document, and you can write an entire book just on formatting. However, I am covering only what I think are the most commonly used formatting tools to get you started making professional-looking documents.

Printing a Document

Now that you have your document looking exactly how you want it to look, it's time to print it out to share with the world—or at least with someone else! There are a few things you need to be aware of when printing out your documents, and I will cover them now.

How to Print

The first thing I suppose you should know (if you don't already) is how you go about printing. If you don't have a print shortcut on your Quick Access Toolbar, then you will need to go to the File tab and then click on Print. As you can see in figure 4.25, you can just click on the Print button and you will be on your way. If you do that though, you will be printing out the entire document with all the default settings, which you might not want to do.

Figure 4.25

Printer Properties

Before you print you have the option to change printer specific settings that are independent of Word and will vary based on the make and model of your printer. I mentioned earlier how I like to print in Draft mode to save on ink and have the printing process go much faster. Here is where you can choose that option (figure 4.26). Clicking on the Advanced button will bring up even more printer-related options such as graphics quality settings and printer hardware options, and, once again, they will vary based on your printer's make and model.

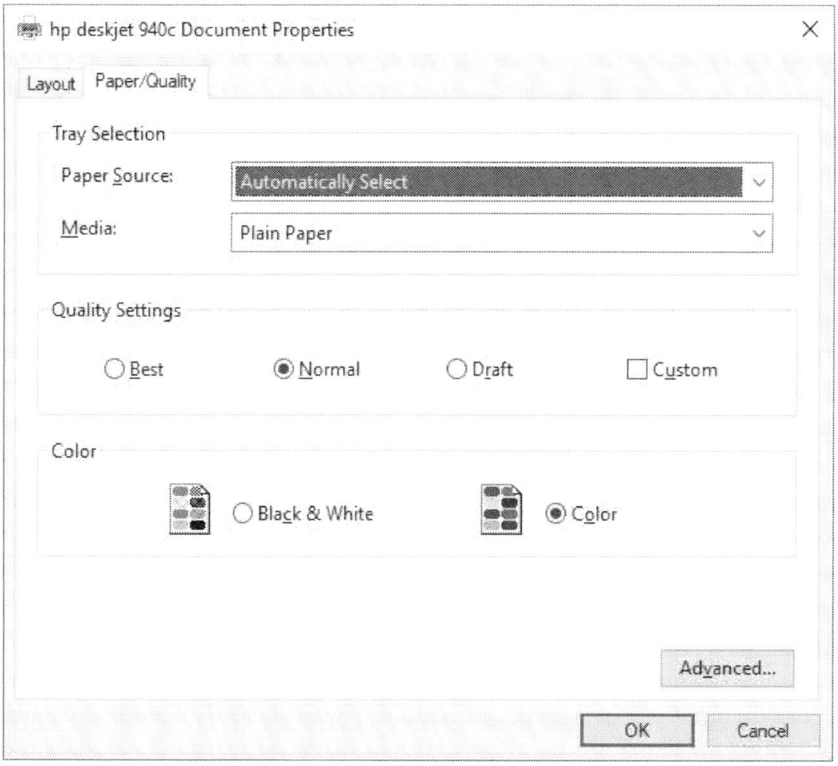

Figure 4.26

Print Settings

There are many settings you can change before printing your document, and these will vary based on what printer you are using and the features that it has available. If you take a look at figure 4.26, you can see that there are many things you can adjust.

The first setting determines what pages are printed when you click on the Print button. The default is to print all the pages, but if you click on the dropdown arrow you will have options for printing just the current page you are on, or just the text you have selected. You can also have it print just odd or just even pages. There is also a box that says *Pages* where you can type in a specific page or a range of pages (such as 5-9) that you want to have printed.

Underneath that there is the setting to print on one side or both sides of the paper. The choices you will have here will vary based on your printer and whether it supports automatic duplexing (printing both sides), or if you have to manually insert the page to have Word print the back side.

If you are printing multiple copies you can have each set be collated or uncollated (based on your needs) by picking the option under the Collated section.

Underneath that there is the setting to print either portrait (up and down) or landscape (long ways). If it doesn't print correctly, make sure your document is set to the same orientation under the Layout tab.

Next we have the size setting. Word should set this to match your document size that you chose under the Layout tab automatically. You can change the paper size for your printout, but keep in mind that it most likely won't print correctly since the document size and the paper size won't match.

For the margin settings, once again Word should match the settings that you configured on the Layout tab under Margins. You can change the setting from here for printing if you want to see how it will print out with different margins.

Finally, the settings will allow you to print multiple pages onto one sheet. So, if you want two or even sixteen pages on a sheet, then that is up to you. Of course, each page will be very small, so don't do too many per sheet!

There is also a Page Setup link on the bottom that will allow you to change margin, paper, and layout settings. The Paper tab will allow you to do things such as choose a different paper tray on your printer, and also change the paper size.

Emailing a Document From Word
One of the neat features that Word and the other Office programs have is the ability to email your document right from the program itself. Keep in mind that you will need to have an email client installed such as Microsoft Outlook, and that this won't work with webmail such as Yahoo and Gmail without some third party software and more advanced configuration.

If you do have an email client installed on your computer and want to attach the current document to an email from Word, be sure to save your current changes, then go to the File tab and click on Share. You will then see a screen like shown in figure 4.27. From there, click on the button that says Send as Attachment.

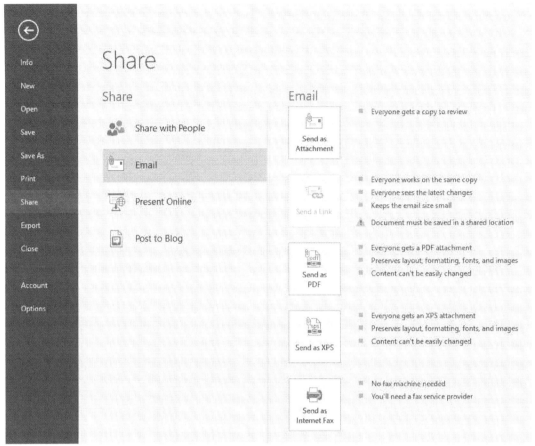

Figure 4.27

Word will open your email client and attach the document to that email (figure 4.28). It will also fill in the subject line with the name of the file, which you can change if you like. Then you just need to choose who you are sending it to and write your email message and you are ready to go.

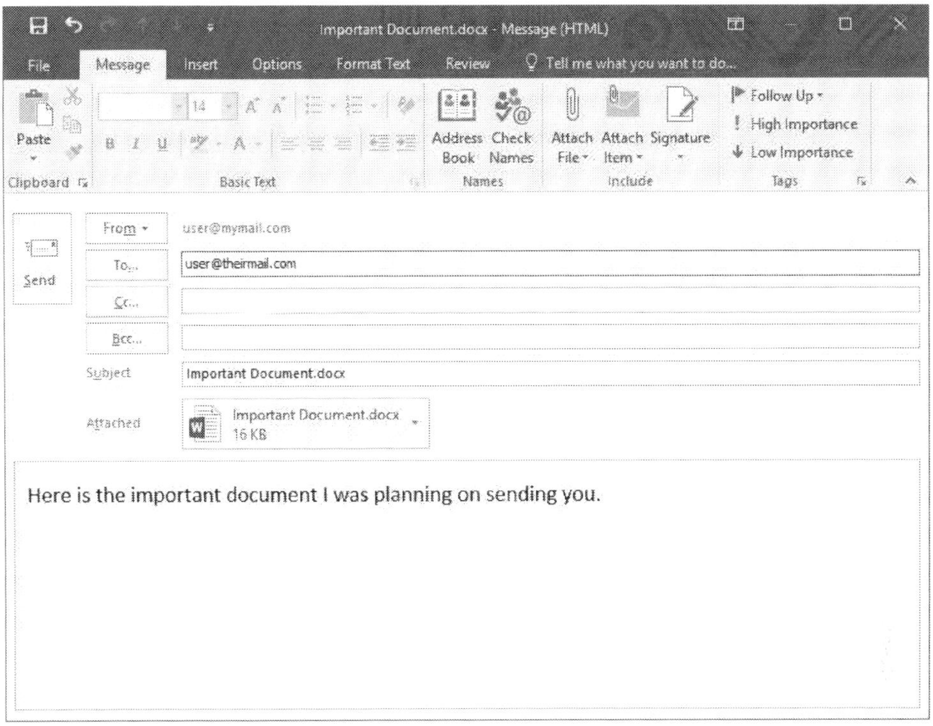

Figure 4.28

Now just because you don't have a mail client installed on your computer doesn't mean that you can't email documents to other people. You will just need to go into your webmail, compose a new email, and find the attachment button (which usually looks like a paperclip). Then you will have to browse to the location where you saved your document and attach it from there. Keep in mind that file size matters when attaching files to email, so make sure your document is not too big, especially if it contains a lot of higher quality images or embedded files (etc.).

Chapter 5– Microsoft Excel

Microsoft Excel is a spreadsheet program that is used to arrange data in cells that form rows and columns so you can enter, store, and manipulate the data with calculations and formulas. They can be used to do things such as tracking spending, creating graphs and charts, analyzing data, and so on. Spreadsheets are used in just about every type of business these days that uses computers. In this chapter I am going to go over the basics of creating and formatting spreadsheets, and also get into some simple formulas as well.

Excel Specific Tabs and Groups

Just like Word, Excel has sets of tabs and groups within these tabs. I mentioned that many of these tabs are universal between Office programs, and I covered most of them in the chapter on Word. Now I want to go over the tabs that are specific to Excel and tell you what they do. I will also mention some of the same tabs that I did before when they have groups that pertain to that program.

Home Tab

There are a few Excel-specific groups on the Home tab that Word doesn't have, so I would like to go over those first.

Styles

The Styles group is where you can add some custom formatting to your spreadsheet to spruce up the way things look or highlight cells that contain important data. The *Conditional Formatting* button will let you do things like highlight cells that contain a certain word or value. With Conditional Formatting, you can add things like data bars and color scales to have a chart-like appearance within your cells or makers to show you alerts (like shown in figure 5.1).

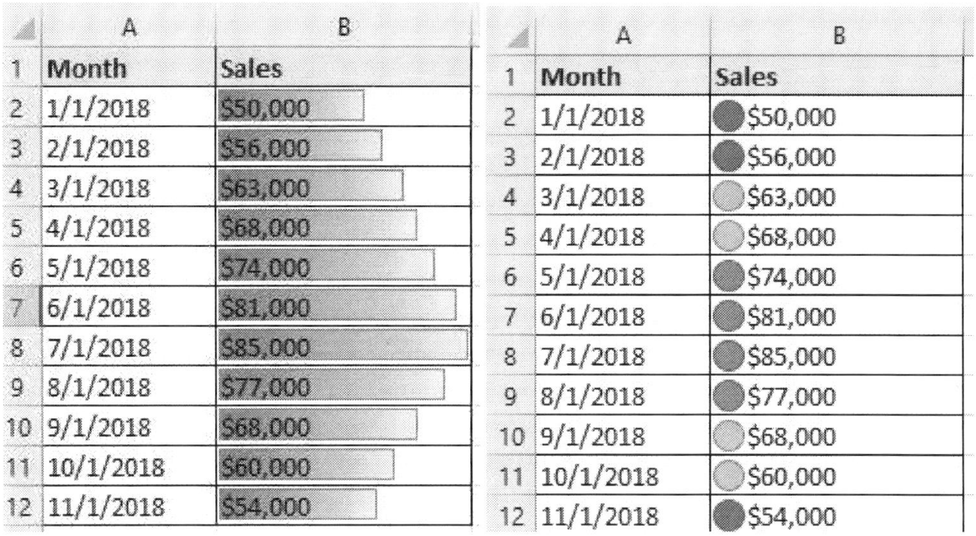

	A	B
1	Month	Sales
2	1/1/2018	$50,000
3	2/1/2018	$56,000
4	3/1/2018	$63,000
5	4/1/2018	$68,000
6	5/1/2018	$74,000
7	6/1/2018	$81,000
8	7/1/2018	$85,000
9	8/1/2018	$77,000
10	9/1/2018	$68,000
11	10/1/2018	$60,000
12	11/1/2018	$54,000

	A	B
1	Month	Sales
2	1/1/2018	$50,000
3	2/1/2018	$56,000
4	3/1/2018	$63,000
5	4/1/2018	$68,000
6	5/1/2018	$74,000
7	6/1/2018	$81,000
8	7/1/2018	$85,000
9	8/1/2018	$77,000
10	9/1/2018	$68,000
11	10/1/2018	$60,000
12	11/1/2018	$54,000

Figure 5.1

The *Format as Table* option lets you choose a color scheme to apply to your table. There are some preconfigured color schemes to choose from, or you can create your own. The *Cell Styles* option (figure 5.2) lets you apply custom formatting to a cell or group of cells based on how you want them to look.

Good, Bad and Neutral					
Normal	Bad	Good	Neutral		
Data and Model					
Calculation	Check Cell	Explanatory ...	Input	Linked Cell	Note
Output	Warning Text				
Titles and Headings					
Heading 1	Heading 2	Heading 3	Heading 4	Title	Total
Themed Cell Styles					
20% - Accent1	20% - Accent2	20% - Accent3	20% - Accent4	20% - Accent5	20% - Accent6
40% - Accent1	40% - Accent2	40% - Accent3	40% - Accent4	40% - Accent5	40% - Accent6
60% - Accent1	60% - Accent2	60% - Accent3	60% - Accent4	60% - Accent5	60% - Accent6
Accent1	Accent2	Accent3	Accent4	Accent5	Accent6
Number Format					
Comma	Comma [0]	Currency	Currency [0]	Percent	

New Cell Style...
Merge Styles...

Figure 5.2

Cells

Cells can contain various types of data from text to dates to currency, and it's always a good idea to make sure your cells use the right format so your data displays correctly. When working on a spreadsheet, you will often find the need to insert or delete cells or even entire sheets. By the way, sheets are additional "pages" you can insert into your workbook to keep information more organized. They are shown on the bottom of the Excel window (like shown in figure 5.3).

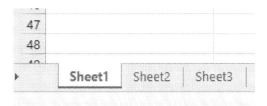

Figure 5.3

To insert a new cell, all you need to do is click on the area where you would like the new cell to be placed and tell Excel what to do with the existing cells in regards to where to move them (figure 5.4). The same goes for deleting a cell.

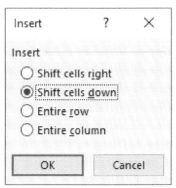

Figure 5.4

Formatting cells and worksheets is something you will be doing often, so it's a good idea to know how to go about doing so and what options you have for formatting. When you click on the *Format* button you will have several options for things like adjusting row height and renaming your sheets. If you click on the Format Cells option you will be presented with many more choices as to what you can do with your cells. As you can see in figure 5.5, there are many format options available to assign to cells, as well as settings for alignment, font, border, fill, and protection. The protection setting allows you to hide and lock cells.

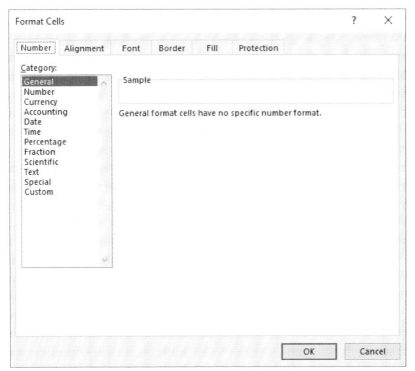

Figure 5.5

Editing

The tools in the Editing group are pretty self-explanatory. There is the *AutoSum* feature, which I will be getting to later in this chapter, as well as the *Fill* option, which can take a series of related values and continue filling the cells to complete the series. For example, if you have a column of months with the first three cells filled in with January, February, and March, you can use the Fill tool to complete the listing of months so you don't have to type them in manually.

I will be going over sorting and filtering later in this chapter, so I will skip that for now, but one last thing I want to discuss in the Editing group is the Find & Select tool. You can use this to search for values in your spreadsheet and have Excel find the next one on your sheet, or all of the matching items in your workbook. If you want to replace one value with another you can do that from here as well (figure 5.6).

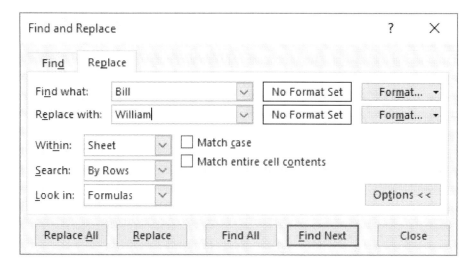

Figure 5.6

Insert Tab
The Insert tab also has some Excel-specific groups that need to be discussed.

Charts
Charts are used to display data that you choose in a specific format in order to make comparisons between fields or values. You can insert various types of charts and have them apply to the entire sheet, or to just a set of data that you choose. After you create your chart, you have the ability to edit what data is in the chart as well as the chart type. (I will be going over creating charts and graphs later in this chapter.)

Tours
Tours is an interesting feature to play with if your spreadsheet has geographical data and you want to have it show on a 3D map. For example, I have the following data in a spreadsheet (figure 5.7) showing some states and how many users (of whatever) there are per state.

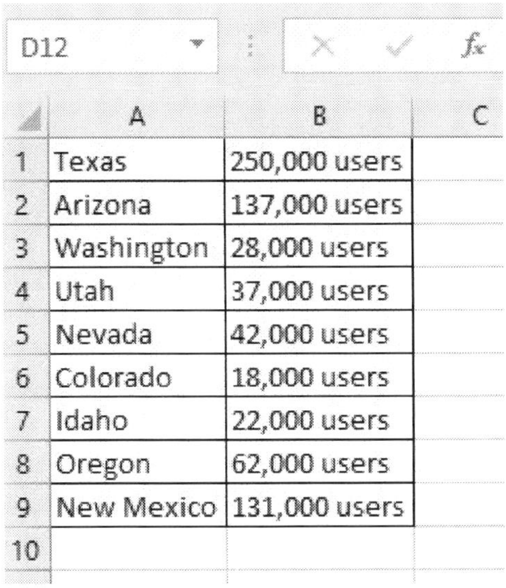

D12	▼	⋮	✕	✓	f_x

◢	A	B	C
1	Texas	250,000 users	
2	Arizona	137,000 users	
3	Washington	28,000 users	
4	Utah	37,000 users	
5	Nevada	42,000 users	
6	Colorado	18,000 users	
7	Idaho	22,000 users	
8	Oregon	62,000 users	
9	New Mexico	131,000 users	
10			

Figure 5.7

Then I can apply it to a Tour and it will display like the map shown in figure 5.8. You can customize the view as well, just like with everything else in Office.

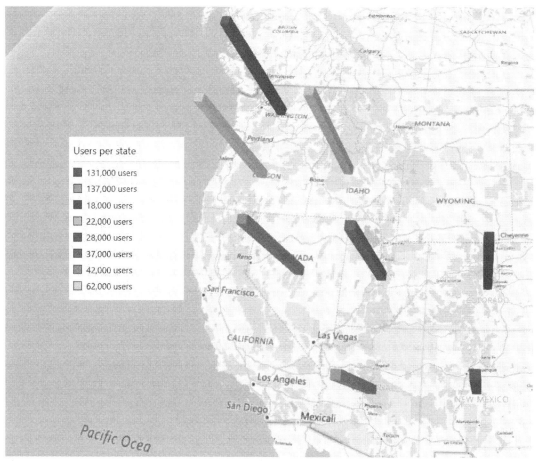

Figure 5.8

Sparklines

Sparklines are small charts inside a single cell that are used to represent a trend in your data. In figure 5.9, I have the yearly sales values from 2015 through 2018. I inserted two different Sparklines to show you what types of charts you can add to a cell. To create a Sparkline, click the cell you want the Sparkline to be in, and then highlight the cells that you want to be represented by the Sparkline. In my case it was the Sales values for all four years.

Year	2015	2016	2017	2018		
Sales	$175,000	$187,000	$162,000	$215,000		

Figure 5.9

Filters

The Filter section in the Insert tab is different from how you would normally filter data in a spreadsheet. One of the options is to use what Microsoft calls *Slicers* to slice out values that you want to filter on. For example, in figure 5.10 I have created slices for the columns labeled Units Sold, Product, and Country, and it shows all of the possible values I have from those columns.

Figure 5.10

Now in figure 5.11, I have filtered on any value for units sold, but only for the product called Paseo that have been sold in France. This will filter my sheet to only show these values under Country, Product, and Units Sold that I selected (figure 5.12). (I have cut off many of the other columns for the sake of making the example fit on the page so you can see it.)

Figure 5.11

	A	B	C	D	E	F	G	H
1	Segment ▼	Country ▼	Product 🔽	Discount Band ▼	Units Sold ▼	Manufacturi ▼	Sale Price ▼	Gross Sales ▼
24	Midmarket	France	Paseo	None	549	$ 10.00	$ 15.00	$ 8,235.00
55	Government	France	Paseo	Low	3945	$ 10.00	$ 7.00	$ 27,615.00
56	Midmarket	France	Paseo	Low	2296	$ 10.00	$ 15.00	$ 34,440.00
57	Government	France	Paseo	Low	1030	$ 10.00	$ 7.00	$ 7,210.00
79	Enterprise	France	Paseo	Low	787	$ 10.00	$ 125.00	$ 98,375.00
84	Government	France	Paseo	Low	2155	$ 10.00	$ 350.00	$ 754,250.00
110	Small Business	France	Paseo	Low	918	$ 10.00	$ 300.00	$ 275,400.00
117	Channel Partners	France	Paseo	Low	1785	$ 10.00	$ 12.00	$ 21,420.00
123	Channel Partners	France	Paseo	Low	1055	$ 10.00	$ 12.00	$ 12,660.00
157	Small Business	France	Paseo	Low	2434.5	$ 10.00	$ 300.00	$ 730,350.00
159	Channel Partners	France	Paseo	Low	1901	$ 10.00	$ 12.00	$ 22,812.00
165	Enterprise	France	Paseo	Low	1287	$ 10.00	$ 125.00	$ 160,875.00
180	Midmarket	France	Paseo	Low	2261	$ 10.00	$ 15.00	$ 33,915.00
195	Enterprise	France	Paseo	Low	2988	$ 10.00	$ 125.00	$ 373,500.00
238	Government	France	Paseo	Medium	1303	$ 10.00	$ 20.00	$ 26,060.00
240	Enterprise	France	Paseo	Medium	2385	$ 10.00	$ 125.00	$ 298,125.00
245	Midmarket	France	Paseo	Medium	2620	$ 10.00	$ 15.00	$ 39,300.00
249	Enterprise	France	Paseo	Medium	704	$ 10.00	$ 125.00	$ 88,000.00
252	Government	France	Paseo	Medium	2136	$ 10.00	$ 7.00	$ 14,952.00
274	Midmarket	France	Paseo	Medium	3801	$ 10.00	$ 15.00	$ 57,015.00
286	Government	France	Paseo	Medium	1496	$ 10.00	$ 350.00	$ 523,600.00
310	Government	France	Paseo	Medium	1757	$ 10.00	$ 20.00	$ 35,140.00
319	Government	France	Paseo	Medium	1031	$ 10.00	$ 7.00	$ 7,217.00
335	Small Business	France	Paseo	Medium	448	$ 10.00	$ 300.00	$ 134,400.00
337	Midmarket	France	Paseo	Medium	2101	$ 10.00	$ 15.00	$ 31,515.00
339	Government	France	Paseo	Medium	1535	$ 10.00	$ 20.00	$ 30,700.00
419	Midmarket	France	Paseo	Medium	1227	$ 10.00	$ 15.00	$ 18,405.00
421	Small Business	France	Paseo	Medium	1324	$ 10.00	$ 300.00	$ 397,200.00
465	Government	France	Paseo	High	1954	$ 10.00	$ 20.00	$ 39,080.00
467	Midmarket	France	Paseo	High	2167	$ 10.00	$ 15.00	$ 32,505.00
497	Government	France	Paseo	High	2532	$ 10.00	$ 7.00	$ 17,724.00
498	Channel Partners	France	Paseo	High	1198	$ 10.00	$ 12.00	$ 14,376.00
518	Channel Partners	France	Paseo	High	2425.5	$ 10.00	$ 12.00	$ 29,106.00
521	Enterprise	France	Paseo	High	2441	$ 10.00	$ 125.00	$ 305,125.00
553	Government	France	Paseo	High	1594	$ 10.00	$ 350.00	$ 557,900.00
595	Government	France	Paseo	High	2696	$ 10.00	$ 7.00	$ 18,872.00
623	Channel Partners	France	Paseo	High	1393	$ 10.00	$ 12.00	$ 16,716.00
644	Government	France	Paseo	High	1731	$ 10.00	$ 7.00	$ 12,117.00
648	Government	France	Paseo	High	1922	$ 10.00	$ 350.00	$ 672,700.00
683	Government	France	Paseo	High	293	$ 10.00	$ 20.00	$ 5,860.00

Figure 5.12

Once you create your Slices, you can click on or off whichever values you choose to filter your data.

The *Timeline* option allows you to do something similar, but it creates a timeline based on your data, allowing you to see trends as they happened. It's based on dates, so if your sheet is not set up correctly, it won't work.

Page Layout Tab

There are only a couple of things on the Page Layout tab that are exclusive to Excel, and the first couple are under the *Page Setup* group:

- **Background** – Here you can specify a background image you can use behind your cells to spruce up your spreadsheet. You can choose them from a file on your computer, or search for one online and have Excel insert it for you.

- **Print Tiles** – With this option you can choose columns or rows that you want to appear on every page when you print your spreadsheet. Think of it as being similar to headers and footers in Word.

Scale to Fit

It's very easy for your spreadsheet to get so big that it won't fit on the paper that you want to print it on. This is where the Scale to Fit option comes into play. You can scale the width or height to the number of pages you like, or you can scale it to a certain percentage.

Sheet Options

Here is where you tell Excel if you want the gridlines and headings to be shown only on the screen, or to have them show when printing. The default is to have them only show on the screen, but sometimes you may want them to print out as well. If you click the arrow for the group you will have even more options for the page setup.

Formulas Tab

Here is where things get interesting in Excel. Formulas are used to make calculations on values within cells. Functions are predefined formulas that are available in Excel for you to use against your data in your spreadsheet. The Formulas tab is broken down into four groups, as you can see in figure 5.13. I will now go over the tools in each group.

Figure 5.13

Insert Function

This is where you can insert one of the many functions that come included with Excel. Remember that a function is a predefined formula that you can use on your data. By default, the function category is set to Most Recently Used (figure 5.14), but you can use the dropdown list to select a category or try the search method to see if you can find what you are looking for.

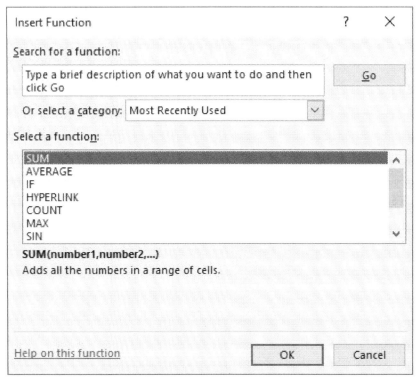

Figure 5.14

Function Library
The Function Library lists your functions and groups them into categories including Financial, Logical, Text, Date & Time, Lookup & Reference, Math & Trig, and More Functions. To use one of these functions, pick your category and then use the down arrow to select the function you would like to use.

Let's do a couple of examples. For the first one we will use the AutoSum feature, since it is one of the most commonly used functions in Excel. In our spreadsheet, we have the yearly salaries of fourteen different employees, and we want to know how much we are paying all of them together each year. We begin by highlighting all of the salaries plus one blank cell at the bottom (figure 5.15) because that is where we want the total to be.

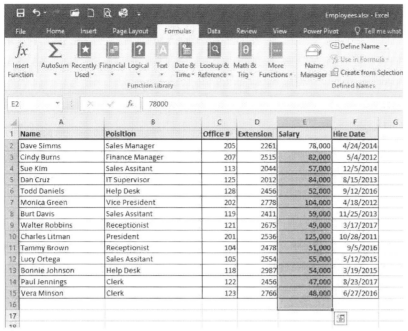

Figure 5.15

Then with the cells highlighted we click on the AutoSum button and we get the results shown in figure 5.16.

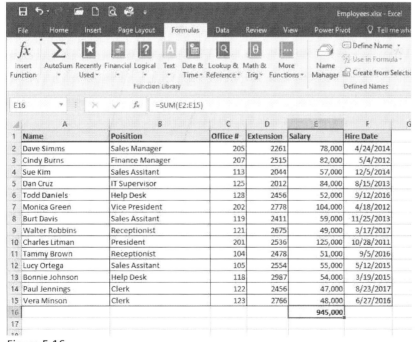

Figure 5.16

When you click on the down arrow under AutoSum, you get additional options besides sum such as average, count numbers, max, and min.

Notice how if you click in the cell with the total it will show the formula in the bar above the cells (figure 5.17). This comes in handy when troubleshooting formulas

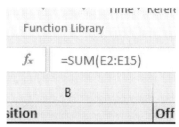

Figure 5.17

For our next example let's insert a date function into a single cell. First we will click on cell A18, and then under the Date & Time function we will choose DATE. Then we will be prompted with an arguments box (as shown in figure 5.18) where we will need to put in the year, month, and the day. I put in 2018 for the year, 11 for the month (November), and 15 for the day.

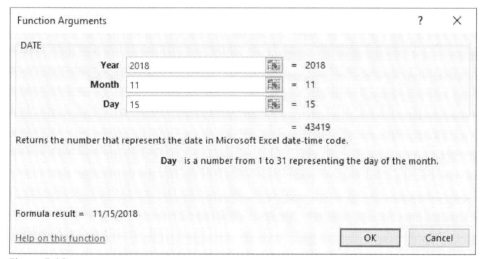

Figure 5.18

When I click OK, I get that date entered in the cell (figure 5.19).

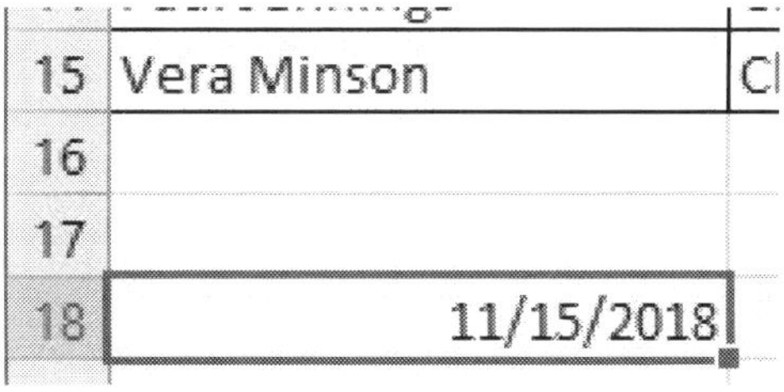

15	Vera Minson	C
16		
17		
18	11/15/2018	

Figure 5.19

Yes, this is a very basic function, but I just wanted to show you how one of the simpler ones worked. If I would have chosen TODAY from the dropdown it would have put today's date in the cell. You can play with these functions and formulas and see for yourself what they do. I will get more detailed on formulas later in the chapter, and we will create our own formulas as well.

Defined Names
You can use Defined Names to name a cell, table, or range of cells so you can then use that defined name later on in a formula so you know exactly what information you are plugging into it. So, if you have a cell with a formula that calculates a 7% sales tax and then adds it to the value of the cell above, you can name it "mytax", and then in a different area of the sheet (or even on another sheet) you can type =*mytax* as part of your formula and have Excel use that defined name in this other calculation. The Name Manager button will show you all of the defined names that you have created and what they refer to.

Formula Auditing
Formula Auditing allows you to see the relationship between formulas and cells. Going back to our employees spreadsheet where we used the AutoSum to get a total for all the yearly salaries, we can click on the cell with the total, then click on *Trace Precedents* to see that the $945,000 value came from cells E2 through E15 (figure 5.20).

| E16 | ▼ | : | × | ✓ | fx | =SUM(E2:E15) |

	A	B	C	D	E	F
1	Name	Poisition	Office #	Extension	Salary	Hire Date
2	Dave Simms	Sales Manager	205	2261	78,000	4/24/2014
3	Cindy Burns	Finance Manager	207	2515	82,000	5/4/2012
4	Sue Kim	Sales Assitant	113	2044	57,000	12/5/2014
5	Dan Cruz	IT Supervisor	125	2012	84,000	8/15/2013
6	Todd Daniels	Help Desk	128	2456	52,000	9/12/2016
7	Monica Green	Vice President	202	2778	104,000	4/18/2012
8	Burt Davis	Sales Assitant	119	2411	59,000	11/25/2013
9	Walter Robbins	Receptionist	121	2675	49,000	3/17/2017
10	Charles Litman	President	201	2536	125,000	10/28/2011
11	Tammy Brown	Receptionist	104	2478	51,000	9/5/2016
12	Lucy Ortega	Sales Assitant	105	2554	55,000	5/12/2015
13	Bonnie Johnson	Help Desk	118	2987	54,000	3/19/2015
14	Paul Jennings	Clerk	122	2456	47,000	8/23/2017
15	Vera Minson	Clerk	123	2766	48,000	6/27/2016
16					945,000	

Figure 5.20

Another thing you can do with formula auditing is look at the dependents of a cell to see which cell depends on the selected cell. In cell A19, we have a formula that tells us the percentage of our 2 million dollar salary budget has been taken by the employees in the list (figure 5.21).

| E16 | ▼ | : | × | ✓ | fx | =SUM(E2:E15) |

	A	B	C	D	E	F
1	Name	Poisition	Office #	Extension	Salary	Hire Date
2	Dave Simms	Sales Manager	205	2261	78,000	4/24/2014
3	Cindy Burns	Finance Manager	207	2515	82,000	5/4/2012
4	Sue Kim	Sales Assitant	113	2044	57,000	12/5/2014
5	Dan Cruz	IT Supervisor	125	2012	84,000	8/15/2013
6	Todd Daniels	Help Desk	128	2456	52,000	9/12/2016
7	Monica Green	Vice President	202	2778	104,000	4/18/2012
8	Burt Davis	Sales Assitant	119	2411	59,000	11/25/2013
9	Walter Robbins	Receptionist	121	2675	49,000	3/17/2017
10	Charles Litman	President	201	2536	125,000	10/28/2011
11	Tammy Brown	Receptionist	104	2478	51,000	9/5/2016
12	Lucy Ortega	Sales Assitant	105	2554	55,000	5/12/2015
13	Bonnie Johnson	Help Desk	118	2987	54,000	3/19/2015
14	Paul Jennings	Clerk	122	2456	47,000	8/23/2017
15	Vera Minson	Clerk	123	2766	48,000	6/27/2016
16					945,000	
17	Yearly Salary Budget - 2M					
18	Percentage of budged used					
19	0.4725					

Figure 5.21

So now when we click on cell E16 and then click the *Trace Dependents* button, we see that cell A19 is dependent on cell E16 to get its value. Here is the formula for cell A19 in case you were wondering (=E16/2000000).

Other things you can do from the Formula Auditing group is click on the *Show Formulas* button to have all the formulas in the sheet displayed in their corresponding cells. The *Error Checking* button will show you any errors you might have in your formulas, which might help you if things are not working the way they should. The *Evaluate Formula* button will look at each part of your formula individually and run it to show you the results. (It's something that you can use for more complex formulas.) The *Watch Window* button lets you add cells to be watched so that when something changes their value, it will be easier to see. For example, I changed Dave Simms' salary from $78,000 to $100,000, and the Watch Window updated the value as well (figure 5.22), making it easier to monitor if you have many cells you need to keep an eye on.

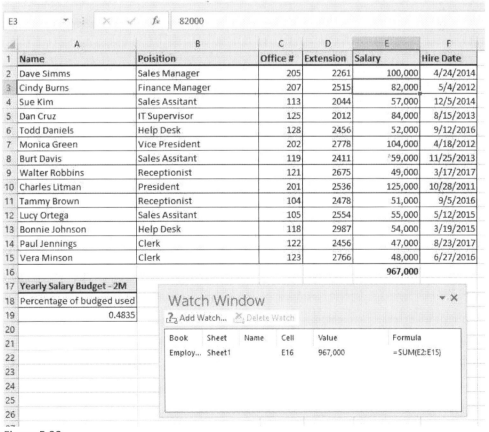

Figure 5.22

Calculation

The last group on the Formulas tab is called Calculation, and here is where you can have Excel perform calculations when you want it to rather than automatically. The *Calculations* button will let you set your calculation options to automatic, manual except for data tables, and manually. If you have automatic calculations turned off, then you can use the *Calculate Now* and *Calculate Sheet* buttons to have Excel run your calculations on demand. The default is to have everything set to automatic.

Data Tab

The Data tab is used to configure data sources and their connections for your spreadsheet, as well as offering filtering and analysis tools (figure 5.23). So let's get started discussing what kinds of tasks you can perform using the tools from this tab.

Figure 5.23

Get External Data

Excel is capable of getting its data from an external source such as a text file, database server, webpage, and so on. By clicking on the *Get External Data* button, you can choose the appropriate data source and then have that data imported directly into your spreadsheet. This comes in handy when someone has, for example, a file with a listing of names and addresses that you want to import into your sheet without having to type them all in manually, or if you want to connect to a database and have your spreadsheet updatable when changes to the database are made.

Get & Transform

This group allows you to gather information from various sources so you can manipulate it to suit your needs. Then you can run queries on this data to get the specific information you are looking for. A "query" is a request for information from a data source that presents the data to you in a specified format such as a table, graph, chart, and so on. These queries can be run against files, databases, and other things.

The *Show Queries* button will list any queries that you have created in the workbook you are working with while the *From Table* button will link a query to a table that you have selected in your workbook.

Sort & Filter

This group is commonly used by new and veteran Excel users because sorting and filtering your data makes it much easier to work with. Sorting is when you organize the data in a consistent way, such as alphabetically or numerically. Filtering is when you have Excel only show you the data you have requested to see.

To sort your data you need to select what information you want sorted, and then you can click the *A to Z* or *Z to A* buttons, which will sort alphabetically. When you have selected cells that have a different type of data, such as numbers or dates, these buttons will sort in numeric or data order, even though they still say A to Z and Z to A.

If you want to get more detailed with your sorting then you can click the *Sort* button and choose the options that will sort the data the way you want it sorted. As you can see in figure 5.24, I have sorted by Position, sorted A to Z, and then by Salary going smallest to largest. To add a new sort category simply click on the *Add Level* button. You can also delete levels and copy them as well.

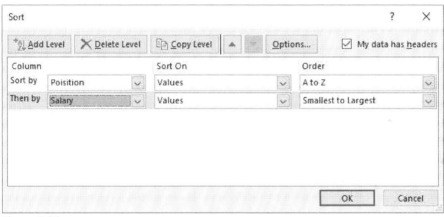

Figure 5.24

As you can see in figure 5.25, the data has been sorted first by position name and then by salary, and our salary total remains the same even when sorted differently.

	A	B	C	D	E	F
1	Name	Position	Office #	Extension	Salary	Hire Date
2	Dave Simms	Sales Manager	205	2261	100,000	4/24/2014
3	Cindy Burns	Finance Manager	207	2515	82,000	5/4/2012
4	Sue Kim	Sales Assitant	113	2044	57,000	12/5/2014
5	Dan Cruz	IT Supervisor	125	2012	84,000	8/15/2013
6	Todd Daniels	Help Desk	128	2456	52,000	9/12/2016
7	Monica Green	Vice President	202	2778	104,000	4/18/2012
8	Burt Davis	Sales Assitant	119	2411	59,000	11/25/2013
9	Walter Robbins	Receptionist	121	2675	49,000	3/17/2017
10	Charles Litman	President	201	2536	125,000	10/28/2011
11	Tammy Brown	Receptionist	104	2478	51,000	9/5/2016
12	Lucy Ortega	Sales Assitant	105	2554	55,000	5/12/2015
13	Bonnie Johnson	Help Desk	118	2987	54,000	3/19/2015
14	Paul Jennings	Clerk	122	2456	47,000	8/23/2017
15	Vera Minson	Clerk	123	2766	48,000	6/27/2016
16					967,000	

Figure 5.25

Now for filtering, which we had a taste of when I discussed the Slicer tool that Excel uses to slice out the pieces of your data that you want to see. (The Slicer was on the Insert tab in the Filters group.)

Another way to filter in Excel is to select the data you want to filter on and then click on the *Filter* button. As you can see in figure 5.26, each column now has a dropdown arrow which will allow you to select which values from that column you want to filter on.

	A	B	C	D	E	F
1	Name	Position	Office #	Extension	Salary	Hire Date
2	Dave Simms	Sales Manager	205	2261	100,000	4/24/2014
3	Cindy Burns	Finance Manager	207	2515	82,000	5/4/2012
4	Sue Kim	Sales Assitant	113	2044	57,000	12/5/2014
5	Dan Cruz	IT Supervisor	125	2012	84,000	8/15/2013
6	Todd Daniels	Help Desk	128	2456	52,000	9/12/2016
7	Monica Green	Vice President	202	2778	104,000	4/18/2012
8	Burt Davis	Sales Assitant	119	2411	59,000	11/25/2013
9	Walter Robbins	Receptionist	121	2675	49,000	3/17/2017
10	Charles Litman	President	201	2536	125,000	10/28/2011
11	Tammy Brown	Receptionist	104	2478	51,000	9/5/2016
12	Lucy Ortega	Sales Assitant	105	2554	55,000	5/12/2015
13	Bonnie Johnson	Help Desk	118	2987	54,000	3/19/2015
14	Paul Jennings	Clerk	122	2456	47,000	8/23/2017
15	Vera Minson	Clerk	123	2766	48,000	6/27/2016

Figure 5.26

Figure 5.27 shows that I clicked the arrow on the Position column and selected the Help Desk and Sales Assistant positions. When I click OK, the results are shown in figure 5.28, and you can see that the only positions shown are now Help Desk and Sales Assitant.

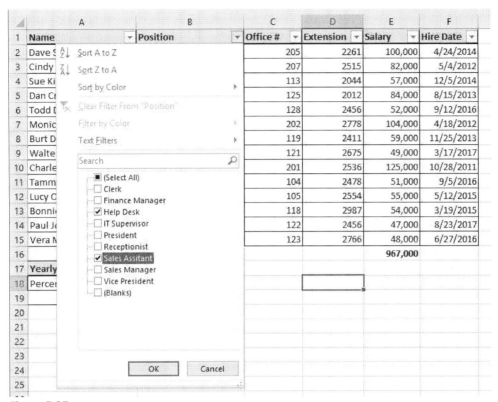

Figure 5.27

	A	B	C	D	E	F
1	Name	Position	Office #	Extension	Salary	Hire Date
4	Sue Kim	Sales Assitant	113	2044	57,000	12/5/2014
6	Todd Daniels	Help Desk	128	2456	52,000	9/12/2016
8	Burt Davis	Sales Assitant	119	2411	59,000	11/25/2013
12	Lucy Ortega	Sales Assitant	105	2554	55,000	5/12/2015
13	Bonnie Johnson	Help Desk	118	2987	54,000	3/19/2015

Figure 5.28

You can filter on multiple columns as well if needed. To remove the filter, simply click on the Clear button and you will be back to normal.

The *Reapply* button is used when you change data in your worksheet and need to reapply the filter to update the results. The *Advanced* button is used to create more advanced filters, which are beyond the scope of the book.

Data Tools

The Data Tools group has some interesting tools that can come in handy when you need to manipulate your data into a format that works better for your spreadsheet.

One very useful feature is called *Text to Columns,* and it will take data in one column and separate it out into multiple columns based on your requirements. For example, in figure 5.29 we have a list of names in column A formatted last name comma first name. Let's say we want to have a separate column for last name and for first name, but don't want to cut and paste each one individually. This is where Text to Columns can help you out. You simply highlight your column, click on the Text to Columns button, and choose the format you want. Excel does the rest.

	A		A	B
1	Simms, Dave	1	Simms	Dave
2	Burns, Cindy	2	Burns	Cindy
3	Kim, Sue	3	Kim	Sue
4	Cruz, Dan	4	Cruz	Dan
5	Daniels, Todd	5	Daniels	Todd
6	Green, Monica	6	Green	Monica
7	Davis, Burt	7	Davis	Burt
8	Robbins, Walter	8	Robbins	Walter
9	Litman, Charles	9	Litman	Charles
10	Brown, Tammy	10	Brown	Tammy
11	Ortega, Lucy	11	Ortega	Lucy
12	Johnson, Bonnie	12	Johnson	Bonnie
13	Jennings, Paul	13	Jennings	Paul
14	Minson, Vera	14	Minson	Vera

Figure 5.29

Flash Fill does something similar in that it will recognize the pattern you are entering data in and try and fill in the rest of the information for you. Going back to our list of names formatted last name comma first, we now want to have them listed first name and then last name in a new column. After entering a couple of them manually to let Excel know what you are doing, you can then click on the next empty cell and click the Flash Fill button. Excel will fill in the rest using the format you stared.

Other tools in this group include the *Remove Duplicates,* which removes duplicate entries in cells when you highlight a range of cells and click the Remove Duplicates button. *Data Validation* lets you set rules as to what kind of data or values can be entered in particular cells. Let's say you only want to allow a certain date range to be entered in certain cells. Once this setting is configured on your cells, when someone tries to enter some data that doesn't match the rule, they will get an error (as shown in figure 5.30).

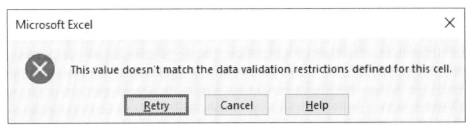

Figure 5.30

The *Consolidate* feature will take data from different ranges and then consolidate that data in one place. Finally, the *Relationships* feature makes a connection between two tables of data based on matching data from each table. Then you can build pivot tables and reports from the matching data in your tables.

Forecast
The Forecast feature in Excel is used to get a prediction of a future value based on the existing data in your spreadsheet. In figure 5.31, I have a table with month values from 1/1/18 through 12/1/19 and their related sales. Then I highlighted the table, clicked on the *Forecast Sheet* button, entered the date I wanted the forecast to end on, and clicked OK. Figure 5.32 shows the results along with a graph of predicted sales. It also created columns for the forecast, as well as the lower and upper confidence bounds which tells you the degree of confidence Excel uses in the forecast. The default setting is 95%, but you can change it if you like.

	A	B
1	1/1/2018	$50,000
2	2/1/2018	$56,000
3	3/1/2018	$63,000
4	4/1/2018	$68,000
5	5/1/2018	$74,000
6	6/1/2018	$81,000
7	7/1/2018	$85,000
8	8/1/2018	$77,000
9	9/1/2018	$68,000
10	10/1/2018	$60,000
11	11/1/2018	$54,000
12	12/1/2018	$51,000
13	1/1/2019	$52,000
14	2/1/2019	$54,000
15	3/1/2019	$65,000
16	4/1/2019	$72,000
17	5/1/2019	$78,000
18	6/1/2019	$84,000
19	7/1/2019	$89,000
20	8/1/2019	$80,000
21	9/1/2019	$72,000
22	10/1/2019	$65,000
23	11/1/2019	$57,000
24	12/1/2019	$53,000

Figure 5.31

Timeline	Values	Forecast	Lower Confidence Bound	Upper Confidence Bound
1/1/2018	$50,000			
2/1/2018	$56,000			
3/1/2018	$63,000			
4/1/2018	$68,000			
5/1/2018	$74,000			
6/1/2018	$81,000			
7/1/2018	$85,000			
8/1/2018	$77,000			
9/1/2018	$68,000			
10/1/2018	$60,000			
11/1/2018	$54,000			
12/1/2018	$51,000			
1/1/2019	$52,000			
2/1/2019	$54,000			
3/1/2019	$65,000			
4/1/2019	$72,000			
5/1/2019	$78,000			
6/1/2019	$84,000			
7/1/2019	$89,000			
8/1/2019	$80,000			
9/1/2019	$72,000			
10/1/2019	$65,000			
11/1/2019	$57,000			
12/1/2019	$53,000	$53,000	$53,000	$53,000
1/1/2020		$53,192	$40,234	$66,150
2/1/2020		$53,384	$35,068	$71,701
3/1/2020		$53,577	$31,140	$76,013
4/1/2020		$53,769	$27,853	$79,685
5/1/2020		$53,961	$24,974	$82,947
6/1/2020		$54,153	$22,386	$85,920
7/1/2020		$54,345	$20,017	$88,673
8/1/2020		$54,537	$17,822	$91,252
9/1/2020		$54,730	$15,769	$93,690
10/1/2020		$54,922	$13,834	$96,009
11/1/2020		$55,114	$12,000	$98,228
12/1/2020		$55,306	$10,253	$100,359

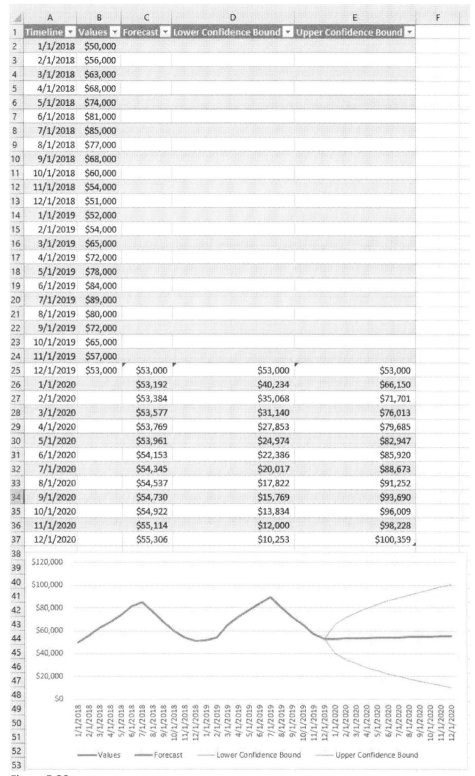

Figure 5.32

My example might not be the best way to show this without using a table with more detailed information, but I just wanted to give you an idea of how forecasting works.

There is also the *What-if Analysis*, which can be used to get an idea of how your results would change if you changed a particular value in your table. You have three options to play with when doing your analysis:

- **Scenario Manager** – If you want to play around with a couple of scenarios to see how each will affect your results, then use the Scenario Manager.

- **Goal Seek** – If you have a goal you want to reach and want to find out what values would need to be adjusted to reach that goal, you would use this option.

- **Data Table** - If you have multiple formulas that all use one common variable, you can use a Data Table to see all the outcomes in one place.

Outline

If you want to arrange your data in a format that is easier to view, then you can try and have Excel create an outline for you. Then you can expand or shrink your table to show only the data you want to look at.

Figure 5.33 shows a table with monthly sales figures from four separate divisions. These sales are totaled once per quarter, and then once at the end of the year for each division. The Outline feature will allow us to change what data is shown with only a click of the mouse.

⬧	A	B	C	D	E
1		2018 Sales Numbers			
2					
3		Division 1	Division 2	Division 3	Division 4
4	January	$5,300	$2,500	$7,800	$2,200
5	February	$5,500	$3,500	$6,500	$2,500
6	March	$4,800	$2,200	$6,800	$2,200
7	Q1 Total	$15,600	$8,200	$21,100	$6,900
8	April	$5,200	$3,400	$6,900	$3,200
9	May	$4,700	$5,100	$7,400	$3,100
10	June	$6,200	$5,300	$7,500	$2,800
11	Q2 Total	$16,100	$13,800	$21,800	$9,100
12	July	$5,500	$2,800	$6,900	$3,500
13	August	$6,300	$1,700	$7,100	$3,700
14	September	$4,800	$1,900	$7,000	$3,000
15	Q3 Total	$16,600	$6,400	$21,000	$10,200
16	October	$5,300	$2,800	$6,900	$2,700
17	November	$5,100	$4,200	$5,500	$3,200
18	December	$5,000	$4,000	$5,700	$3,100
19	Q4 Total	$15,400	$11,000	$18,100	$9,000
20	Yearly Total	$63,700	$39,400	$82,000	$35,200

Figure 5.33

The first thing we need to do is click on the *Group* button and then select *Auto Outline*. Figure 5.34 shows the results of this, and you can see that things look pretty much the same except there are some markers on the side and three boxes labeled 1,2, and 3.

1 2 3		A	B	C	D	E
	1		**2018 Sales Numbers**			
	2					
	3		Division 1	Division 2	Division 3	Division 4
	4	January	$5,300	$2,500	$7,800	$2,200
	5	February	$5,500	$3,500	$6,500	$2,500
	6	March	$4,800	$2,200	$6,800	$2,200
	7	**Q1 Total**	**$15,600**	**$8,200**	**$21,100**	**$6,900**
	8	April	$5,200	$3,400	$6,900	$3,200
	9	May	$4,700	$5,100	$7,400	$3,100
	10	June	$6,200	$5,300	$7,500	$2,800
	11	**Q2 Total**	**$16,100**	**$13,800**	**$21,800**	**$9,100**
	12	July	$5,500	$2,800	$6,900	$3,500
	13	August	$6,300	$1,700	$7,100	$3,700
	14	September	$4,800	$1,900	$7,000	$3,000
	15	**Q3 Total**	**$16,600**	**$6,400**	**$21,000**	**$10,200**
	16	October	$5,300	$2,800	$6,900	$2,700
	17	November	$5,100	$4,200	$5,500	$3,200
	18	December	$5,000	$4,000	$5,700	$3,100
	19	**Q4 Total**	**$15,400**	**$11,000**	**$18,100**	**$9,000**
	20	**Yearly Total**	**$63,700**	**$39,400**	**$82,000**	**$35,200**

Figure 5.34

If we click on the box labeled 2, it will shrink our data into only the quarterly and yearly sales numbers (figure 5.35).

1 2 3		A	B	C	D	E
	1		**2018 Sales Numbers**			
	2					
	3		Division 1	Division 2	Division 3	Division 4
+	7	**Q1 Total**	**$15,600**	**$8,200**	**$21,100**	**$6,900**
+	11	**Q2 Total**	**$16,100**	**$13,800**	**$21,800**	**$9,100**
+	15	**Q3 Total**	**$16,600**	**$6,400**	**$21,000**	**$10,200**
+	19	**Q4 Total**	**$15,400**	**$11,000**	**$18,100**	**$9,000**
–	20	**Yearly Total**	**$63,700**	**$39,400**	**$82,000**	**$35,200**

Figure 5.35

Then clicking on the box labeled 1 shrinks it down even further, so only the Yearly Total results are shown (figure 5.36).

1 2 3		A	B	C	D	E
	1		**2018 Sales Numbers**			
	2					
	3		Division 1	Division 2	Division 3	Division 4
+	20	Yearly Total	$63,700	$39,400	$82,000	$35,200

Figure 5.36

You can use the + and – buttons to expand and shrink the data in the table as well.

View Tab

The View tab in Excel has many of the same groups as it does for other programs, but it does have a couple of groups specific to Excel which I would now like to go over.

Show

This group is pretty self-explanatory, and it gives you options as to what you want to display on the screen as you are working in Excel. The options include the ruler, formula bar, gridlines, and headings, and they are all enabled by default. If you don't want one or more of these items showing, then all you need to do is uncheck the box next to it.

Window

The options here are pretty much the same as with other Office programs, but one thing I do want to mention because it's commonly used is the *Freeze Panes* tool. This is used when you want to keep a portion of your sheet visible while scrolling through the rest. Let's say you have a row on the top of your spreadsheet with column titles and the data below spans hundreds of rows. Normally when you scroll down the sheet the title row will disappear out of view. If you freeze the pane on that row, then it will stick at the top of the sheet as you are scrolling down so you always know what column name goes with what data.

Power Pivot Tab

This tab gets us into the advanced features of Excel, therefore, I'm just going to give you the quick overview in case you want to turn yourself into an Excel power user in the future. As you can see from figure 5.37, the Power Pivot tab doesn't have as many options as the other tabs, but it's still a very powerful area in Excel.

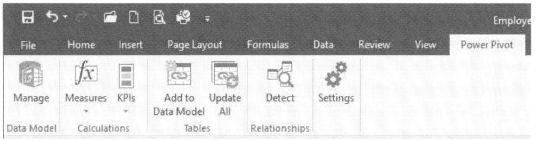

Figure 5.37

Power Pivot is used for data modeling to create complex calculations and working with larger than normal data sets. In fact, you can import hundreds of millions of rows of data from many different data sources into a single Excel workbook to build things such as Pivot Tables and Pivot Charts. Without Power Pivot, you are limited to how much data you can import, and having too much data can start to slow down Excel because it can't handle the load.

Creating a Spreadsheet

Now that you have a better understanding of what all the tabs and groups in Excel do, it's time to make a spreadsheet and put your newfound knowledge to work. When you click on New from the Quick Access Toolbar, Excel will open a new blank workbook. If you click on new from the File tab, then Excel will give you a selection of templates that you can use to build your spreadsheet on (figure 5.38). You will also get the option to create a new blank workbook as well.

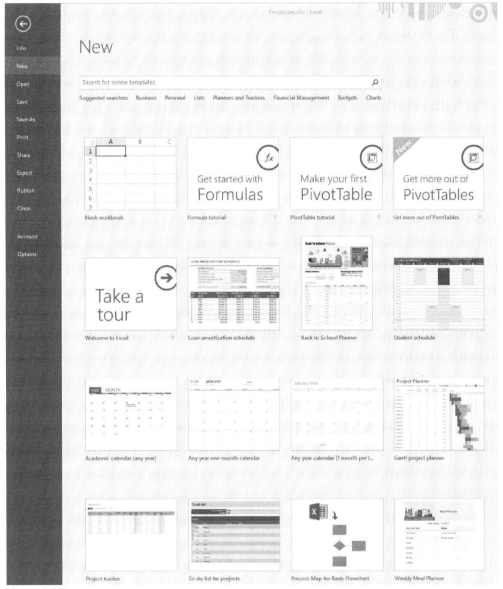

Figure 5.38

For our tasks, we are going to start with a blank workbook so we can customize everything ourselves. Once you have the blank workbook open, you are free to start adding or importing data and then formatting it the way that works best for you.

Let's begin by creating a table for the number of hits our make believe webpage gets per month so we can track any loss or gain of website visits. First, we will enter our heading information in row A. Let's add Month, Hits, and Hits Lost or Gained so it looks like figure 5.39.

	A	B	C	D
1	Month	Hits	Hits Lost or Gained	
2				
3				

Figure 5.39

You might have noticed that the Hits Lost or Gained heading goes into cell D as well. We will fix that when we get to formatting.

Next, we will add in the months of the year starting with January. Type the word January into cell A2. Now, instead of typing the rest of the months manually, click on cell A2 and put your mouse cursor in the lower right hand corner of the cell until it turns into a black cross (as shown in figure 5.40).

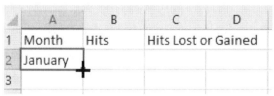

	A	B	C	D
1	Month	Hits	Hits Lost or Gained	
2	January			
3				

Figure 5.40

Then, while holding down the mouse button, drag the box down until column A is filled from January to December. Then, for the number of hits, add the following to match my example (figure 5.41) if you are playing along on your computer.

	A	B	C	D
1	Month	Hits	Hits Lost or Gained	
2	January	4500		
3	February	4800		
4	March	4100		
5	April	4000		
6	May	3500		
7	June	3800		
8	July	4900		
9	August	3800		
10	Septembe	5000		
11	October	4800		
12	Novembe	4100		
13	December	3700		

Figure 5.41

Now we need to have Excel calculate the hits lost or gained each month so we don't have to do the math ourselves. I will be going over formulas in more detail later in the chapter, but for now we will make a simple one for this column. To find the hits lost or gained, we need to subtract the first number from the one after that. So for February we would subtract February's hits from January's hits to get 300 hits gained for February (figure5.42).

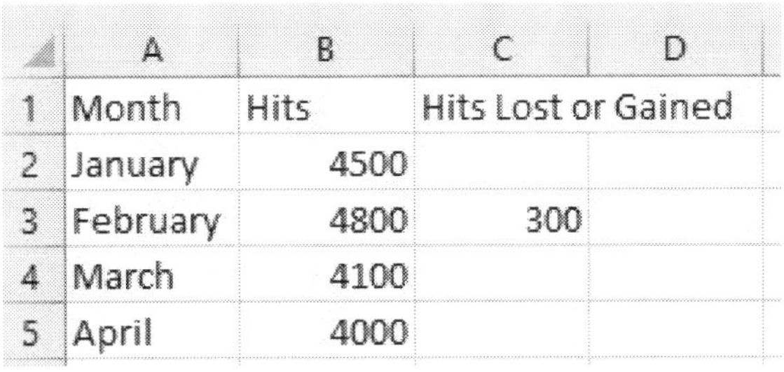

	A	B	C	D
1	Month	Hits	Hits Lost or Gained	
2	January	4500		
3	February	4800	300	
4	March	4100		
5	April	4000		

Figure 5.42

The formula I used to get this number was =B3-B2, which means 4800-4500, which equals 300. You can either type that formula in the cell, or type in an equals sign (=) and then click on cell B3. Then type a minus sign (-) and click on cell B2 and press enter. It should look like figure 5.43 before you press enter.

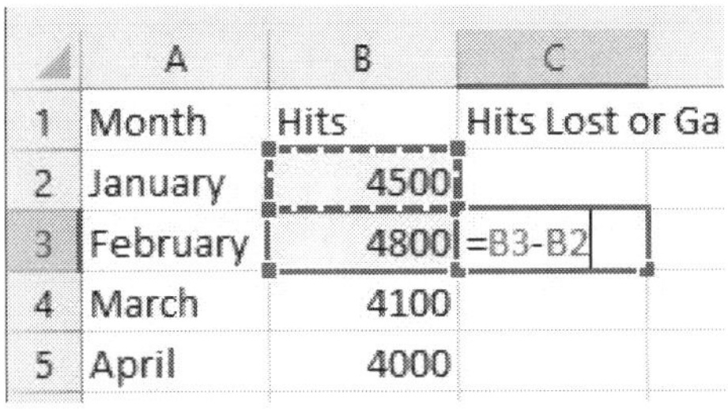

	A	B	C
1	Month	Hits	Hits Lost or Ga
2	January	4500	
3	February	4800	=B3-B2
4	March	4100	
5	April	4000	

Figure 5.43

Now you can use the autofill method like you did for the month to have Excel fill in the rest of the cells with that formula. As you can see in figure 5.44, all the values are there and the loss of hits have a minus sign in front of them.

	A	B	C	D
1	Month	Hits	Hits Lost or Gained	
2	January	4500		
3	February	4800	300	
4	March	4100	-700	
5	April	4000	-100	
6	May	3500	-500	
7	June	3800	300	
8	July	4900	1100	
9	August	3800	-1100	
10	Septembe	5000	1200	
11	October	4800	-200	
12	Novembe	4100	-700	
13	December	3700	-400	

Figure 5.44

Now before we move on to formatting our sheet, let's add a new sheet so we can use that later on. If you look down at the bottom of you sheet you should have a tab that says Sheet1, and there should be a + sign next to it. To add another sheet simply click on the + sign and Excel will add a new sheet named Sheet2 (like shown in figure 5.45).

Figure 5.45

You can also right click on an existing sheet and choose the *Insert* option to add another sheet. Other things you can do from the right click menu is delete a sheet and rename a sheet. If you want to rearrange the order of your sheets simply click on the one you want to move and drag it to the left or right of whatever sheet you want it next to.

Formatting a Spreadsheet
Now that we have our spreadsheet created, it's time to start formatting it to make it look more presentable and to make people think we know what we're doing!

Formatting will also make your spreadsheet easier to read and make certain data stand out more than others (if that's what you are going for).

Let's begin by fixing our column width so our headers line up correctly. The Month and Hits Lost or Gained columns need to be widened a little to make all the text fit the way we like. In order to do so, we can put our mouse cursor on the grey line between columns A and B until it makes that familiar black cross. Then we can drag to the right until the column is as wide as we need it to be. We can do the same for the Hits Lost or Gained column by clicking and dragging between columns B and C. Just because the text goes into Column D doesn't mean that it's actually in that column, but rather it's just overlapping on the screen.

If you have a lot of columns that need to be adjusted, there is a way to do it all at once. Simply click on the upper left corner of the sheet to highlight the entire thing (as shown in figure 5.46), then you can simply choose any column you like, make the cross with the cursor, and double click. This will auto fit every column on the sheet.

	A	B	C	D	E	F
1	Month	Hits	Hits Lost or Gained			
2	January	4500				
3	February	4800	300			
4	March	4100	-700			
5	April	4000	-100			
6	May	3500	-500			
7	June	3800	300			
8	July	4900	1100			
9	August	3800	-1100			
10	September	5000	1200			
11	October	4800	-200			
12	November	4100	-700			
13	December	3700	-400			
14						
15						

Figure 5.46

Notice in figure 5.47 that it shrunk down the Hits column because it adjusts it to the size of the largest cell entry. If you don't like the way it looks, simply adjust the Hits column manually to make it a little bigger.

	A	B	C
1	Month	Hits	Hits Lost or Gained
2	January	4500	
3	February	4800	300
4	March	4100	-700
5	April	4000	-100
6	May	3500	-500
7	June	3800	300
8	July	4900	1100
9	August	3800	-1100
10	September	5000	1200
11	October	4800	-200
12	November	4100	-700
13	December	3700	-400

Figure 5.47

Another way to make the data fit better in the table is to adjust the row height. You can use the same method for increasing the row height as you do for the column width. To make sure all rows are exactly the same, you can highlight them all at once by clicking on the numbers you want to change, right clicking anywhere on the selected rows, choosing *Row Height,* and then typing in a larger number.

Next we want to adjust the numbers in the Hits and also the Hits Lost or Gained column so they are left justified (just like the month column). You can do this one column at a time or both at once, which makes more sense. To do this simply select all the cells in both columns, go to the Insert tab, and under the Alignment group click on the Align Left button to have all the cells aligned to the left.

Tip

To make it so all future entries in a column are aligned the same way as the existing data you can click on the column letter to highlight the entire column itself and format it the way you like.

Now we are going to add a little color to our sheet to make things stand out better, but first let's make the header text a little bigger and bolder. To do this, highlight cells A1, B1, and C1 and click the B for bold under the *Font* group on the insert tab. (Or press Ctrl-b on your keyboard.) Then from the same Font group make the text size 16, and then readjust the width for column C. Now, with the cells highlighted again, click on the *Fill Color* bucket to fill in the cells. If you don't like the default yellow, you can choose a different color from the dropdown arrow.

You might have noticed that we don't have any lines on our sheet except for the grey background lines. Let's fix that by highlighting all of the cells with data in them, going to the *Border* tool in the Font group, and selecting the one called All Borders. If you don't remember which is the Border tool, simply hold your mouse over the various icons to see the tool tip. Your table should now look similar to figure 5.48.

	A	B	C	D
1	**Month**	**Hits**	**Hits Lost or Gained**	
2	January	4500		
3	February	4800	300	
4	March	4100	-700	
5	April	4000	-100	
6	May	3500	-500	
7	June	3800	300	
8	July	4900	1100	
9	August	3800	-1100	
10	September	5000	1200	
11	October	4800	-200	
12	November	4100	-700	
13	December	3700	-400	
14				
15				

Figure 5.48

Another thing I think needs to be changed is rather than having the negative numbers showing with the minus sign in front of them, I would rather have them appear in red. To do this we need to highlight all the cells in the Hits Lost or Gained column that have numbers, right click anywhere in that highlighted range, and choose *Format Cells*.

Next go to the Number tab (figure 5.49) and choose the Number category, change the Decimal places to 0, and choose the second choice for Negative numbers, which is to show them in red. (You will have to take my word that it's red if you are reading this book in black and white.)

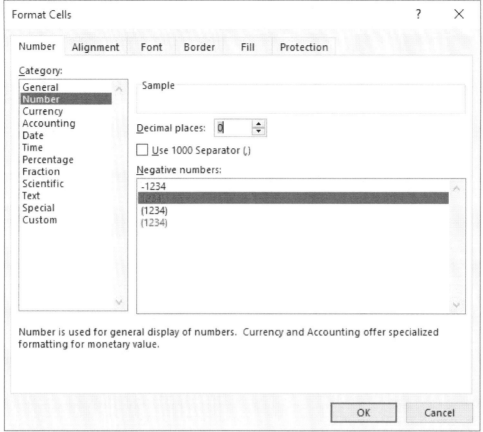

Figure 5.49

Then click OK, and now the negative numbers in column C will show in red and without the minus sign next to them.

Formulas

Now that things are looking good, it's time to add some more formulas to our spreadsheet to get some more useful information out of our data. Let's start with something easy and get a total of all the hits for the year. The easiest way to do this is to use the *AutoSum* feature, which uses one of the most commonly used formulas in Excel.

Highlight cell B14, because that is where we want the total to be. Then drag up all the way to cell B2, which is our first number on the list. Click on the AutoSum button on the Home tab or Formulas tab and you will see the results right away. You should have got 51,000 for your result.

Now we will get the average of the same numbers. To begin, delete the 51,000 from the cell (because that is where we are going to put our average) and highlight cells B14 up through B2. Then on the Formulas tab click the down arrow under AutoSum and choose Average. You should now have 4250 showing in cell B14.

These types of formulas are easy because you are simply highlighting a range of cells and telling Excel what to do with them. But what if you want to have the results in a different place? One way to do this is by doing the same process and then dragging that cell to a new location because the formula will follow along with it. If you look at figure 5.50, you will see that I moved the 4250 average to cell D1, but the formula remains the same as shown in the formula box above the cells (=AVERAGE(B2:B13)).

D2					f_x	=AVERAGE(B2:B13)	

	A	B	C	D
1	**Month**	**Hits**	**Hits Lost or Gained**	
2	January	4500		4250
3	February	4800	300	
4	March	4100	700	
5	April	4000	100	
6	May	3500	500	
7	June	3800	300	
8	July	4900	1100	
9	August	3800	1100	
10	September	5000	1200	
11	October	4800	200	
12	November	4100	700	
13	December	3700	400	

Figure 5.50

To drag the cell and keep its contents intact, you need to position the mouse cursor on the edge of the cell until it makes a cross with arrows on each end and then drag the cell to where you want it to go.

Now we will create a simple formula by hand in a cell of our choosing. For the next example we want to get the average hits for the first six months of the year and then the average hits for the last six months. So, to do that, we need to add up all the values in column B for January through June and divide it by 6 for the number of months in the first half of the year. We will put this number in cell D14. Then we need to do the same for the last six months of the year. We will put that number in cell D15. As you can see in figure 5.51, we get 4116.67 hits for the average for the first six months of the year. The formula used was **=SUM(B2:B7)/6** which says to add up the numbers in cells B2 through B7 and then divide that number by 6. Then for the second half of the year the formula would be **=SUM(B7:B13)/6**.

	A	B	C	D
	Month	Hits	Hits Lost or Gained	
2	January	4500		
3	February	4800	300	
4	March	4100	700	
5	April	4000	100	
6	May	3500	500	
7	June	3800	300	
8	July	4900	1100	
9	August	3800	1100	
10	September	5000	1200	
11	October	4800	200	
12	November	4100	700	
13	December	3700	400	
14				4116.67
15				5016.67

D14 — fx =SUM(B2:B7)/6

Figure 5.51

I also right clicked the cell and chose Format Cells, and from the Number tab and Number category chose to only show two decimal places.

Of course, there are far more advanced formulas you can create that can actually span sheets within your workbook, but for the purposes of this book, I just wanted to introduce you to formulas and show you where you can find the ones included with Excel, and how you can create your own once you figure out the syntax.

Creating Graphs and Charts

Once you have your data entered into your tables it's nice to be able to create a graph or chart showing that data in a format that makes it easier to see or analyze. Excel has many graph and chart options built-in, plus you can customize them once you add them to your workbook.

Under the Insert tab you will find the Charts group, where you can choose from a variety of charts. If you click on the Recommended Charts button, Excel will show you the types of charts it thinks will work best with your data. I chose a bar chart that shows the hits in blue and then the hits lost or gained in orange (figure 5.52). For the hits lost, it shows the bar going under the base of the chart.

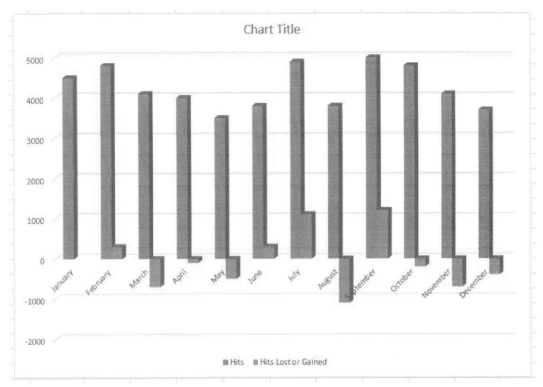

Figure 5.52

Notice when you click on your chart that you have some options pop up that you can click on. These options will let you do things such as add, remove, and change chart elements, set a chart style, and also filter your chart so it only shows the data you want to see. I went through some of the settings and added some labels, renamed the chart, added an informational table, and changed the coloring. You can see the results in figure 5.53.

Not all data translates well into a chart or graph so keep that in mind when creating them. If it looks wrong or doesn't make sense then it might be the data you are using rather than Excel not formatting it correctly.

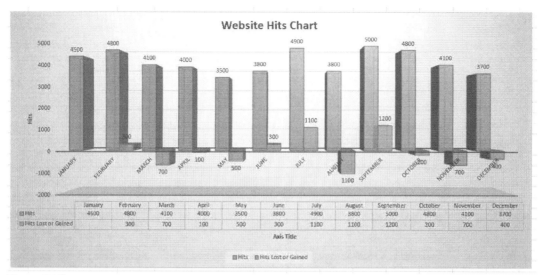

Figure 5.53

After you create your chart you can move it wherever you like on the sheet and resize it so it looks right on the page. You can even cut and paste it into a different sheet within your workbook and all the values will stay with the chart.

Importing Data

Sometimes you will want to import some data into your spreadsheet from another source, such as a different Excel file, text document, database, web file, and so on. Depending on what type of data you are trying to import and its source will determine how smoothly the process goes.

Many times Excel users will have to import data from a text file that was actually exported from another program. Many times the text file will be comma or tab delimited, meaning the entries are separated by tabs or commas.

For my next example I will import some data from a text file. I have a text file called Car Import.txt that has the year, make, model, and value for some selected cars that we need to import into our spreadsheet (figure 5.54).

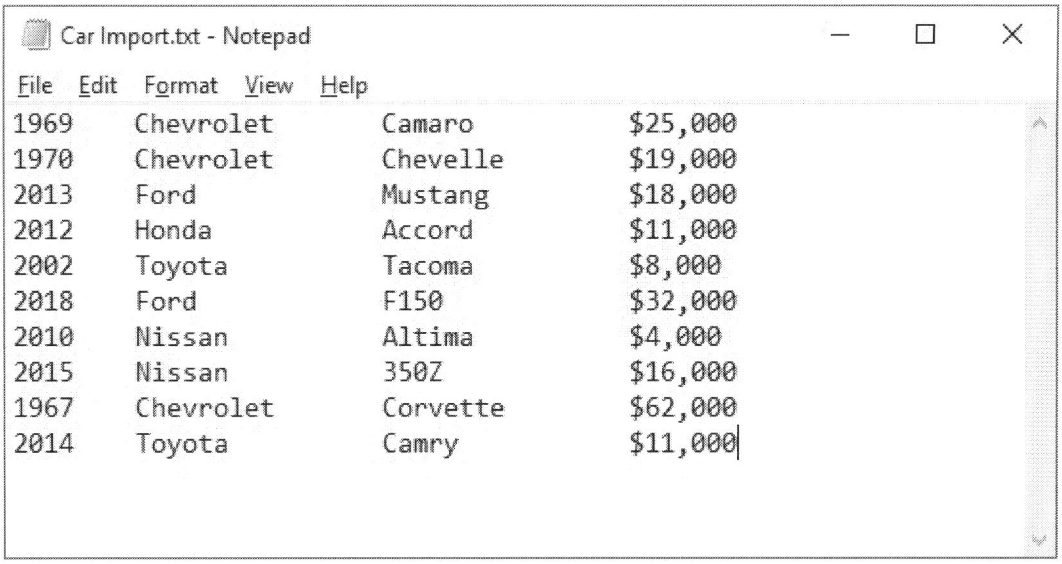

1969	Chevrolet	Camaro	$25,000
1970	Chevrolet	Chevelle	$19,000
2013	Ford	Mustang	$18,000
2012	Honda	Accord	$11,000
2002	Toyota	Tacoma	$8,000
2018	Ford	F150	$32,000
2010	Nissan	Altima	$4,000
2015	Nissan	350Z	$16,000
1967	Chevrolet	Corvette	$62,000
2014	Toyota	Camry	$11,000

Figure 5.54

The way we do this is to go to the Data tab, click the button that says *Get External Data,* choose *From Text,* and then browse to the location of our text file. Then in Step 1 we choose if the file is delimited or a fixed width. In our case it is tab delimited, and Excel has determined that as well (figure 5.55). If our text file had headers then we would check the box that says *My data has headers*.

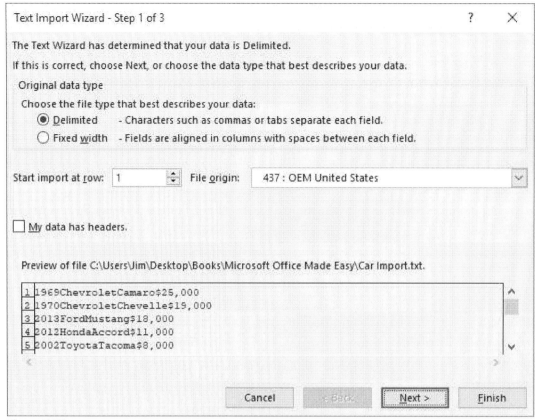

Figure 5.55

Then we need to tell the import wizard what the file is using for its delimiter. In our case it's tab, but I had to also choose Space to make Excel read the data correctly (figure 5.56). You might have to play around with different options as well when importing text documents to make it work right. When things line up correctly between the lines in the Data preview section, then you know you are on the right path.

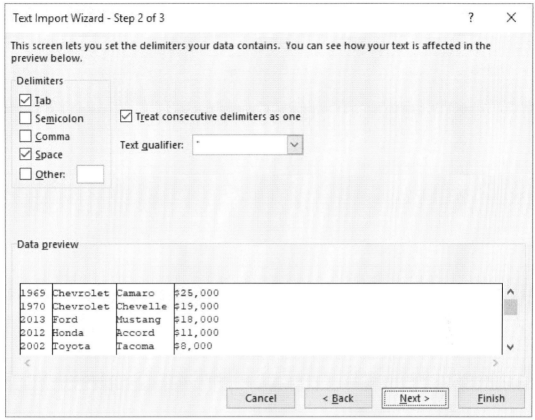

Figure 5.56

From here we can either click on Finish to import the data, or Next to format the data to match the type of data we are importing (figure 5.57).

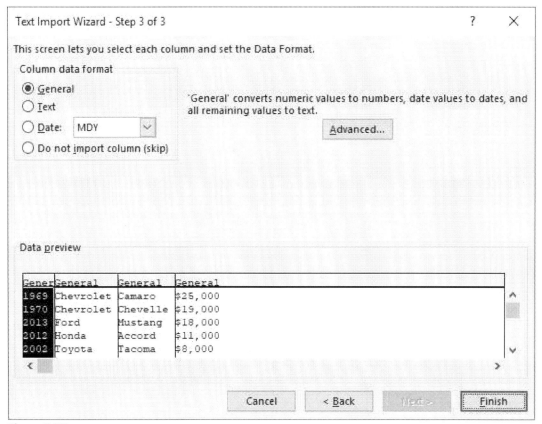

Figure 5.57

Finally, we need to tell the wizard where we want to place the imported data in our workbook (figure 5.58). If you click on the cell where you want the data imported before starting the wizard, then it will pick that cell for you automatically.

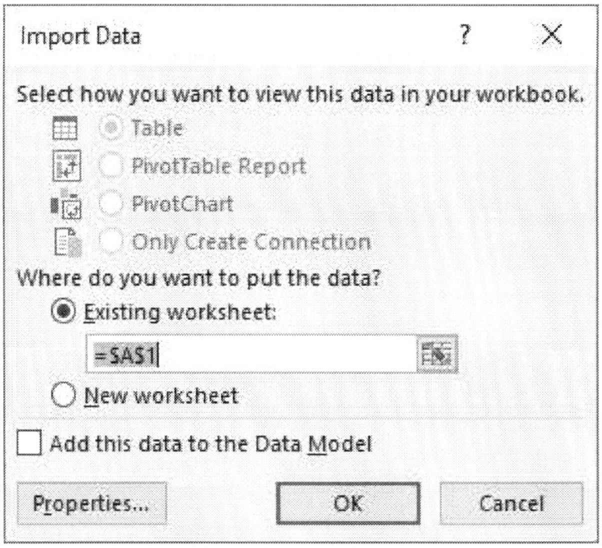

Import Data   ?   X

Select how you want to view this data in your workbook.
- ⊙ Table
- ○ PivotTable Report
- ○ PivotChart
- ○ Only Create Connection

Where do you want to put the data?
- ⊙ Existing worksheet:
  =A1
- ○ New worksheet

☐ Add this data to the Data Model

Properties...   OK   Cancel

Figure 5.58

As you can see in figure 5.59, we now have the data imported into our worksheet and all the values have been placed in their own columns.

	A	B	C	D
1	1969	Chevrolet	Camaro	$25,000
2	1970	Chevrolet	Chevelle	$19,000
3	2013	Ford	Mustang	$18,000
4	2012	Honda	Accord	$11,000
5	2002	Toyota	Tacoma	$8,000
6	2018	Ford	F150	$32,000
7	2010	Nissan	Altima	$4,000
8	2015	Nissan	350Z	$16,000
9	1967	Chevrolet	Corvette	$62,000
10	2014	Toyota	Camry	$11,000

Figure 5.59

Printing a Spreadsheet

I went over printing in the chapter on Microsoft Word, but Excel has some different methods you can use to print what you need, and sometimes it can be tricky to make things fit on the page. So, on that note, I will now go over some things you need to watch for while printing spreadsheets.

When you go to the File tab and click on Print, you have the same settings that we saw with Word with a few different options that will help you get your spreadsheet printed correctly.

As you can see in figure 5.60, when you look at the print preview the chart is cut off on the right side of the page, even though it fits on the screen when looking at it in Excel itself. It also shows page 1 of 2 at the bottom, indicating it will print the other half of the chart on page 2, which is not what we want.

Figure 5.60

If you look closely at figure 5.61, you will see the dotted line going through the graph by column H and also the one horizontally below the graph. These indicate the edges of the page based on what size you set your workbook to be from the Page Layout tab. For this spreadsheet it's set to 8.5x11. If I change the layout to landscape that will allow the sheet to fit on my page (assuming that's acceptable).

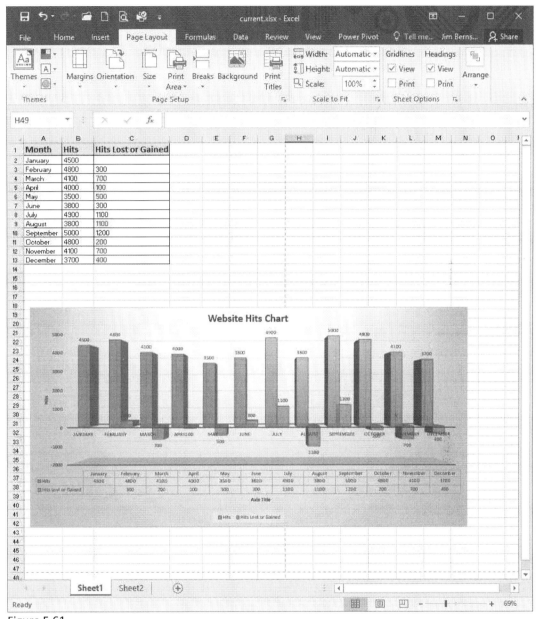

Figure 5.61

Another option is to go back to the Print settings and change the scaling to the **Fit Sheet on One Page setting** (figure 5.62) so Excel will shrink the page to make it fit our paper size. One problem you might run into is it could shrink it so much to make it fit that everything looks too small.

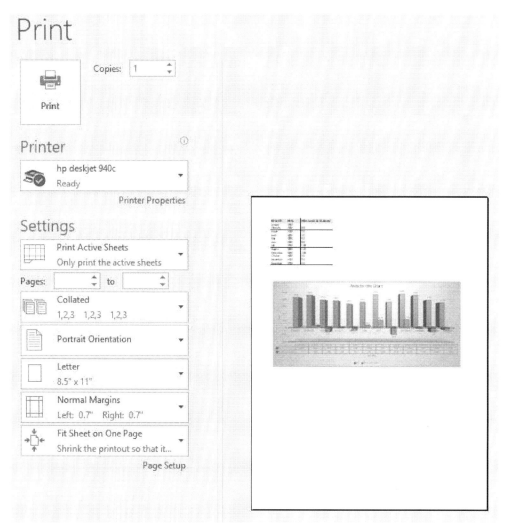

Figure 5.62

You can also try to reduce the margins to give you a little more room, or adjust your column width and make them smaller if you can spare the space.

One nice feature of Excel is that you can print out only what you want to print by selecting it on your worksheet. Let's say in our example we only want to print out the table and not the chart. All you need to do is highlight the chart, then go to the print settings and choose **Print Selection** from the list. Then it will only print what you have highlighted.

Chapter 6 – Microsoft PowerPoint

Although it may not be as popular as Word and Excel, PowerPoint is used by many people at the workplace to make professional looking presentations with a minimal learning curve. PowerPoint is fairly easy to learn compared to other Office programs like Excel and Access, and once you get the basics down then you will be off and running making your own flashy presentations.

PowerPoint Specific Tabs and Groups
PowerPoint has its own unique tabs, plus there are also some different groups within the tabs that are common to the other Office programs. I want to begin this chapter by going over these unique tabs and also the PowerPoint related groups in the common tabs.

Home Tab
Like all the other Office programs, the Home tab is the default tab that is displayed when you open the program (figure 6.1). It has many of the same groups as the other Office programs, but there are a few that are specific to PowerPoint.

Figure 6.1

The Slides group is where you can add new slides and keep things organized. There are four man tools you can use in this group:

- **New Slide** – If you want to add another slide into your presentation, simply click the New Slide button to add a new blank slide, or you can click the down arrow to choose from preconfigured slide templates. You can also choose to duplicate the slide you have selected or reuse a slide from a different PowerPoint file.

- **Layout** – Here you can change the layout of an existing slide to one of the preconfigured layouts included with PowerPoint.

- **Reset** – This setting will reset the position, size, and formatting of the slide placeholders to their default setting. So, if you make a bunch of changes and want to start over, then you can use the Reset feature.

- **Section** – When you have a lot of slides sometimes it's a good idea to break them up into sections to keep them more organized. In figure 6.2, you can see how the slides are broken up into sections called Day One and Day Two.

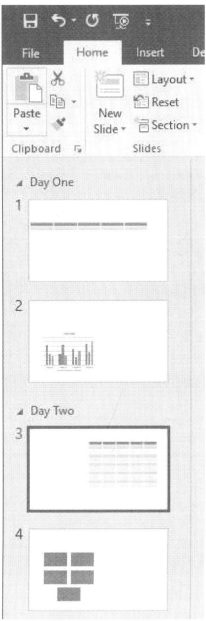

Figure 6.2

Paragraph
The Paragraph group has many of the same settings such as text alignment and list making features, but there are some other things you can do here as well. For example, the *Text Direction* tool will let you change the direction of your text. So, if you want it vertical instead of horizontal, then that's easy to do. You can also have the letters stacked on top of each other if you choose so.

Another cool feature is the *Convert to SmartArt* tool, which will take your text and insert it into one of the many available shapes built into PowerPoint (figure 6.3).

Converted to SmartArt

Figure 6.3

Drawing
Once you start using PowerPoint you will find yourself using the Drawing group quite a bit. When people make presentations, they like to include lots of arrows, lines, boxes, and so on to get their point across. Once you draw your shape, you can click on it to highlight it (like shown in figure 6.4). Then you can resize it and rotate it to suit your needs.

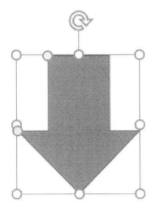

Figure 6.4

If you click on the arrow at the bottom right of the Drawing group it will bring up the Format Shape settings (figure 6.5), where you can change things such as fill color, line color and size, effects, and so on. There are also some buttons for these features in the Drawing group itself.

Figure 6.5

If you are looking for a quick way to add some color to your drawing, PowerPoint also has some built-in styles that you can apply to your drawing from the *Quick Styles* button.

Insert Tab

There are only a couple of things here that are different and worth mentioning, and one of them is the *Photo Album* tool. If you have a bunch of pictures that you would like to make a slide show from, simply click the Photo Album button, browse to your pictures, select the ones you want, click Insert, and then click Create. PowerPoint will then create a new presentation with each picture on its own slide.

The other feature I wanted to mention from the Insert tab is the *Screen Recording* option under media. This is really cool because you can have PowerPoint take a video recording of what you are doing on your screen and then insert it into your presentation as a movie that you can play back. So, if you need to demonstrate something for training purposes, it's a great way to do so.

Design Tab

There aren't really too many things to do here except change the way your overall slides look when it comes to their design. There are a bunch of built-in themes you can choose from, and as you click on each one it will change your whole presentation and give you a preview of what it will look like (figure 6.6).

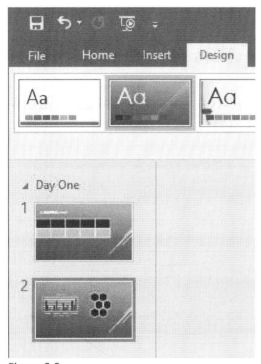

Figure 6.6

By default, PowerPoint uses a widescreen (16:9) size for its slides, but if you want something a little more square you can choose the standard (4:3), or create your own custom size from the Customize group.

Clicking the *Format Background* button in the Customize group will bring up settings to change your background in regards to color, transparency, brightness, gradients, and so on.

Transitions Tab

Transitions are used to create effects that take place in between your slides. There are many built-in transitions you can apply (as shown in figure 6.7), and once you choose one of these transitions you can customize it even further.

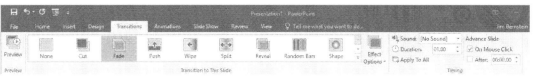

Figure 6.7

To use transitions, select the slide you want the transition to take place on. Then choose a transition you like and click on the Preview button to see how it will look when applied. Then, under Effect Options, choose whether you want the transition to happen smoothly, or if you want it to fade to black between the slides.

Timing
The Timing group is where you can go to set how fast and with what action your slides will transition from one to the other. The Duration setting is set at one second by default, but if you want to be more dramatic and extend that time period, then enter however many seconds you like. There is also an option to have a sound play in between each slide, such as a drumroll. Keep in mind that using sounds might get annoying after a while unless you do it for just a couple of slides to make a point.

By default, PowerPoint won't advance to the next slide during a slide show unless you click the mouse, but if you want your slide show to run automatically, then you can check the box labeled *After* and enter the time interval between slides.

Once you get things looking the way you want them, you can click on the *Apply To All* button to have your settings be applied to your entire presentation.

Animations Tab

Animations are a big part of PowerPoint slide shows, and you will find yourself on the Animations tab on a regular basis. Animations are when you have one aspect of your slide show change into another, such as some text sliding off the screen and an image appearing in its place.

As you can see from figure 6.8, the Animations tab looks similar to the Transition tab, and it functions the same way (to some degree).

Figure 6.8

Animation

Under the Animation group there are many built-in animations that you can apply to your slides, and there is also the *Preview* button like we saw on the Transitions tab. The *Effect Options* button will let you fine tune how the animation you chose will look. The options will be different based on your choice of animation. (I will go over how to apply an animation later on in this chapter.)

Advanced Animation

If you click on the *Animation Pane* button it will open up an area on the side of your slide where you will have a listing of all the animations you have applied to that slide (figure 6.9). From here you can fine tune the way each one of your animations work. You can also change the order of your animations with in the *Reorder Animation* section.

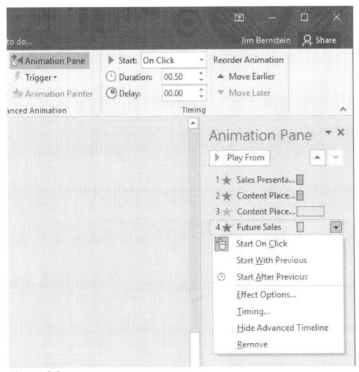

Figure 6.9

Timing

The settings in the Timing group include options to control when the animation begins, the duration of the animation, and also its delay.

Slide Show Tab

The whole point to making a PowerPoint presentation is so you can show it to other people in the form of a slide show, so it makes sense to have a tab dedicated to how your slide show will appear when you play it.

Start Slide Show

This group will allow you to decide how the slide show is presented and when it starts. The *From Begging* button will start the slide show from the first slide while the *From Current Slide* button will start it from whatever slide you are on while in editing mode. If you have access to the Office Presentation Service (which is free, by the way), then you can upload your slide show so it can be viewed via a web browser by other people who might not be in your office. Finally, the *Custom Slide Show* option will let you choose which slides you want to appear in your slide show just in case there are some you want to omit.

Set Up

This group is where you adjust your settings for showing how the slide show will start, and how it will play once you get it going. There are several settings you can adjust here:

- **Set Up Slide Show** – When you click on this button you will be presented with the options shown in figure 6.10, and from here you can choose the type of show, the show options, what slides will be shown, how the slides will be advanced, and if the show will be presented on multiple monitors.

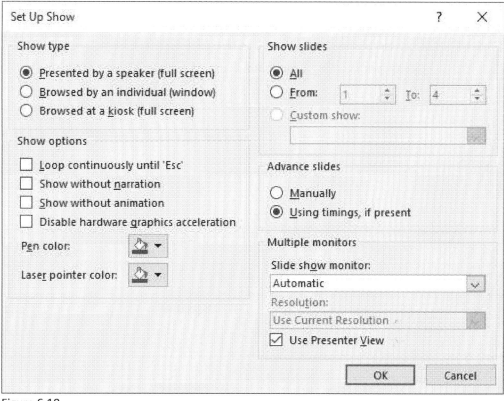

Figure 6.10

- **Hide Slide** – If there's a particular slide you don't want to appear when you run your slide show then select that slide and click on the Hide Slide button to prevent it from showing.

- **Rehearse Timings** – If you plan on running your slide show automatically, then you will want to have an idea of how much time you'll need to spend on each slide. With the Rehearse Timings option you can run through your slides and PowerPoint will track how much time you spend between each one (figure 6.11). Then you can save the timing and have it applied to your automatic slide show.

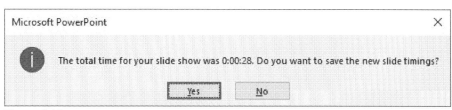

Figure 6.11

- **Record Slide Show** – With this option you can have PowerPoint record your slide show along with any voice narrations and webcam footage so you can show it later. While recording the slide show you will have a Recording box in the upper left hand corner (figure 6.12) where you can pause the recording or advance to the next slide or animation if needed. You can also click with the mouse to advance the slides.

Figure 6.12

- While recording you can right click anywhere on the slide, choose *Pointer Options,* and select from tools such as a laser pointer, pen, or highlighter. Then you can play your slide show back with your narrations and highlights to see how it looks.

Monitors
The final group in the Slide Show tab is the Monitors group, and here is where you can tell PowerPoint how you want the slide show to be presented if you have more than one monitor. The options are Automatic or Primary Monitor, which will allow you to select which one of your monitors the slide show plays on. Presenter View allows you to have the slide show on one monitor while showing things like notes and a preview of the next slide (etc.) on the other monitor.

Review Tab
The only thing that's really different in the PowerPoint Review tab is the Ink group, which allows you to mark up your slides with various colors and pen types. Once you click on the Start Inking button, the Ribbon changes to the Ink Tools tab where you have various options for drawing (figure 6.13).

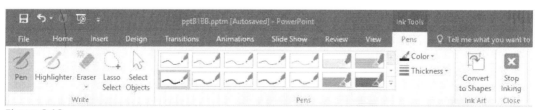

Figure 6.13

The Convert to Shapes button will take something you drew and convert it to a geometric shape. So, if you draw a rough looking circle, and with the Convert to

Shapes button selected, PowerPoint will make a nicer looking shape for you. Take a look at figure 6.14 to see the difference between having the button turned off and turned on when drawing.

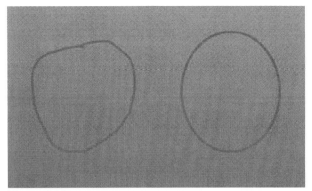

Figure 6.14

View Tab

The View tab has a few groups on it that are specific to PowerPoint, but also has some groups on it that I have already gone over in the chapter on Word (figure 6.15).

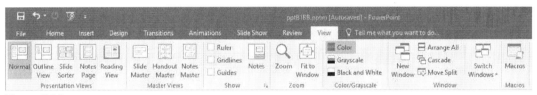

Figure 6.15

Presentation Views

Just like with the other Office programs, PowerPoint has its own set of views that you can choose from to change how your presentation looks on the screen. Most of the time you will be using *Normal View,* which shows the slide previews on the left of the screen and the slide you are working on in the center. In *Outline View* you can do things like add notes to your slides and create outlines that you can edit from this view by right clicking on the outline and choosing one of the available options (figure 6.16).

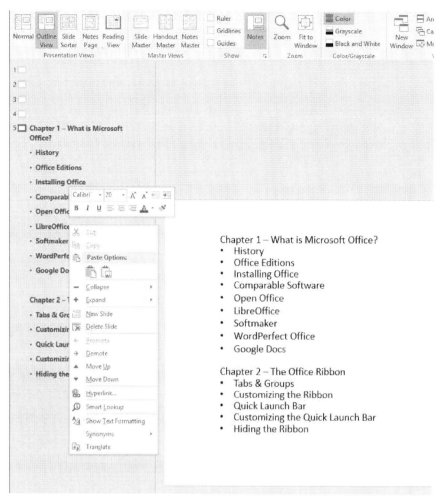

Figure 6.16

After you create your slides, you might need to rearrange them, and the best way to do that is to use the *Slide Sorter* view. Then you can drag and drop the slides in the order you want them to appear (figure 6.17).

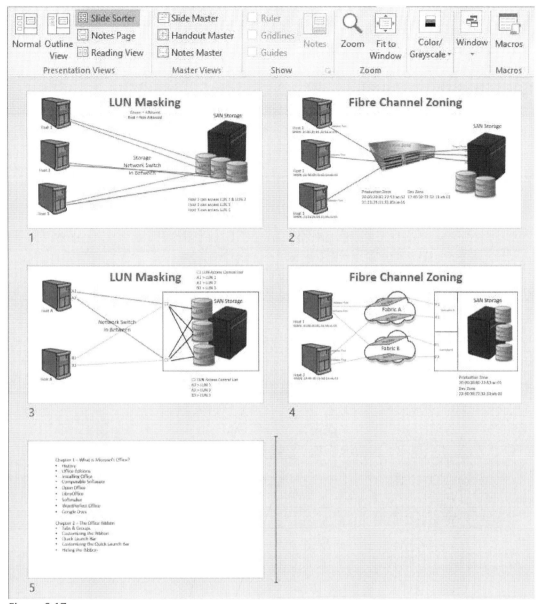

Figure 6.17

After you make some notes on your slides you can see how they will look when printed out with the presentation by using the *Notes Page* view.

Finally, you can use the *Reading View* to see how your slide show will play out in the current window without having to switch to the full screen slide show mode.

Master Views

When creating PowerPoint files it's important to retain consistency among your slides when it comes to fonts, colors, logos, and so on to keep things looking professional. The *Slide Master* controls how all these visual features look throughout the entire presentation. Once you are in the Slide Master view, you will have the master slide listed on top with sub slides showing below. When you make a change to the Slide Master, it will take effect on all of the other slides below it. It won't change the content of the slides, but only their appearance. When you click on Close Master View, these changes will be applied to your slides.

If you plan on printing out your slide show to hand out to viewers then you can click the *Handout Master* button to see how it will look when printed. You can also make changes here, as well as change the page setup options. The *Notes Master* does a similar thing, but will let you adjust how things will look when printed out with any notes you might have with your slides. The *Notes* button in the Show group will toggle the note box on or off for the slide.

Creating a Presentation

Now it's time to start working on a new presentation and getting our data added to it so we can format it and add some effects to it later. When you go to the File tab and click on New, you will be presented with some templates that you can use to get things started (figure 6.18). We are going to start from scratch and add our own custom touches, so we will choose Blank Presentation.

I often use PowerPoint to create graphics for my website and my books. It's very easy to move things around and resize them to make some professional looking graphics. Just remember the send to front and send to back options are your friends when using PowerPoint if you have things that overlap.

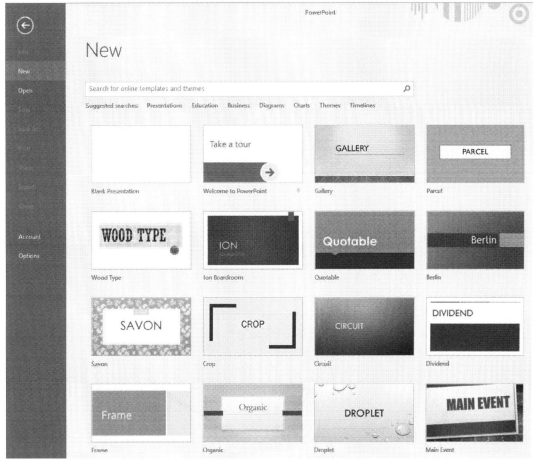

Figure 6.18

A blank presentation will give you a single slide with no backgrounds, but will have a couple of text boxes added for you so you can add a title and a subtitle. These can be deleted if you really want to start with a blank canvas, or you can use them to start adding some text. For this presentation I am going to delete them so we can start from scratch.

Now let's add some text by going to the Insert tab and choosing Text Box. You won't see anything happen, but you will be able to draw a box on the blank page to create your text box. Once the box is there, you can start typing in the text you want. I will type in *Yearly Sales Figures,* and you can see in figure 6.19 that the text is now inside our text box.

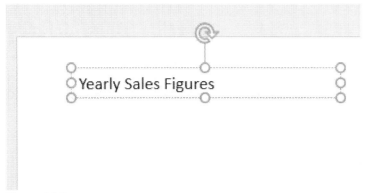

Figure 6.19

Notice how there are round points around the box? These are meant to be clicked on and dragged to resized the text box. The curved arrow can be used to rotate the text box around.

Next, I increased the font size, changed the color to red, and added the shadow effect on the text all from the Home tab (figure 6.20). Then I selected the text and centered it from the Home tab as well. Now, when I stretch out the text box, the text within it will stay centered to the box.

Figure 6.20

When you click off of the text box the outline of the box will go away, but if you like to have a box around your text, you can add one by right clicking it and choosing Format Shape. Then you can do things like add a fill or line and change the fill and line colors.

Next I am going to insert our company logo on the top right of the slide. It's an image file that I have on my computer, so I will go to the Insert tab and choose Pictures, then browse to where I have the picture stored and click on Insert. Then I will drag it to the position I want and resize it so it looks good on the slide (as shown in figure 6.21).

Yearly Sales Figures

Figure 6.21

Next I will insert a chart that was made in Excel by going to the Insert tab and then to the Text group. From there I will select Object and choose the Create from file option, browse to the location of my spreadsheet, and insert it into the slide. Then I can move it and resize it to suit my needs (figure 6.22).

Yearly Sales Figures

Month	Sales	Last Years Sales
January	$52,000	$50,000
February	$58,000	$55,000
March	$63,000	$64,000
April	$59,000	$60,000
May	$57,000	$55,000
June	$61,000	$60,000
July	$60,000	$57,000
August	$57,000	$58,000
September	$60,000	$60,000
October	$64,000	$61,000
November	$62,000	$59,000
December	$59,000	$55,000

Figure 6.22

Now I want to add another slide to show next year's projected sales, but rather than start from a blank slide, I'm going to right click on the slide preview on the left and choose Duplicate Slide to have PowerPoint make an exact copy of the current slide. Then I will just delete the chart and change the text from Yearly Sales Figures to Projected Sales Figures. As you can see in figure 6.23, we now have two slides with the information I just mentioned.

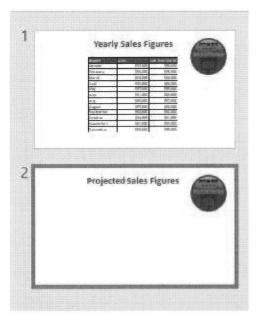

Figure 6.23

For the Projected Sales Figures slide I am going to insert a chart from the Insert menu. I chose a standard bar chart. Figure 6.24 shows that when you insert a chart, it also brings up an Excel-like box that you will use to enter the information about the chart. I will fill in the cells with the projected sales information so it looks like figure 6.25.

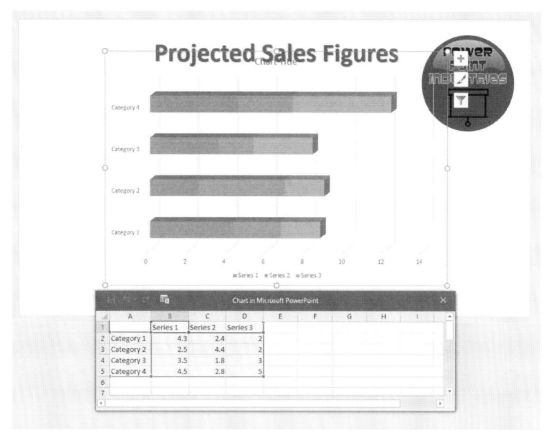

Figure 6.24

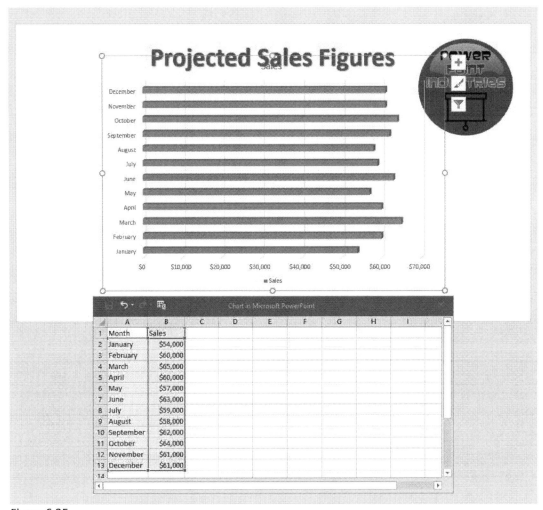

Figure 6.25

Once I get into formatting we will worry about making the chart a little more pleasing to the eye. And speaking of formatting, that's coming up right now!

Formatting a Presentation

When it comes to PowerPoint presentations, the look of the presentation is almost as important as its contents. If you can't keep your audience interested, then they will start tuning out and maybe even fall asleep! This is where formatting can help you out, especially the animations, because people seem to pay more attention to flashy stuff like that.

Themes

The first thing I want to do to the presentation is add a theme so we don't have the boring white background to look at. However, make sure not to add a theme that will overtake the content on the slide or make the information it too hard to see. Since there is purple and red in the slides, I don't want to use a background with those colors because they might make the text or company logo too hard to see.

If you go to the Design tab you can start clicking on the various built-in themes to see how they look with your slides. Once you find one you like, it will be applied to all the slides and be ready to go for additional slides. Figure 6.26 shows an example of a bad choice of a theme.

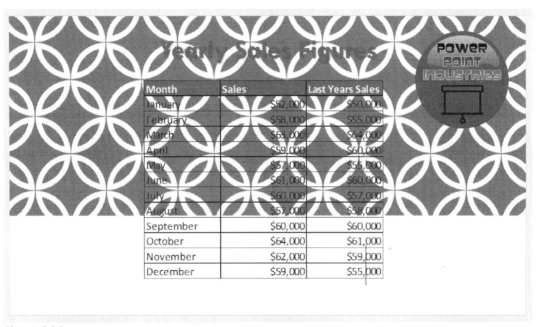

Figure 6.26

I decided to go with the theme shown in figure 6.27. Originally it was green, so I chose a blue look from the Variants group.

Yearly Sales Figures

Month	Sales	Last Years Sales
January	$52,000	$50,000
February	$58,000	$55,000
March	$63,000	$64,000
April	$59,000	$60,000
May	$57,000	$55,000
June	$61,000	$60,000
July	$60,000	$57,000
August	$57,000	$58,000
September	$60,000	$60,000
October	$64,000	$61,000
November	$62,000	$59,000
December	$59,000	$55,000

Figure 6.27

Fonts

Another way to spice up your slide show is by changing the fonts and font colors around to make it a little more exciting to look at. Sure, the basic fonts are easy to read, but they look pretty boring. Just be sure not to use anything too crazy so that people will still be able to read the text on your slide.

If you take a look at figure 6.28, you will see that I changed the heading font for Yearly Sales Figures to something with a little more style. I also changed the font in the table to something a little bolder to make it easier to read, and also adjusted the column size, left justified the text, and added a blue background behind all of the months. (If you were reading this in color, you would actually see how good it looks!)

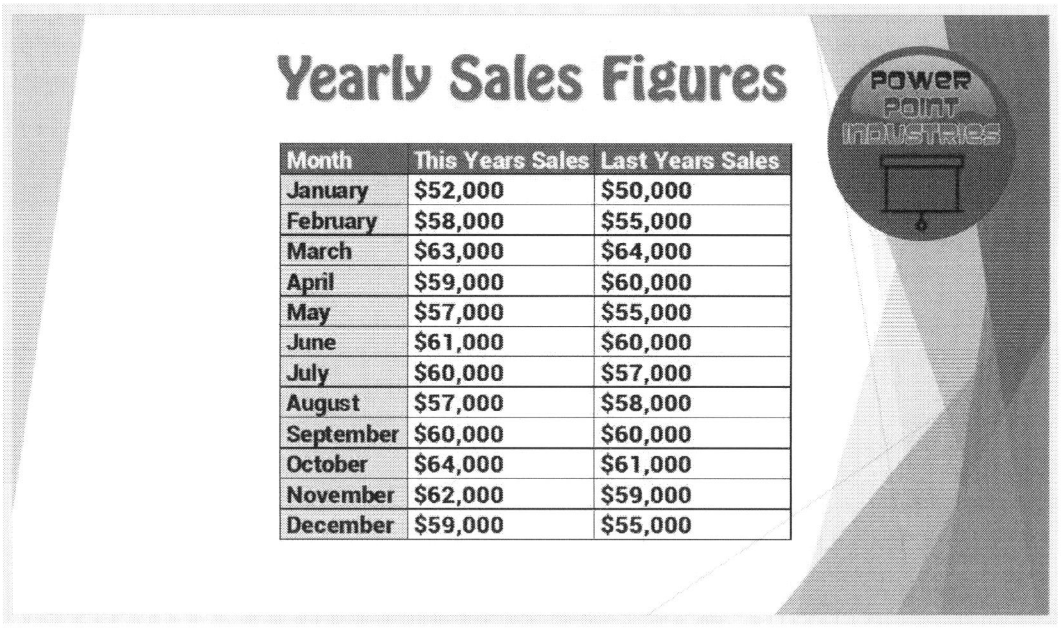

Figure 6.28

Background Formatting

Another option you have to spice up your presentation is to format the background. You can add things as simple as a solid color, or even a photo from your computer or the Internet. Other options include gradient fills, texture fills, and pattern fills. Figure 6.29 shows you the options you have to choose from when clicking on the *Format Background* button from the Design tab and Customize group.

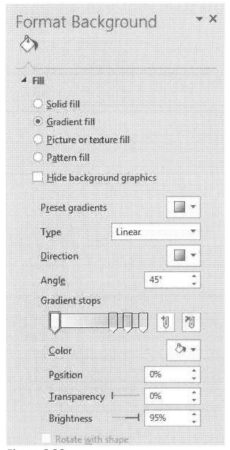

Figure 6.29

Using Transitions and Animations

One of the most widely used features of PowerPoint is the ability to create custom transitions between your slides and custom animations within your slides. Using these features helps add some life to your presentation, and can actually help the way it flows. Plus, they are good to use to keep people's attention!

Transitions

The Transition tab has many built-in transitions you can apply to your slides, but these are used *in between* slides rather than *on* your slides. If you don't use transitions, then when you advance to the next slide it will just simply appear after you click the mouse button.

Figure 6.30 shows you all of the available transitions that you can apply to your slides. When you select a transtion, then the Effects Options you will have with that transition will change based on the transition you choose (figure 6.31).

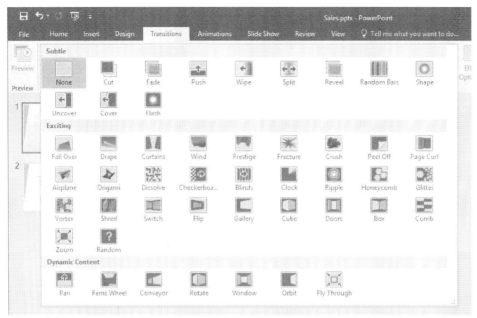

Figure 6.30

Figure 6.31

After you choose your transition and effects options, you then need to decide if it will apply only to the slide you have selected (the default), or if you want to have that transition apply to *all* the slides. If you want it to apply to all the slides simply click the *Apply to All button* in the Timing group. The *Duration* setting will determine how long the transition takes to apply and move to the next slide. Of course, I can't show you a demonstration since this is a book and all, but it's very easy to play around with transitions on your own.

Animations
Animations are what you use within your slides to make custom effects and control how your presentation moves along. They can be used to have text, images, charts,

etc. appear on command with the click of the mouse. They can do things like slide in or appear out of thin air, and you can choose what order all of your animations happen in.

To create an animation, select the item you want it to apply to and then click the Animations tab. As you can see from figure 6.32, there are many animations to choose from, and even more if you click the options at the bottom.

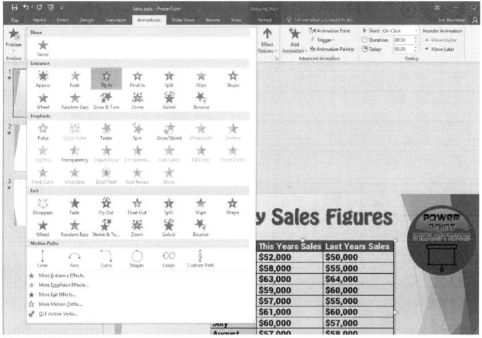

Figure 6.32

The Animations tab has the same Effect Option button as the Transition tab, and the options will vary based on what animation you choose. There is also a Duration setting like the transitions have, and also a Delay setting in case you don't want the animation to happen immediately.

The Reorder Animation setting under the Timing group will let you change the order of the animations that you have applied. To use this feature simply click the object that you have applied the animation to and then choose either Move Earlier or Move Later from that setting.

To fine tune your animations you can adjust the settings from the Start option. Here you can determine when the animation takes place. Many people just leave the default setting of On Click, but you can also have it take place after a different animation finishes, as well as with or after the previous animation.

As I mentioned earlier in the chapter, you can use the Animation Pan in the Advanced Animation group to see your animations and to change their order, as well as change other settings such as their timing and effect options.

When you are all ready to go remember that there is the Preview button at the left of the Ribbon that will play your slideshow within the PowerPoint window. It will play the animations automatically so you don't have to actually click through each one. Pressing F5 on the keyboard will start the presentation in slide show mode full screen and allow you to click through it as if you were actually giving the presentation.

Saving and Showing a Presentation
Just like with all the other office programs, there is a need to save your work in case you want to go back to it and continue later. With PowerPoint there are many choices you can use to save your files (depending on what you are planning on doing with them) even though there are really only two that most people commonly use. There is one save option you really need to know about if you plan on showing your presentation to others or sending it for someone else to show.

There are many ways to save your PowerPoint presentation. If you just want to save it so you can edit later, you would stick with the default *PowerPoint Presentation (.pptx)* file. Other save options include saving it as a PDF, older PowerPoint version, video file, image file, and so on. You might want to try using the *Save As* option to see what these other types of saves can do for you.

When it comes to showing your presentation on the screen after you have it ready to go, you can use the From Beginning or From Current Slide option on the Slide Show tab to have it play full screen as an actual slide show. But if you save the file as a *PowerPoint Show (.ppsx)* file, then when you or someone else clicks the file it will open as a slide show rather than display your work with all the individual slide previews etc. And when the show is over and you exit, it will simply close the file and not take you back to editing mode like the preview option will. This is good for when you just want someone to show the presentation and not make any changes.

Printing a Presentation

Some people like to include handouts of their slide show for people to look at during the show or take back to the office with them for later reference. PowerPoint has its own set of print settings that you can alter to print your presentation the way you want it to appear on paper.

When you go to the File tab and then to Print, you will see that the print options look similar to other Office programs, yet a little different at the same time (figure 6.33). I will now go over the settings that are PowerPoint specific.

Figure 6.33

The first option that says Print All Slides is the same type of setting you would see in Word where you would print only the pages you want, but in this case it's only the slides that you want. There is even a Print Selection option like Excel has which will only print the slide or slides that you have selected on the left slide preview part of PowerPoint. You can use the *Shift* or *Ctrl* keys while clicking to select the slides you want to print.

The next option will determine if you are printing the slide to take up the full page or if you are just printing the notes or outline content. As you can see in figure 6.34, there is an option to print handouts where you will have multiple slides on each sheet of paper rather than using a whole sheet per slide.

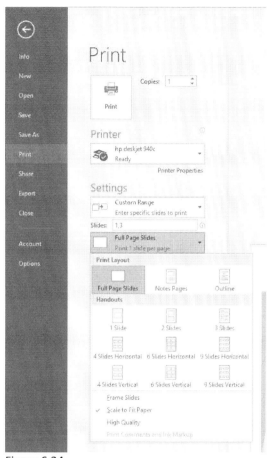

Figure 6.34

Finally, at the bottom there is an option to put a frame around each slide while printing, which will help it look better when you have a white background in your slide. The *Scale to Fit Paper* setting will reduce the size of the slide so it fits on the sheet.

If you want to save on ink you can use the last option to choose between color, greyscale, or black and white. Of course, you will need to have a color printer to print in color, and greyscale is pretty much the same as black and white except it will have more shades of grey to differentiate your colors when you are not actually printing in color.

 Remember that I mentioned using Draft mode earlier in the book to save ink. You can use this mode on pretty much anything you print within Windows, so if you need to print out a bunch of copies of your presentation and don't want to go broke buying ink for it, give it a try.

I have always like playing around with PowerPoint, and find that it is the best way to learn how to use it. It doesn't hurt to create a new file or even use a template and start adding text and graphics so you can get a feel for how things work. Just remember that you aren't going to break your computer by doing this, so have at it!

Chapter 7 – Microsoft Publisher

Microsoft Publisher has been around for a long time, and is used to create publications such as greeting cards, business cards, flyers, calendars, newsletters, brochures, and anything else you might need to create. To me it's kind of like PowerPoint, but without the slide show feature, since you kind of use it the same way.

Publisher Specific Tabs and Groups
Just like with the other chapters, I will begin by discussing the tabs and groups that are exclusive to Publisher so you can have an idea of where you need to go to do what you need to do.

Home Tab
The Home tab in Publisher is very similar to the Home tab in Word, and only has a few differences. If you look at the *Objects* group in figure 7.1, you will see that it has the same options that are on the *Insert* tab in Word.

Figure 7.1

Also notice in figure 7.1 that there are two *Format* tabs with a darker color to them. These only appear when you highlight an object on the page that has formatting options. I just happened to have a text box on the page with the text highlighted, and that's why these tabs appeared.

Arrange
The only other group that I want to mention from the Home tab is the Arrange group. When you start adding things like photos and graphics to your document, they will start overlapping each other and many times you get something like an image stuck in front of your text or behind another graphic and you need to move things around to make them look right.

To do this, you will use the *Bring Forward* button to move an object in front of another, or use the *Bring to Front* option to have it brought in front of everything else on the page. The *Send Backwards* option does the opposite and sends the object back a level, and of course the *Send to Back* option sends it all the way to the back.

Using the *Align* button will give you choices of how to align that object on the page, and you can see in figure 7.2 there are many choices available. This tool can help you get things aligned to each other so they look right on the page.

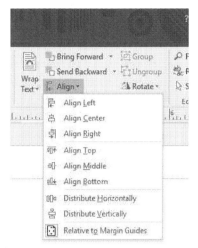

Figure 7.2

Insert Tab
The Publisher Insert tab is also very similar to the Word Insert tab and has many of the same tools and settings, so I will now go over the ones that I haven't discussed already.

Pages
The Pages group only has a couple of options, and the one called *Page* is similar to what you saw in PowerPoint with the New Slide button on the Insert tab. You have three options to choose from when using the Page button. First, you can insert a blank page, which is exactly how it sounds. Next, you have the option to insert a duplicate page of the one you are on, which will copy all the work you have done to a new page. Finally, there is the Insert Page option which gives you a dialog box (figure 7.3) where you can enter the number of pages, where you want them to go, and what type of pages they will be.

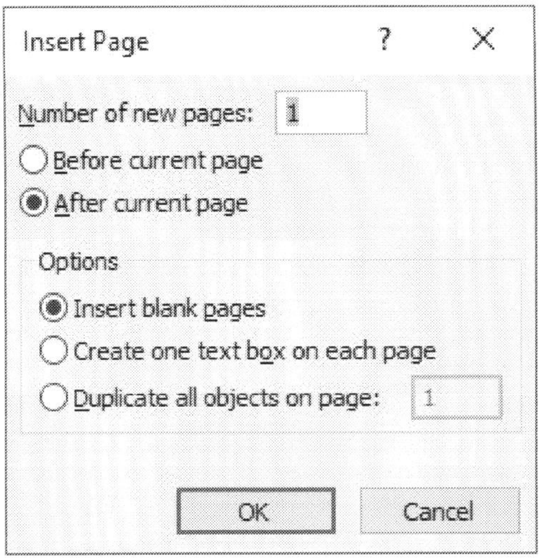

Figure 7.3

Building Blocks

This group is where you can add some custom touches to your publication without having to do a lot of manual design work. There are four main tools in the Building Blocks group:

- **Page Parts** – Page Parts consist of preformatted content such as sidebars, headings, and quote boxes (figure 7.4). Then all you need to do is add your own text and you are ready to go.

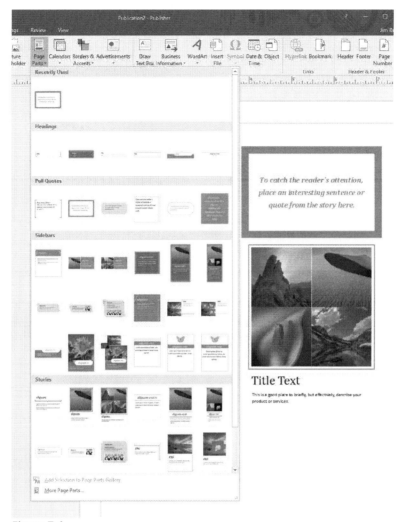

Figure 7.4

- **Calendars** – Here you can add a custom looking calendar to your publication without having to make one from scratch or copy one from another program.

- **Borders & Accents** – This is similar to the Page Parts tool, but instead you can add various types of borders, accent lines, frames, lines, and so on (figure 7.5). Once you add your object you can move it to wherever you like and resize it so it fits your publication correctly.

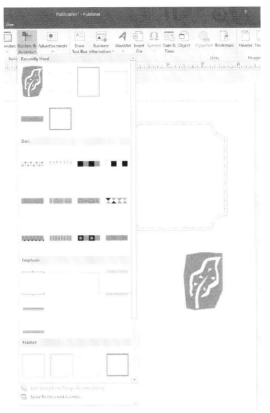

Figure 7.5

- **Advertisements** – If you are creating a publication that is for advertising purposes, then you can use one of the premade advertising graphics included with Publisher (figure 7.6) and then just change the text to suit your needs.

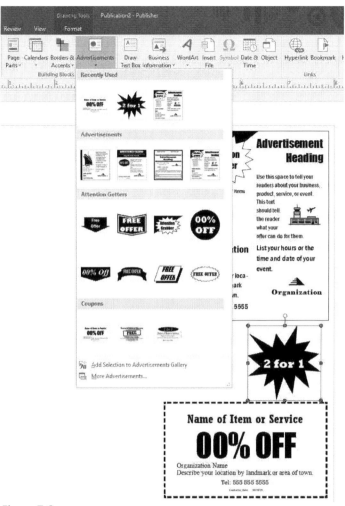

Figure 7.6

Page Design Tab

The Page Design tab (figure 7.7) has many Publisher specific groups that you can use to help design your publication in regards to its layout, color schemes, and font choices.

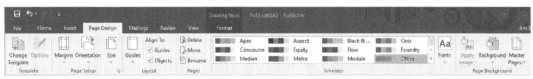

Figure 7.7

Template

Publisher offers many preconfigured templates that you can apply to your publication. Once you choose the one you like, you will be prompted to apply it to the current publication or create a new publication based on that template. If you choose to apply it to the current publication, you might run into an issue where your current content does not fit into that template (figure 7.8). If that is the case, then you will have the option to drag the content that didn't fit back into the publication somewhere that does fit.

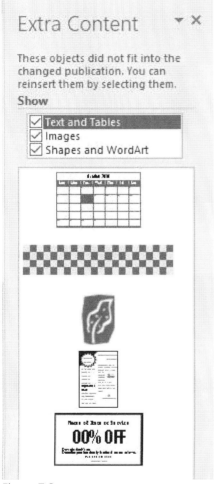

Figure 7.8

So, if you plan on using a template, it might be a good idea to select the template before you start adding anything to your publication.

Depending on what type of template you use, you will have some options available to alter the settings for that template. If the *Options* button is greyed out, that means that there are no additional options for that template. Usually options are reserved for things like newsletters, catalogs, greeting cards, and invitation templates.

Layout

When designing a publication, you may find the use of guidelines to be very helpful, especially when trying to make things evenly spaced and for items that get repeated (such as labels and business cards). When you click on Guides in the Layout group, there are several built-in options to choose from, or you can add your own guidelines wherever you like. Figure 7.9 shows how guidelines are used when creating a sheet of mailing labels so they are all spaced out evenly on the page.

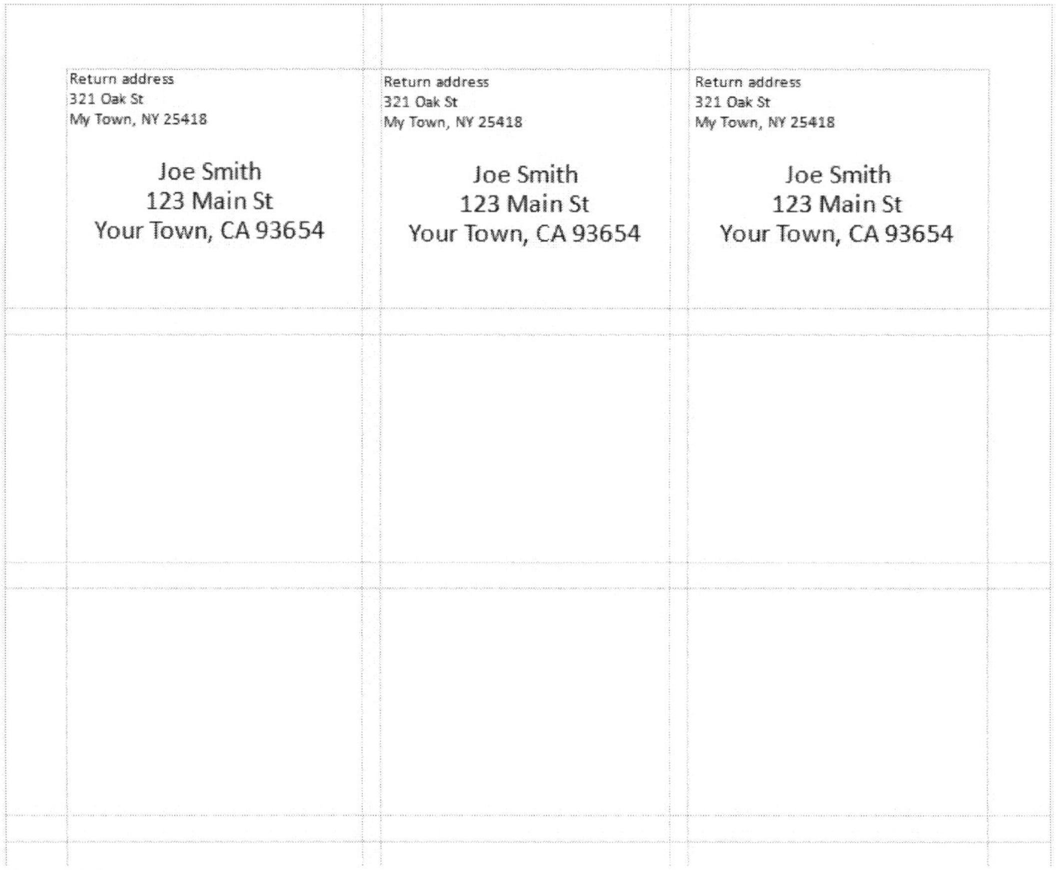

Figure 7.9

The *Align To* boxes will help you get things in the right place on the page. When they are checked and you drag an item close to a gridline, it will automatically snap into place at the gridline. You can also have items self-align to each other when the Objects box is checked.

Schemes

Schemes are used to add a consistent look and feel to your publication by applying the same color attributes to all of your items throughout the publication. Publisher has many built-in schemes, and you can also create your own by clicking the down arrow in the Schemes list and choosing *Create New Color Scheme.*

The *Fonts* button will apply a common font scheme to your publication so that everything looks consistent. Once again, you can use one of the many built-in schemes, or create your own.

Page Background

This group has settings that allow you to customize the background look of your publications. These settings are very similar to the ones we saw in the PowerPoint chapter, so let's review them again.

- **Apply Image** – If you have an image in your publication that you want to be the background image, then all you need to do is select it and then click on the Apply Image button. Then you will choose to fill the entire page with the image, or have it tiled multiple times to fill the page.

- **Background** – From here you can select things like solid colors, gradient fills, patterns, images, and so on to apply use for your background.

- **Master Pages** – If you have aspects that you want to repeat throughout the entire publication, then you can edit your master page with the design features you like, and then apply it to some or all of the pages in your publication.

Mailings

If you are creating a publication with items such as mailing labels, then you have the option to perform mail merge functions just like you can with Word (figure 7.10).

Figure 7.10

You can do a *Mail Merge* or *E-mail Merge* by running the wizard under each one in the Start group, or you can begin by selecting recipients from things such as Outlook contacts or an Excel spreadsheet. Or you can create a new list right on the spot.

Then you would click on the Insert *Merge Field* button to choose from fields in your list (such as name and address). You can also add things like greeting lines or pictures to personalize your list.

Then, when everything is looking good, you can click on the *Preview Results* button to see how everything is going to look. If everything looks good, you will click on the *Finish & Merge* button to kick things off.

Review Tab
There aren't too many things you can do from the Review tab besides check your spelling or use the thesaurus, but there are a couple of cool features that I really like.

One of those features is the Research button. You can highlight some text within your publication, click the Research button, and Publisher will research that text for you using the Encarta Dictionary or the thesaurus. It will then show you results that you can use within your publication.

The other feature I like is the Translate Selected Text button. You can use this by highlighting the text you want to translate and then choose a *from* and *to* language to have Publisher give you the translated text (figure 7.11). Then you can have the translated text inserted directly into your publication, or you can have it copied to the clipboard to use elsewhere.

The *Language* button also deserves a little attention because if you are using more than one language in your publication, you can choose another one from this area to be used for proofing. You can also get to the Publisher Language options by clicking on *Language Preferences*.

Figure 7.11

View Tab

This tab is also similar to the View tab from Word (with a few exceptions). There are more options that you can check in the Show group, such as boundaries, guides, fields, page navigation, scratch area, graphics manager, and baselines. Not all of them are checked by default, but you can play around with each one to see what they do.

In the Zoom group there is a button called *Selected Objects,* and what that does is makes whatever object you have selected take up the whole screen so you can get a better look at it. To reduce it back to normal, simply click a smaller zoom percentage from the zoom box above.

Other than that, it's pretty much the same things I talked about earlier, such as changing the page layout view and arranging your windows.

Format Tabs

When you select certain items on the page (such as objects, text, and pictures) you will get a Format tab that appears giving you additional options for that item you have selected.

As you can see in figure 7.12, each Format tab has its own settings based on the type of item you are formatting. There are the Drawing Tools, Text Box Tools, and Picture Tools formatting tabs. Most of the tools in these tabs we have already seen from the other Office programs, and it's pretty obvious what each one does by looking at the names of the buttons and group names.

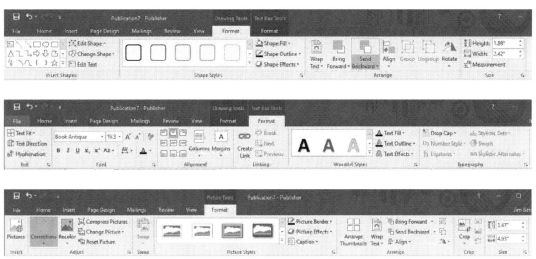

Figure 7.12

Creating and Formatting a Publisher Publication

If you haven't figured it out already, Publisher files are called Publications, just like Word files are called documents and Excel files are called workbooks or spreadsheets. The process for creating a Publisher publication is similar to the other program we talked about, but let's get started creating one and see if there any noticeable differences. For this section I'm going to cover the creation and formatting together since it's nice to format as you go along to see how things work together.

Just like with the other Office programs, when you go to the File tab and click on New, you get presented with a bunch of templates to choose from to start your publication with in case you don't feel like starting from scratch (figure 7.13). But just like with the other Office programs, we are going to create a new Publisher file from scratch, so we will pick the *Blank* option.

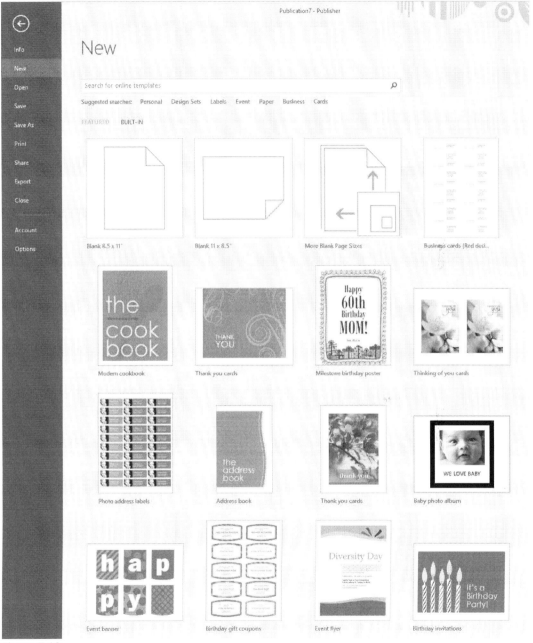

Figure 7.13

The first thing we are going to do is add a border to our Master Page so that it will apply to any additional pages we create. From the Page Design tab click on *Master Pages,* and then click on *Edit Master Pages*.

You will notice that the background behind the page turns yellow, and that you have a Close Master Pages button that you will use after you are done editing the page (figure 7.14). I have added a border from the Insert tab under the *Building Blocks group* and then *Borders & Accents*. Then I will go back to the Master Page tab and click on Close Master Page.

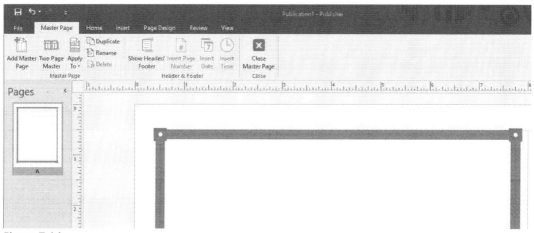

Figure 7.14

Now every time I add a new page to the publication it will automatically include this border. Of course, if you only want something like this to be on one page, you would not add it to the Master Page.

Next let's add some text to our publication so we can work on formatting it to make it look the way we want. The first thing we need to do to add text is go to either the Home tab or the Insert tab and click on the *Draw Text Box* button. It will do the same thing from either tab.

When you click the Draw Text Box button, it will change the mouse pointer to a cross. Then you simply draw a box on the page which will contain your text. Don't worry about getting the size perfect, because you can change that later. Also, be sure to notice that the box will only show when you have clicked inside of it (figure 7.15). If you click outside the box it will disappear until you click back into it. Also notice that when you do click into the box the Format tab for the Text Box Tools group will show in the Ribbon.

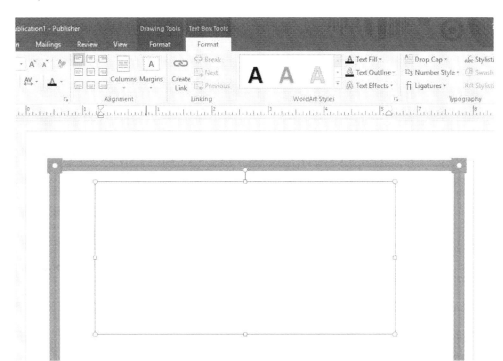

Figure 7.15

Next I added some text, changed the font and size, and then used a WordArt feature with the font. I then right clicked on the text box itself and chose Format Text Box. From here I added a gradient fill color to the text box as well as a border (figure 7.16). This was all done from the Format tab for the Text Box Tools, and you can see the results in figure 7.17.

Figure 7.16

Figure 7.17

By the way, we are creating a flyer for a mountain bike race, so that explains my choice of text! Next I want to add a background image to the flyer to spruce it up a bit. To do that, I will go to the Insert tab and then *Pictures* or *Online Pictures* if you want to find something online. Notice how I didn't go to the Background option from the Page Design tab, because that will make the image take up the entire page even outside of our border (and we don't want that).

I chose to find an image online by clicking the Online Pictures button, which will bring up a Bing Image Search box for you to search with. You can also search your personal OneDrive cloud storage account if you have one (figure 7.18). (I will be going over OneDrive later in this book.)

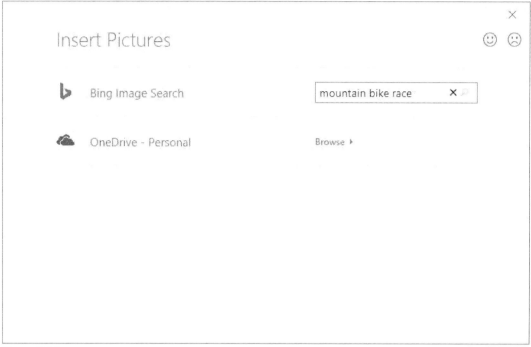

Figure 7.18

As you can see in figure 7.19, it shows me the results of my search for "mountain bike race", and I chose the third image from the results.

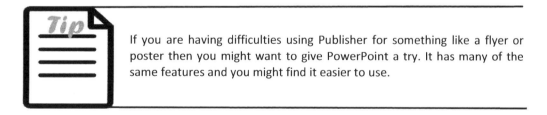

If you are having difficulties using Publisher for something like a flyer or poster then you might want to give PowerPoint a try. It has many of the same features and you might find it easier to use.

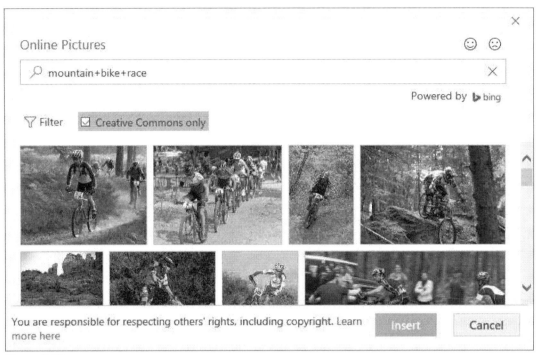

Figure 7.19

Now when I place it on the page, the picture is too big and covers up the text box. Sure I can resize it, but I want the image to take up all the space within the border, and that means it will have to show behind the text box as well (figure 7.20).

Figure 7.20

In order to fix this, I need to select the picture, and from the Format tab for Picture Tools click on *Send Backward*, then choose *Send to Back* so the picture is behind everything—including the text box and the border. Then I can resize the picture to make it fit within the border (figure 7.21). Keep in mind that you should start with a picture that is roughly the same shape as the space you need it to take up, as you might make it look funny if you stretch it too much. Otherwise you can get one that's too big and crop out the part you want to use.

Figure 7.21

Finally, I inserted some advertisement objects from the Insert tab and Building Block groups, and then edited the fill colors by right clicking each one and choosing the format option. Then I changed the text from the default sample to make it fit with the content of the flyer (as shown in figure 7.22).

Figure 7.22

Saving Your Publication
Just like with all the other Office programs, there are many ways you can save your publication depending on what you plan on doing with it. The default file type is a Publisher file with the .pub file extension on the end of it. This is what you will be saving as for the most part.

However, if you have a need to save your file in another format, then there are various options to choose from. For example, if you need to send it to someone that either doesn't have Publisher or that you don't want to be able to edit your file, then you can save it as a PDF file or even a Microsoft XPS document. XPS (XML Paper Specification) documents are a Microsoft file format similar to PDF files, but they are based on XML rather than PostScript (but for what you need to know they pretty much do the same thing). You just need a program that can open XPS files on your computer to view the publication if you save it this way. The same goes for PDF files, but most people have that covered.

If you try and use some of the options like save as a Word file, you will get error messages saying that format only supports text, and it won't save the images from your publication, which most of the time doesn't do you any good.

One great way to save your publication is to email it to someone to look over as a JPEG file (which is an image file). Most pictures you view on your computer or get from your camera or smartphone are in JPEG format. Using this option will create an image file of your publication that will be nice and small for easy emailing, and won't be able to be edited. Other image formats you can save as include TIF, PNG, BMP, and GIF.

One last file type that you can save as that I want to mention is the Single File Web Page (.mht or .mhtl). If you want to be able to open your publication in a web browser, then you can save it as this type of file. There is another option for saving as a web page in HTML format, but the problem with that is it will save the images in a separate folder rather than keeping everything all in one file like the Single File Web Page does.

Printing Your Publication
Most people will want to print their publication when they are finished with it. After all, that's really the point of making one in Publisher. Printing a publication from Publisher is pretty much like printing a Word document. There are not too many options to worry about or that you can even change.

If you look at the print options (as shown in figure 7.33) you will see that they are very similar to the Word print options, and are actually a little simpler.

Figure 7.23

As for the page printing settings, you have the usual print all the pages, print the current page, print selected pages, and enter custom pages to print. Beneath that you can type in the pages you want to print. For a range of pages, use a dash (so to print pages 5 through 10 you would type 5-10). To print certain pages, use a comma to separate them (such as 3,5,10). You can even combine the two for a custom range (such as 2,4,7-10).

You can also have Publisher print each page on an entire sheet, or fit multiple pages on one sheet. The reason you would do this is to show it to someone for proofing or have a copy of all your pages on one page for easy reviewing.

When you first setup your publication, you should choose the page size that matches the paper you plan to print on. This way things will look the same on the screen as they do when they print. If you want to print on a different size paper than what your publication is setup as, you can still do that by choosing a different paper size.

Finally, you have options to print one sided or two sided, as well as to print in color or greyscale. The checkbox at the bottom that says *Save settings with publication* will keep your preferences saved with the file so that when you open it later and go to print, they will be the same.

Chapter 8 – Microsoft Outlook

Outlook is Microsoft's email and calendar program that is the most commonly used email program in existence. If your work uses Windows computers, then there is a good chance you have the Outlook email client installed on your office computer. Even for home users, Outlook is a very popular program, and since it comes with some versions of Office, many people end up using it.

If you don't know what an email client is, I will give you the quick rundown. When someone sends you an email it needs to go to an email server either hosted somewhere on the Internet or housed in your company's server room and connected to the Internet. For many companies that email server is called Microsoft Exchange, which Outlook was designed to work with. Then to get the email from that email server, you need an email client, which is what Outlook is.

Outlook also has a built-in calendar that can be used for more than just adding reminders for appointments. In the corporate world, it can be used to reserve conference rooms, equipment, and schedule meetings with other people. Plus, Outlook is a great place to store your contacts in its built-in address book.

Outlook Specific Tabs and Groups
Outlook doesn't have as many tabs as the other Office programs, but the ones it does have are quite different than what we have seen so far. Let's take a little time and go over them now.

Home Tab for Mail
Once again, Outlook has a Home tab, just like all the other Office programs (figure 8.1), but it's very different than the other Home tabs I discussed earlier in the book. There are actually two versions of the Home tab in Outlook, depending on if you are working with mail or with the calendar. I'm going to start with the Home tab for email and then discuss the Home tab for the calendar.

Figure 8.1

New

Under the New group you have *New Email* and *New Items*. If you want to write a new email, then you obviously click the New Email button. But, if you want to do other things like make a new appointment, meeting, task, or contact, you can pick one of those options from the New Item button.

Delete

In order to keep your inbox and other folders clean you should delete emails you will never read again, or that you never wanted in the first place (such as spam messages). To delete an email or several emails, highlight them and then click the Delete button to have them sent to your trash. (By the way, I will be using the terms *email* and *messages* throughout this chapter, and they refer to the same thing.)

 If you want to delete an email message without sending it to your trash you can hold down the Shift key while clicking on the Delete button or pressing the Delete key on your keyboard. You will get a prompt telling you that the item will be permanently deleted, so keep in mind that if you want it back, you are out of luck.

There are three other buttons in the Delete group that you can use to keep your mailbox clean.

- **Ignore** – Use this option when you have a current email conversation going that you don't want to see in your inbox anymore. It will send any future updates to that conversation to your trash.

- **Clean Up** – If you have redundant messages in your inbox or other folders, you can use the Clean Up tool to remove the extra copies of the messages.

- **Junk** – Anyone who has an email account knows what junk mail is. It's that annoying email you get from people advertising things like Viagra or from the prince who wants to leave you his fortune. Outlook gives you a few options as to what you can do with email you consider junk. You can choose to block the sender, or never block the sender or their domain if you don't want the email considered junk. Sometimes you will get email in your Junk E-mail folder that shouldn't be there, and this way you can have it marked as okay.

If you click on Junk E-mail Options, you can fine tune how you want Outlook to filter your email (figure 8.2). Notice the tabs for Safe Senders, Safe Recipients, Blocked Senders, and International as well.

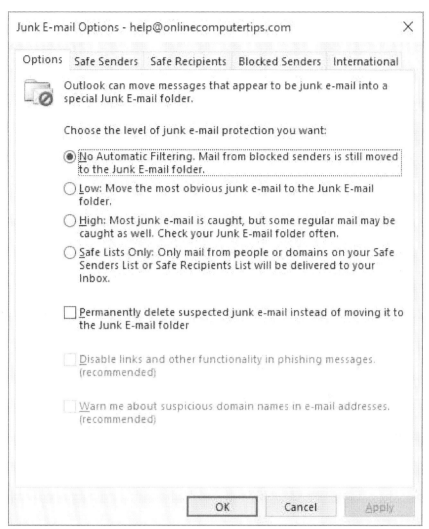

Figure 8.2

Respond

When you receive an email, many times you will need to respond to that message in some way or send it to someone else who needs to view it. There are several ways you can respond to an email:

- Reply – Clicking this button will open a new message addressed to the sender of the message so you can send them a reply.

- Reply All – If you received an email that was sent to you as well as other people and you want to reply to everyone who got a copy of that email, then you can do so with this button.

- Forward – When someone sends you an email that you want to send to someone else to read, then click the Forward button and type in their email address to send them a copy of the message.

- Meeting – This button, when clicked, will open up the meeting scheduler tool and allow you to set up a meeting with the sender of the email, and then send off an invitation via email to the person who sent you the original email.

- More – This option lets you forward an email to someone as a file attachment rather than forwarding just the email itself.

Quick Steps

Quick Steps are used to perform an action on an email by simply selecting that email and clicking on one of the options from the Quick Step list. There are some built-in Quick Steps, such as Move to (which will move an email to a specific folder and mark it as read) and To Manager (which will forward an email to your manager). Figure 8.3 shows the options when you click the arrow in the Quick Steps group. From here you can see all of your configured quick steps as well as edit, duplicate, and delete them. The New button will let you create your own custom quick step.

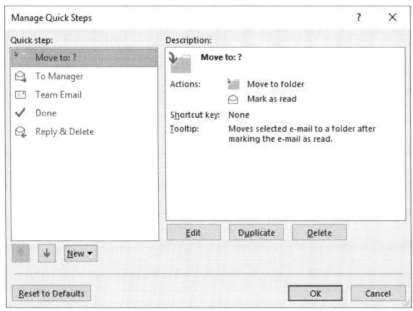

Figure 8.3

Move

Part of using Outlook successfully is knowing how to organize your emails so they are easy to find and you don't just have a big mess with all of your messages in your Inbox. I will cover creating folders later in this chapter, but for now you should know that the Move button will allow you to move an email to a different folder within Outlook, or even create a calendar event from it.

Rules are a little more complicated, but come in handy when you want Outlook to perform an action on an email without having to do it manually. For example, you can set up a rule that sends any emails from joe@joemail.com to a folder called Joe every time one comes in. Figure 8.4 shows the rule wizard that will walk you through creating a rule based on your requirements. It takes a little playing with to get used to how it works, but overall it's pretty easy to create a rule.

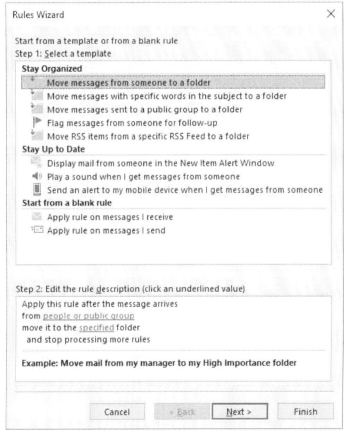

Figure 8.4

The OneNote option can be used to send an email to a OneNote notebook to reference later. If you don't have OneNote or don't plan on ever using it, then you don't need to worry about this option.

Tags

Tags are used to mark your emails so you know what has been done to them or what needs to be done to them. There are three tag types to choose from.

- **Unread/Read** – When you have an unread email in Outlook it will be shown with bold type, indicating it has not been read. After you open it, the bold font turns to normal, showing that it has been opened. The *Unread/Read* button can be used to mark an email as unread or read in case you want to change its status manually.

- **Categorize** – Outlook lets you categorize emails based on things like importance or any other category you want to use on your messages. When you have an email selected, you can click on the *Categorize* button to choose one of the preconfigured colored categories. The colors themselves don't mean anything, but it's up to you want color you want for what category. For example, in figure 8.5 I selected an email, clicked the Categorize button, and will choose Red Category from the list.

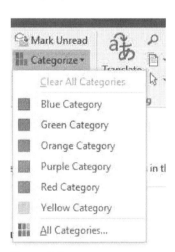

Figure 8.5

It will then ask me if I want to rename Red Category to something more useful, since it's the first time I have used Red Category (figure 8.6). I decided to name it *Important!*

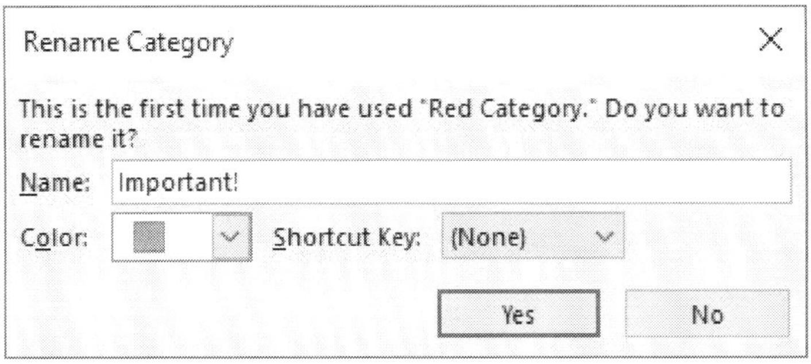

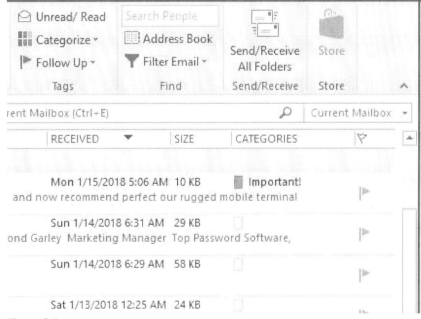

Figure 8.6

Now when I go back to my Inbox (figure 8.7), I can see that I have the red *Important!* category showing next to the email I assigned it to.

Figure 8.7

- **Follow Up** – Here is where you can set reminders as to when you need to act on a particular email. When you click the Follow Up button, there are several choices such as Today, Tomorrow, This Week, Next Week, Mark Complete, and so on. When you choose one of the options, the flag icon (which you can see on the right side of each message in figure 8.7) will change according to how you marked it.

Find

The Find group is pretty easy to understand since its purpose is to find things such as people and emails. The *Search People* box is used to search for people in your contacts (which I will get to later in this chapter). You can also click the *Address Book* button to bring up your address book, which contains people you have entered into it. Finally the *Filter Email* button is used to only display emails based on criteria such as unread, has attachments, flagged, and so on.

Send/Receive

This button is used to do a manual send and receive of your email accounts. Normally you have Outlook configured to do automatic send and receives at the interval you specify in the options. There is also a dedicated Send/Receive tab (which I will go over next).

Send/Receive Tab for Mail

If you can't send and receive email in your email client, then obviously it doesn't do you any good. Therefore, the Send/Receive tab has some options that you can configure to help you with these tasks (figure 8.8).

Send & Receive

This group has a few options you can use to configure how you send and receive email as well as allow you to do immediate sending and receiving of your messages. The big *Send/Receive All Folders* button will send out any emails you have waiting in your Outbox, as well as check for any new messages. This will be done for all of the email accounts you have configured. (By the way, if you didn't already know you can use more than one email account with Outlook, now you do!)

If you want to update messages only in the folder you happen to be working in, then you can click the *Update Folder* button to do so. The *Send All* button will send any emails you have waiting to go out for all of your accounts. Finally the *Send/Receive Groups* option will let you choose which specific email account you want to perform a send and receive on rather than doing it for all accounts.

Download

When your email is getting checked, technically your messages are being "downloaded" to Outlook, and Outlook has a stats box which you can view to check the progress or check for any possible errors. Figure 8.9 shows an example of what this progress box looks like.

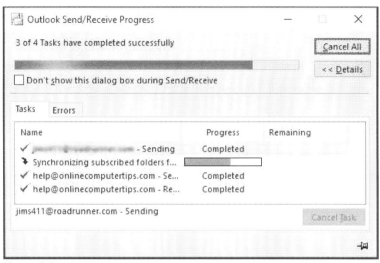

Figure 8.9

Sometimes while Outlook is checking messages it takes a long time to complete, especially if you are having connection issues or have to download a large number of messages or emails with large attachments. If you need to stop the process, then you can click on the *Cancel All* button to do so.

Server

The Server group has some options for downloading headers with your email. Headers are extra lines in the email that identify routing information such as the sender, recipient, email server, date, and so on. Header information comes in handy when troubleshooting email issues and also to help see where an email really came from (in case the sender is trying to cover their tracks and hide that information). An example of an email header can be seen in the bottom box of figure 8.10.

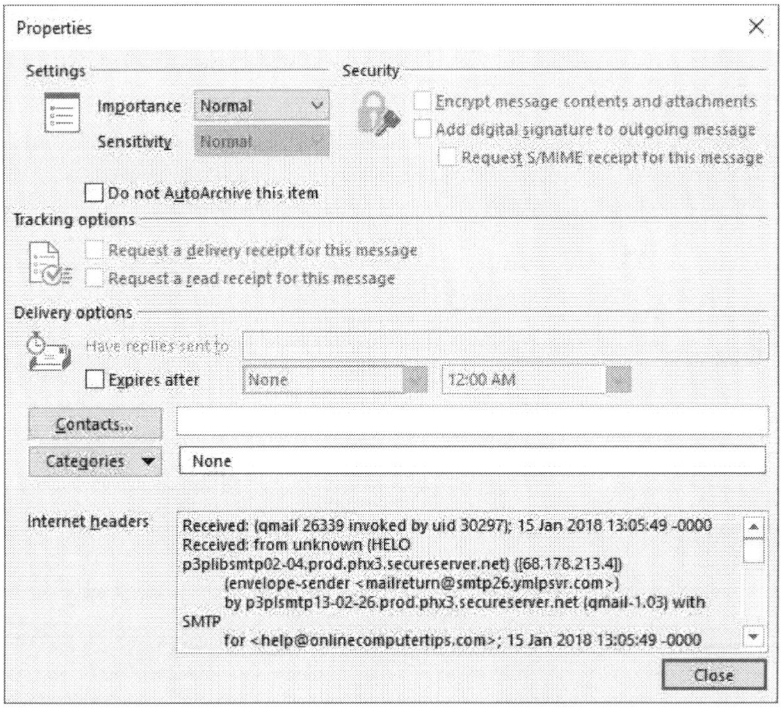

Properties
Settings
Importance Normal
Sensitivity Normal
Security
Encrypt message contents and attachments
Add digital signature to outgoing message
Request S/MIME receipt for this message
Do not AutoArchive this item
Tracking options
Request a delivery receipt for this message
Request a read receipt for this message
Delivery options
Have replies sent to
Expires after None 12:00 AM
Contacts...
Categories
None
Internet headers
Received: (qmail 26339 invoked by uid 30297); 15 Jan 2018 13:05:49 -0000
Received: from unknown (HELO
p3plibsmtp02-04.prod.phx3.secureserver.net) ([68.178.213.4])
(envelope-sender <mailreturn@smtp26.ymlpsvr.com>)
by p3plsmtp13-02-26.prod.phx3.secureserver.net (qmail-1.03) with
SMTP
for <help@onlinecomputertips.com>; 15 Jan 2018 13:05:49 -0000
Close
Figure 8.10

Work Offline

The Work Offline has one button, and that is also called Work Offline. This is used if you want to disconnect from your email server and not get any new messages. I have never had the need to use this feature, and you probably won't either!

Folders Tab for Mail

Folders are an important part of using Outlook because they let you organize your email, just like you use folders on your computer to organize your files (figure 8.11). The Folder tab has many options and settings to help keep your email organized.

Inbox - help@onlinecomputertips.com - Outlook
File
Home
Send / Receive
Folder
View
Tell me what you want to do...
New Folder
New Search Folder
New
Rename Folder
Copy Folder
Move Folder
Delete Folder
Actions
Mark All as Read
Run Rules Now
Show All Folders A to Z
Clean Up Folder
Delete All
Recover Deleted Items
Clean Up
Show in Favorites
Favorites
AutoArchive Settings
Folder Permissions
Folder Properties
Properties
Figure 8.11

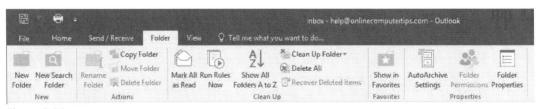

New

Here you can create a new folder in a location that you choose to add emails to as you see fit. When you click on *New Folder* you will be prompted to choose a location for that folder as well as tell Outlook what type of folder you wish to create (figure 8.12). Most of the time it will be Mail and Post Items.

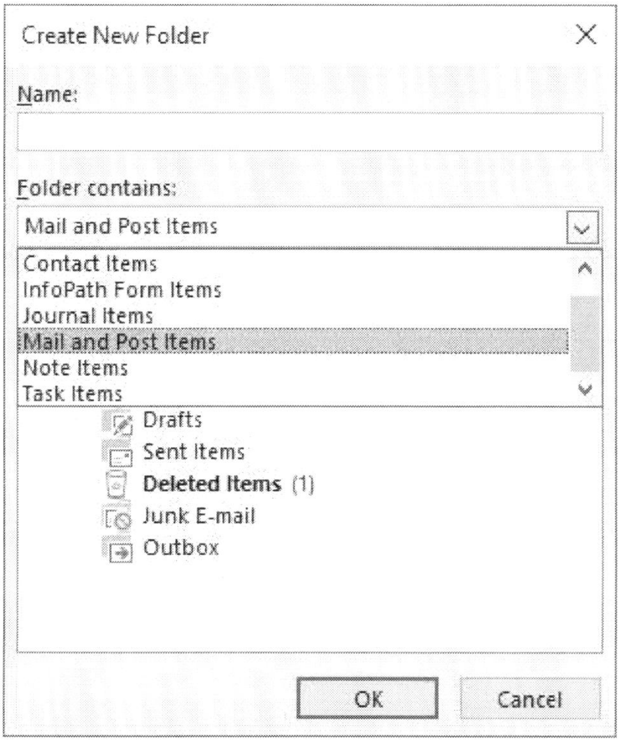

Figure 8.12

A *Search Folder* is used to display messages based on a specific criteria that you configure when creating the folder. The process for creating a Search Folder is kind of like making a rule, where you tell it what you want it to do and show. Figure 8.13 shows some of the choices you have when creating a Search Folder. Going back to the email we flagged for follow up, if we create a Search Folder and choose the *Mail marked for follow up* option, then when the folder is created, the email that we flagged will appear in that folder.

Figure 8.13

Actions
This group is pretty self-explanatory, and it allows you to perform several common actions on your folders just like you would with the folders on your computer that contain your files. You can do things such as rename, copy, move, and delete a folder simply by selecting that folder and clicking the appropriate button.

Clean Up
This group is where you come when it's time to clean up some of the clutter that you have accumulated in Outlook. The first button called *Mark As Read* simply marks any email in that folder that is showing bold for unread, to normal to show that it has been read.

The *Run Rules* Now button will run any of the rules that you configured from the Move group on the Home tab. So, if you have any items in your mailbox that haven't had your rules applied to them yet, you can do this right on the spot.

Many people like to have their files and folders in alphabetical order, which makes sense since I like to as well. If you are like this too, then clicking on *Show All Folders A to Z* will sort your folder list alphabetically, making things easier to find.

The *Clean Up Folder* button will let Outlook clean up redundant messages from conversations in the folder or from both the folder and its subfolders. *Delete all* will do exactly what it says, delete all the emails in the folder, so be careful if you ever use this! Finally the *Recover Deleted Items* button will attempt to restore emails that you have deleted from this folder, assuming they haven't already been purged from your email server.

Favorites
The Favorites in Outlook is an area where you can place shortcuts to your most commonly used folders that you access. Outlook places your Inbox, Sent, and Trash in the Favorites automatically (figure 8.14), but you can easily add your own.

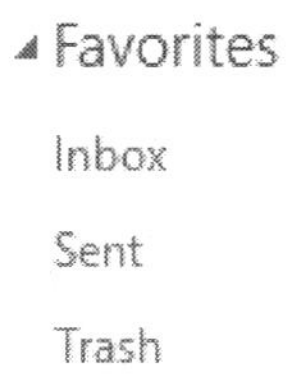

⊿ Favorites

Inbox

Sent

Trash

Figure 8.14

To add a new folder to the Favorites section, select that folder and then click the *Show in Favorites* button to have it added (like seen in figure 8.15).

⊿ Favorites

Inbox

Sent

Trash

Sales

Figure 8.15

Properties
Here is where you can go to check the details on folders and also set archiving settings (if that is a feature you are using).

- **AutoArchive Settings** – When you use an archive in Outlook, it will take older emails and move them to an archive folder to keep your folders clean and up to date. You can also set the interval and location for your archived emails.

- **Folder Permissions** – You have the ability to share your email folders with other users in your organization if you have an Exchange email server configured on your network.

- **Folder Properties** – This will show you information about the type of folder you are looking at, its location, its size, and will also let you get to the archive settings.

View Tab for Mail

The main purpose of the View tab is to change how Outlook looks on the screen to make it easier to find what you are looking for. Figure 8.16 shows all the groups and the options you have for changing views.

Figure 8.16

Current View

Here you can configure how Outlook displays your message in your folders. The *Change View* button allows you to pick from several different views, such as IMAP messages, hide messages that are marked to be deleted, group messages marked to be deleted, and preview messages. The choices you have here will vary based on what type of email account you have. You might also see options such as Compact, Single, and Preview, which changes what shows for your mail folder.

Outlook has many columns, such as From, Subject, and Received, but there are many other columns you can add to your view, such as Created, Due Date, and Sensitivity. Clicking on the *View Settings* button will let you add and remove these columns from Outlook, as well as change the way email is grouped, sorted, filtered, and so on.

If you make some changes and realize you don't like what you have done, you can click on the Reset View button to set everything back to their defaults.

Messages
When you have many back and forth replies in an email chain, then you might want to have your messages shown as conversations more like how a text message thread would look like. When you enable this option, then the *Conversation Settings* button will become active and you can change things such as showing the senders above the subject and so on.

Arrangement
Another way to organize your messages is to sort them by a certain category. This is what the Arrangement group will let you do, but one other thing it does is sets the display preview lines for each message. So, when you look at your list of emails, they will usually have part of the message itself showing underneath the subject. If you click on the *Message Preview* button you can change the number of lines from 0 to 3. Figure 8.17 shows it sent with 1 line showing while figure 8.18 show an email with 3 lines showing.

Figure 8.17

Figure 8.18

The main box in the Arrangement group has several categories that you can sort your emails by, including Date, From, To, Subject, Importance, and so on. You also have the option to group your emails based on the category you choose.

If you want a quick way to reverse the sort order that you are currently using then click the *Reverse Sort* button. The Add Columns button will do the same thing as the View Settings button did in the Current View group.

Finally you can use the *Expand/Collapse* button to expand or collapse items within groups. So, if you have a bunch of emails that are grouped by subject, then you can use this button to expand or collapse that group depending on whether you want to see the emails or not.

Layout

I find this group very useful because it allows you to change the overall look of Outlook and can hide things you don't need and enable things you want to see. There are three types of view settings you can change from here.

- **Folder Pane** – Here you can configure the Outlook folders on the left side of the screen to display in various configurations. Figure 8.18 shows some samples of how the different settings look.

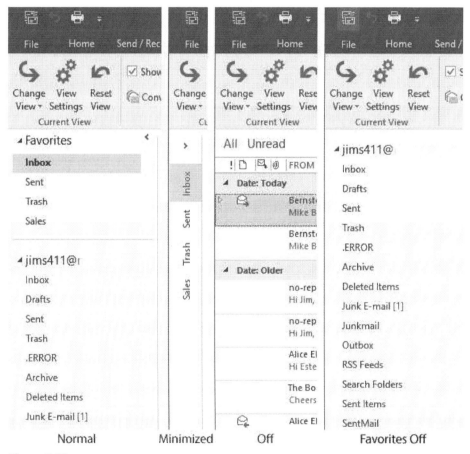

Figure 8.19

- **Reading Pane** – This is the preview window that shows the contents of the email when you click on one. You can have Outlook show it on the bottom, right side, or off altogether.

- **To-Do Bar** – If you use the calendar or tasks features of Outlook, then you can have your tasks show up on the To-Do Bar so you can see what you have coming up. Figure 8.20 shows the To-Do Bar enabled and showing the outstanding tasks that need to be completed.

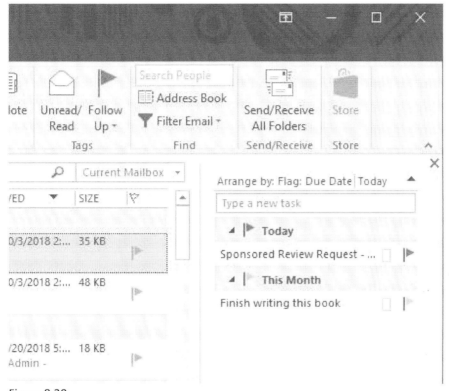

Figure 8.20

Window

The Window group does a couple of things, and the one you will use the most is the *Reminders Window* button. This will bring up any upcoming reminders in one place so you can either dismiss or snooze them based on your needs.

The *Open in New Window* button will open the selected email account\mailbox in its own window. This can come in handy if you want a quick way to switch back and forth between separate accounts without losing your place. The *Close All Items* button will close any extra windows that you might have opened.

Home Tab for the Calendar

Now that we've covered how the tabs work for when you are looking at your email, let's now take a look at how they differ when you're looking at your calendar. If you take a look at figure 8.21, you should notice that the groups and buttons are quite a bit different than what we were just looking at. If you don't know how to switch over to your calendar, there are icons on the bottom left of your screen for each Outlook feature (figure 8.22)

Figure 8.21

Figure 8.22

New

The New group is pretty self-explanatory. You can click on *New Appointment* or *New Meeting* depending on what you need to accomplish. An appointment is just a way to set a reminder with details for yourself and also show that you're busy on your calendar if you share it with others. A meeting is when you want to schedule a meeting with other people in a predetermined place at a predetermined time. You can send out meeting invitations, and when the recipients accept them it will place the meeting information in their Outlook calendar.

Go To

If you click on *Today* in this group, then Outlook will bring the active day of your calendar to the current day. If you click on *Next 7 Days* then Outlook will give you a 7 day view of your calendar starting from the current day.

Arrange

This group is what you would use to change the view of your calendar depending on how many days you want to see and what days of the week you want to see. The *Day* button will show only today's meetings and appointments etc. *Work Week* will show Monday through Friday while Week will show Sunday through Saturday. *Month* will display the entire month so you can get a complete overview of the whole month. Then you can double click any specific day to create a new event for that day. The *Schedule View* comes in handy when you can see other people's calendars and want to know what days or times they have available. It will open the day in a horizontal view and show the additional calendars that you have shared with you in the same view.

Manage Calendars

If you have access to additional calendars besides your own, you can open them by clicking the *Open Calendar* button. This usually applies to your corporate account with an email server, but if you have access to an Internet calendar you can open it from here as well. There is also an option to create a new blank calendar from here. Calendar Groups are used to group together frequently used calendars so you can see them all from one view, making it easy to see schedules and available resources from all of them at once.

Share

Outlook makes it possible to share your calendar with other users, making it easier to collaborate on projects since you will be able to see each other's schedules. There are four ways to share your calendar in Outlook:

- **E-mail Calendar** – This option will add your calendar to an email as an attachment that you can send to other people. You have many options as to what you can include on your calendar and what will be available for the other person to see (as shown in figure 8.23).

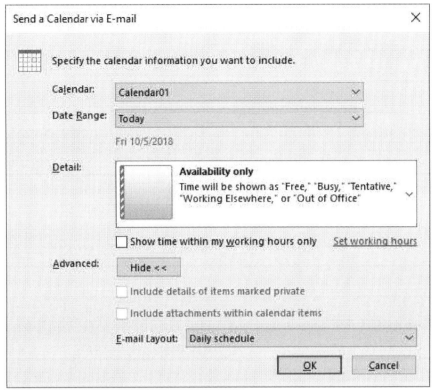

Figure 8.23

- **Share Calendar** – If you are using a Microsoft Exchange email server for your mail, then you can use the *Share Calendar* feature to share your calendar with other Exchange users in the office.

- **Publish Online** – This option will let you publish your calendar on a supported website so that other people can view it online.

- **Calendar Permissions** – When sharing your calendar, you can assign various levels of permissions to various people who you have granted access to it. To use this feature you must be using a Microsoft Exchange email server.

Find

Some users have many contacts, making it hard to find who they are looking for. You can use the *Search People* box to type in a name or other details about a contact to help you find it. Clicking the *Address Book* button will bring up your Outlook Address Book, which shows your contacts all in one place. You can have more than one Address Book as well.

Send / Receive Tab for the Calendar

This tab is identical to the Send / Receive tab for mail, but actually has less options. You can use either one, but if you need more mail related options use the Send / Receive tab for mail.

Folder Tab for the Calendar

The calendar has its own tab as well, but, once again, it's not as involved as the Folder tab for mail, and has less items on the Ribbon (figure 8.24). But that doesn't mean there are not important things you can do from here, so let's get started going over the groups in this tab.

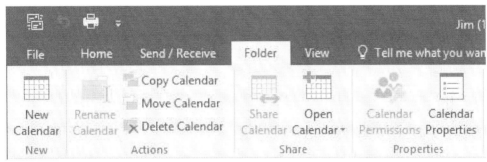

Figure 8.24

New

You are not limited to only having one calendar in Outlook, and can create as many as you like for different purposes. If you click on *New Calendar* you will be prompted to name the calendar and tell Outlook where you want to place it within your Outlook folders (as shown in figure 8.25).

Figure 8.25

Actions

When you want to organize your calendars (assuming you have more than one) you can use the options in the Action group to do so. The available options are pretty self-explanatory, and you can do things such as rename, copy, move, and delete your calendars if you choose to do so. When you click on either copy or move, you will see a box similar to figure 8.25 asking you to specify where you want the calendar to go.

Share

You might remember that we talked about sharing and opening calendars when discussing the Home tab for the calendar. Well, the Folder tab has the same *Share Calendar* and *Open Calendar* buttons that will do the same thing.

Properties

Once again, we have an option that has been repeated with the *Calendar Permissions* button, which is just like the one on the Home tab. But we do have another setting in the Properties group, and that is to see the properties of your calendar by clicking on the *Calendar Properties* button. This will show you information regarding things like the type of calendar you are using, its location, description, and folder size.

View Tab for the Calendar

Once again, the View tab for the calendar (figure 8.26) has some of the same items that it did when we were looking at mail, but it does have some additional options that I will now go over while ignoring the duplicate items (since I have already discussed them).

Figure 8.26

Arrangement

I talked about the different calendar views that you can use, such as day, week and month, but there are a few more things in the Arrangement group that I would like to go over. The *Time Scale* button can be used to change the view area of your calendar and allow you more space for seeing appointments and meetings. You can change the scale from five minutes to sixty minutes, and the larger the number the less space you have per time slot (as seen in figure 8.27). (This option is not available when having the calendar in the month view.)

Figure 8.27

If you use multiple calendars and want to see how things line up, then you can use the *Overlay* button to have a different calendar on top of your current calendar. Each calendrer will be shown in a different color, making it easy to tell them apart. This is an alternative to using the side-by-side mode, where each calendar appears next to the other.

When at the office, your hours are different from when you are at home. Outlook has an option to only display the working hours on your calendar so you don't need to even see times when you are not in the office. To get this view click on the *Working Hours* button. To change your calendar working hours, go to the File tab, then click on Options and go to the Calendar setting. Then under *Work time* change the hours to whatever they should be.

Color
Outlook has a default color scheme for your calendar, but that can be changed if it's not your thing. Simply click on the Color button and choose a new color for your calendar. You can't create your own colors here, and can only use the choices Outlook provides for you.

A couple more tabs that I want to mention are the Calendar Tools for Appointments and for Meetings. When you click on an appointment or meeting on your calendar, it will bring up a special tab where you can adjust settings for that specific appointment or meeting. As you can see in figures 8.28 and 8.29, the options are a little different for each one, but you can do things like add additional attendees, cancel meetings, or delete appointments, and forward them to other people.

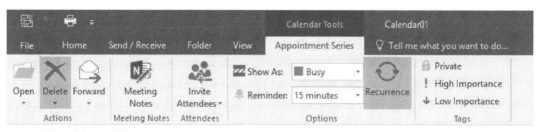

Figure 8.28

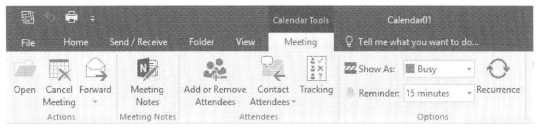

Figure 8.29

Default Outlook Folders

Outlook comes with many folders built-in to help you organize your mail, and also allows you to create your own folders to organize things even further. (I will get into creating folders later in this chapter.)

Figure 8.30 shows the folders that I have in my copy of Outlook 2016. If you have a different version, the folders may vary a little, or even if you have the same version they may vary a little based on your configuration. I will now go over the basics of what these folders do.

Figure 8.30

- **Inbox** – This is where all your new mail will arrive unless you create a rule that places certain types of emails into other folders. New emails will show in bold, and after you read them the bold will be removed.

- **Drafts** – When you are working on an email and want to come back to it later, you can save it as a draft. It's kind of like working on a Word document and then saving it to work on later. When you save an email as a draft, it will be stored in this folder until you send it.

- **Sent** – Outlook, by default, will save a copy of all emails that you have sent out in the Sent folder. If you need to refer back to something you previously sent someone or that you wish to forward to someone else, you can find it here. One thing to keep in mind is that this folder can get rather full, so you might want to purge or archive your sent items at some point. Sometimes this folder will be called Sent Items or Sent Mail.

- **Trash** – This is where any emails that you delete will go, even if it's from your draft or sent folder. Think of it like the Windows Recycle Bin where you delete the emails but they are not really deleted until you empty them out of the trash.

- **Archive** – If you have old emails you would like to archive, then you can click on the Archive button from the Home tab and Delete group if you have that option available to you.

- **Deleted Items** – This does the same thing as the Trash folder, and which one Outlook will use depends on the type of email account you have (such as a corporate Exchange account vs. a Gmail account).

- **Junk E-mail** – Outlook has a junk mail filter that will try and determine when you get any spam emails and then put them in this folder. If you get something in this folder that is not junk, you can right click it and choose *Junk>Not Junk* to have it sent to your inbox.

- **Outbox** – If you have Outlook configured not to automatically send your email when you click the Send button, then it will go to the Outbox and wait for you to click the Send / Receive button to send it out manually. This way you can work on a bunch of emails and send them to the Outbox, then send them all at once when you're ready.

- **RSS Feeds** – RSS (or Really Simple Syndication) is a way that publishers get their content to your email when you subscribe to things like blogs or online magazines. You subscribe to the ones you want, and then they will show up in this folder. To add an RSS feed to Outlook, simply right click the RSS Feeds folder, choose Add a New RSS Feed, and enter in the location\address of the feed (like shown in figure 8.31). Many sites will have the RSS Feed icon on them, allowing you to click on it to subscribe.

Figure 8.31

- **Search Folder** – These are used to set up a specific folder that you can base a search on and have the results show up in that folder so you can then refer to them later on when you need to. The folder itself doesn't do anything until you right click it and it and choose New Search Folder. (I discussed this feature earlier in this chapter.)

- **Favorites** – One last thing I wanted to mention again was the Favorites group. Even though it's not technically a folder, it's a place where you can store your favorite or most commonly used folders. When you right click a folder and choose *Show In Favorites,* it just puts a shortcut to that folder there and doesn't actually copy or move it there. So whatever you do in the real folder or the favorites shortcut will affect the other one.

Creating and Managing Folders

Now that I went over the default folders, you should know that they are not the only folders that you can use in Outlook. You can create multiple folders as well as subfolders within those folders so you can keep all of your emails organized.

Creating a folder is very easy, and all you need to do is decide where you want that folder to be, and then right click there and choose *New Folder*. If you do this procedure on an existing folder, then it will make the new folder a subfolder of the one you clicked on. So, if you want a new folder in the same place as the main folders, then you will need to right click on your email address and do the new folder process from there. Then you will have your new folder shown in "the root" of your folder tree (as seen in figure 8.32).

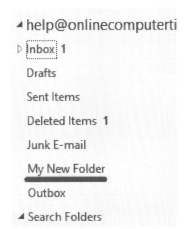

Figure 8.32

Going to the Folder tab will give you a way to create a new folder as well from the New group.

I always like to create subfolders in Outlook when I have a lot of email because your Inbox can get full really quick and it makes it hard to find what you are looking for. Of course you can always do a search but that takes more time than going to the folder where you know your email is located.

When you right click a folder there are several other options besides creating a new folder that you can use to manage your folders, such as renaming, deleting, moving them, and so on (figure 8.33).

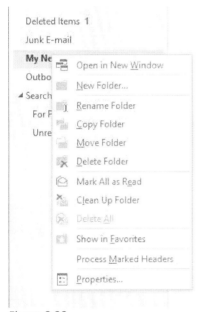

Figure 8.33

I would like to discuss some of the options that might not be totally obvious as to what they do. For example, if you choose the *Move Folder* or *Copy Folder* option, it will bring up a box asking you where you would like to move the folder to. You need to select that location and then click OK.

The *Mark All as Read* choice will simply mark all the emails in that folder as read, meaning taking the bold formatting off all of them. This comes in handy if you want to mark all of your emails as read without having to do so one at a time.

The *Clean Up Folder* option (which I mentioned before) will let Outlook clean up redundant messages from conversations in the folder or from both the folder and its subfolders.

The *Delete all* option will delete all of the emails in that folder, but not the folder itself. You would choose the *Delete Folder* option if you wanted the folder removed as well. When you delete a folder, it will go to your Trash or Deleted Items folder just like your email does.

I mentioned email headers earlier, and the *Process Marked Headers* option is used to download an email header once you have examined it and marked it for download within Outlook.

Outlook allows you to drag and drop your folders to different locations as well. All you need to is click and hold the one you want to move, drag it to its new location, release the mouse button, and it will be moved there.

Setting Up an Email Account

Now that you hopefully have a better idea of how Outlook is configured, it's time to setup an email account so you can finally start using it. Like I mentioned before, there are several types of email accounts (such as a corporate Exchange account and POP3 or IMAP accounts and so on), so this affects how you add an email account to Outlook.

To begin, we need to go to the File tab and then click on the *Account Settings* button, and then on *Account Settings* under that (figure 8.34).

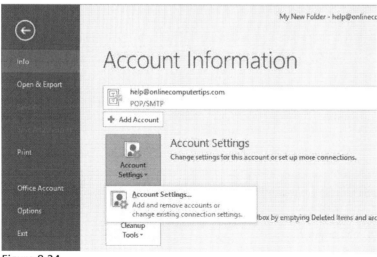

Figure 8.34

Then, from the *E-mail* tab, click the *New* button to start the email account setup process. Now you have two choices as to how you are going to setup your email account. There is the automatic method and the manual method (as shown in figure 8.35). If you are lucky, you can use the automatic method to have Outlook configure everything for you. The automatic method has improved over the years, so there's a much better chance of it working for you so you don't have to use the manual method.

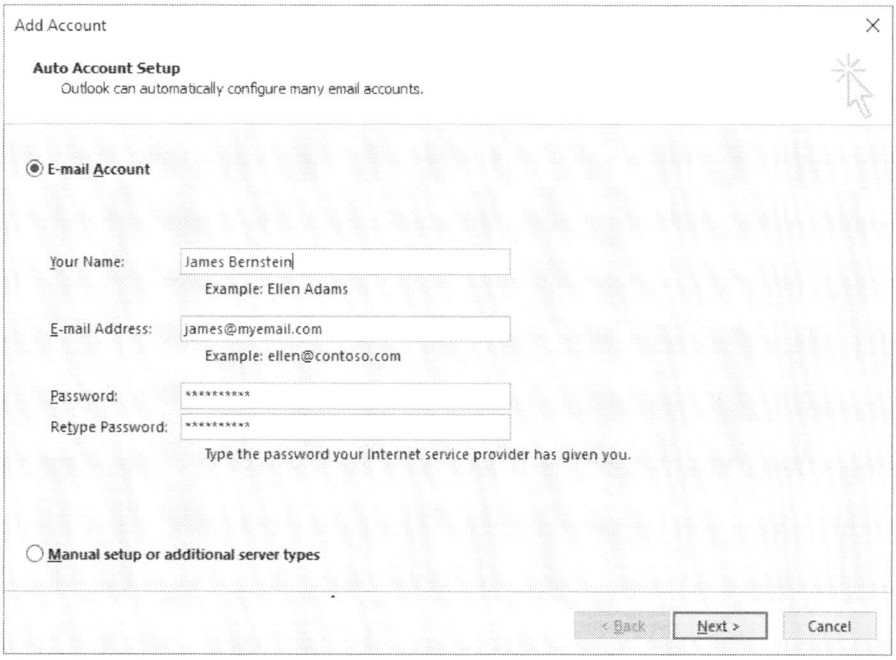

Figure 8.35

All you need to do is put your name in the first box and then your email address and password in the other boxes. Then click on Next. Outlook will then go out and find your email account settings for you and configure your account. If you have an email provider that is not well known (like Gmail or Yahoo) you have less of a chance of Outlook being able to configure itself automatically.

If that doesn't work, then you are stuck configuring your email account manually, and you will need to obtain certain information from your email provider to do so. (This can usually be found on their website if you search for Outlook email setup.)

The first thing you will need to determine is if you are using an outlook.com or Exchange compatible service, or whether you are using a standard POP or IMAP account. Once again, this information should be available on your providers website. If this is a corporate account and your company has its own Exchange email server, then you would choose the first option in figure 8.36, but for my example I choose the second option to setup a personal POP3 email account.

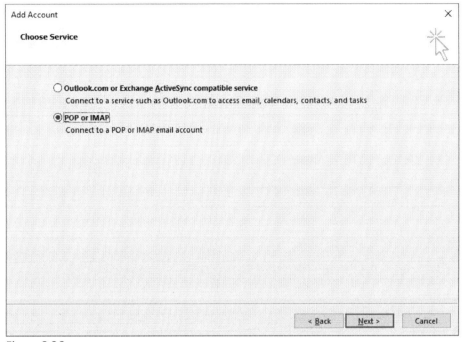

Figure 8.36

To add your account manually you will need to know your email address, password, account type, incoming mail server, and outgoing mail server. The default is to configure this new email account in a new Outlook data file, which is what you will most likely want to do (figure 8.37). Once you have the settings in place, you can click on the Test Account Settings button and see if everything checks out okay.

Figure 8.37

If you get any errors, it may require you to click on the More Settings button to configure additional settings such as checking the box that says *My outgoing server (SMTP) requires authentication,* which is something that is commonly required (figure 8.38). Your email provider might also use different port numbers for the incoming and outgoing servers besides the default 25 and 110 as shown in figure 8.39.

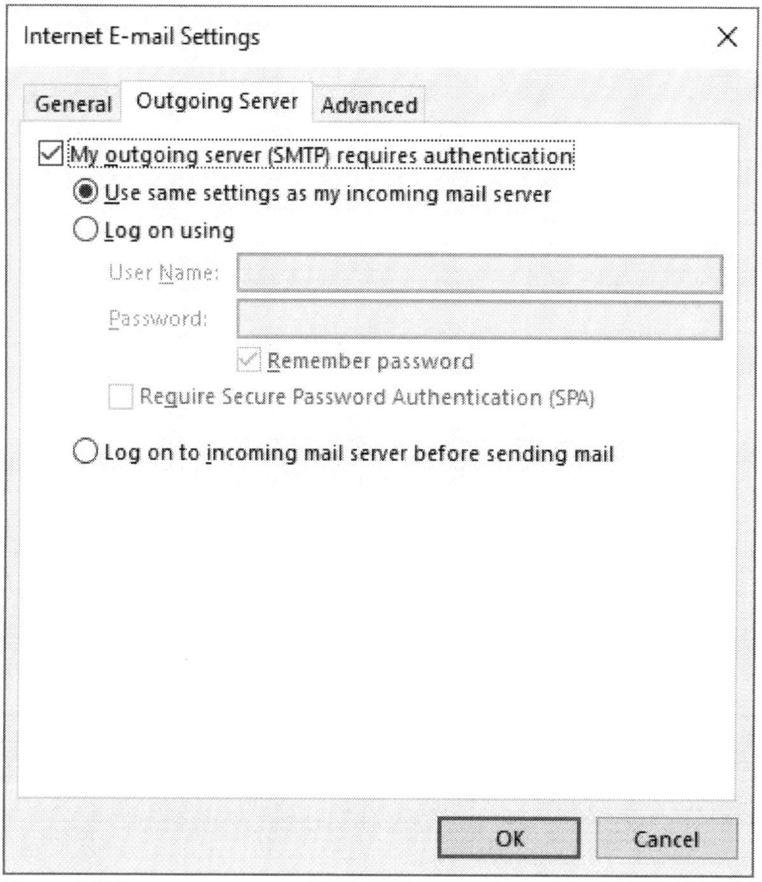

Internet E-mail Settings ✕

General | Outgoing Server | Advanced

☑ My outgoing server (SMTP) requires authentication
    ◉ Use same settings as my incoming mail server
    ○ Log on using
        User Name: [   ]
        Password: [   ]
        ☑ Remember password
        ☐ Require Secure Password Authentication (SPA)

    ○ Log on to incoming mail server before sending mail

[OK] [Cancel]

Figure 8.38

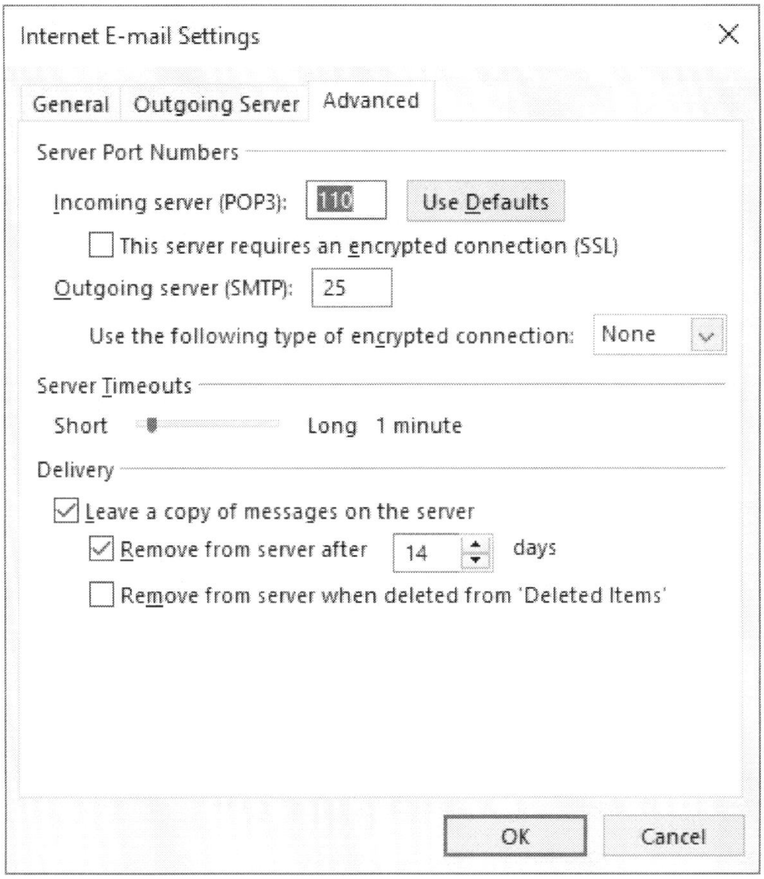

Figure 8.39

Once you get everything configured correctly, you will have your new email account listed in Outlook. If you already have an account configured then it will be added beneath any other previous accounts (figure 8.40). If you want to change the order of how they are listed, simply drag and drop the email account to where you want it to be listed within Outlook. To remove an email account all you need to do is go back to the original account settings section, highlight the account, and click on the *Remove* button.

Figure 8.40

Composing and Reading Email

Now that you have your email account set up and ready to go (hopefully) it's time to start composing some new emails while waiting for the flood of incoming email you will certainly be waiting for.

Creating a new email is a pretty simple process, but there are ways you can customize your email to personalize it. Plus, you might want to attach a file like a picture or document to your email to send off with it, so I will go over that as well.

To create a new email you can click on the New Email button on the Home tab and the new email box will appear, allowing you to compose your email. Let's begin by going over the main areas of the new email box (figure 8.41).

- **From** – This is where you pick which email account you want to send the email from. If you only have one, then you don't need to worry about it, but if you have others you can select them by clicking the small down arrow in the From button.

- **To** – This is where you enter the email address of who you are sending the email to. If you want to enter multiple people, just separate their email addresses with a semicolon. Clicking the To button will bring up the address book, where you can select recipients from your contacts.

- **Cc** – The Carbon Copy button will send the email to additional people of your choosing, but mark it a carbon copied, indicating the email is just for informational purposes and not really something they need to act on.

- **Bcc** – Blind Carbon Copy will copy other recipients on the email, but nobody will see who else was copied on the email. Think of it as a way to send the email to other people without them knowing who else was copied on it.

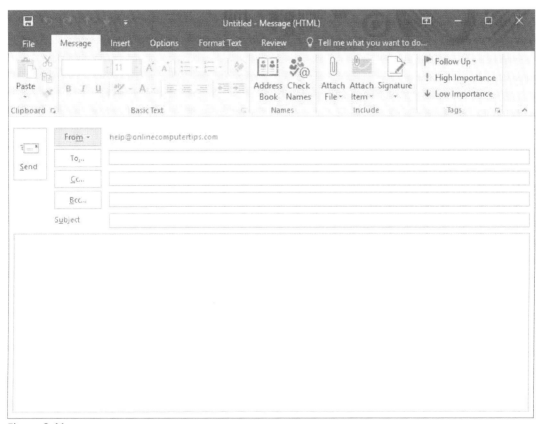

Figure 8.41

Now I will quickly go over the available tabs you can choose from when composing a new email.

Message
Here you can change things like the font type, size, and color, as well as paragraph formatting. There is also a button to open your Address Book, which will list your Outlook contacts. The *Include* group gives you choices to attach files, business cards, calendars, and so on. I will be going over email signatures in a bit, so I will skip that part for now. Finally, the *Tags* group lets you label your email with various levels of importance.

Insert
This tab will also let you attach files (etc.) to your document from the *Include* group. Other things you can do here is create tables, insert pictures, and draw shapes and charts from the *Illustrations* group. The other groups on the Insert tab allow you to insert links to websites, draw text boxes, add WordArt, and even insert the date and time (figure 8.42).

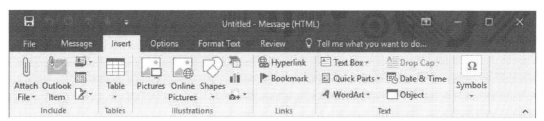

Figure 8.42

Options
If you want to spruce up your email, you can use the Options tab (figure 8.43) to add things like themes and change colors to something a little fancier. One thing I want to point out is the *Show Fields* group because this is where you enable the Bcc box (which is hidden by default). The *Tracking* group has settings to request delivery and read receipts, which will tell you when the person on the other end has read your email (assuming they choose to have the read receipt sent back to you). One nice feature on the Options tab is the Delay Delivery setting, which lets you specify the date and time your email will be sent so you can just walk away and have Outlook send it for you (assuming you leave it running).

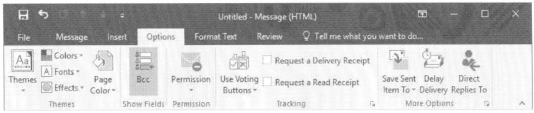

Figure 8.43

Format Text

The Format Text tab has many of the options I already went over in regards to formatting your text to give it a personal touch (figure 8.44). One thing I want to mention here is the *Format* group because it's here where you will determine how text is formatted. *HTML* allows you to insert pictures, backgrounds, and do custom formatting like you would see on a webpage. *Plain Text* will not format anything at all, and just show basic black text. *Rich Text* lets you do things like make the text bold and change its color.

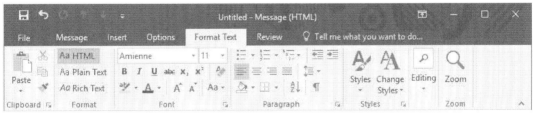

Figure 8.44

Review

This tab also has many of the same options I have already discussed (figure 8.45), but I wanted to point out the *Word Count* feature (which is nice) and also the *Translate* feature (which I already mentioned, but want to mention again because it can come in very handy). It will let you translate your typed text from one language to the other.

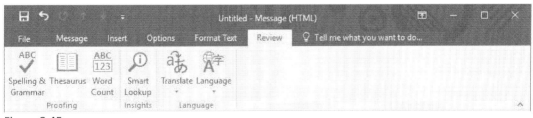

Figure 8.45

Formatting Your Email

Rather than just using the bland white background and plain text that is the default for new messages, you might want to brighten things up a bit by using a theme and changing around the fonts and colors in your email. For my email in figure 8.46, I have changed the font, text color, text size, and added a background texture. (Yes, I realize it's ugly, but I just wanted to show some of the things you can change in your email!)

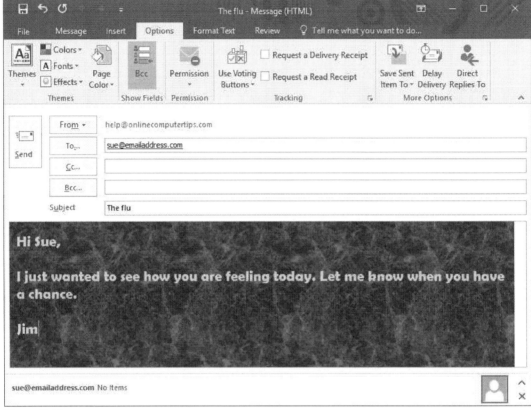

Figure 8.46

One thing to take note of is when I do the next new email, it will not look like the one in figure 8.46 because Outlook won't save my changes. But, if I create an email signature, I can add some custom touches that will be used every time I compose a new email.

To create a signature click on *New Email,* and then on the *Signature* button on the Message tab. From here you can create your email signature and apply it to a specific account (if you have more than one). In my example, I am creating a signature for the help@onlinecomputertips.com account and applying it to new messages, but not when I reply to a message or forward one (figure 8.47).

To begin, click on *New* and then give your signature a name. For my signature I decided to call it *Help Signature*. Then type in what message you want included in your email every time you compose a new one. You can format the text any way you like with fonts and colors etc.

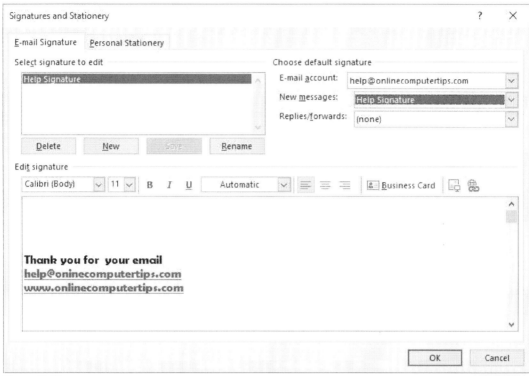

Figure 8.47

Next I want to add a background theme to my email, so I'll click the *Personal Stationary* tab, select the Compass theme (figure 8.48), and then click OK.

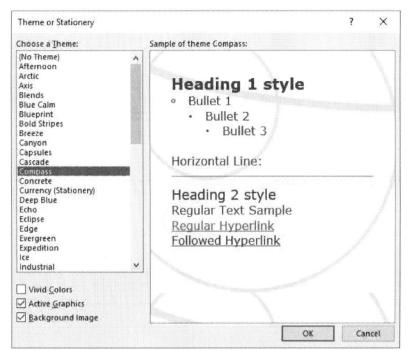

Figure 8.48

Now, when I click on New Email, I get my signature text and background automatically inserted into the new email (figure 8.49). All I need to do is add any additional information and I'm ready to go!

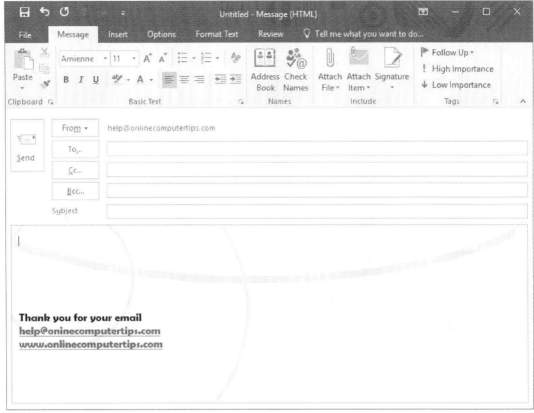

Figure 8.49

Reading Email

If you plan on sending out emails using Outlook then of course you plan on receiving them as well. Like I mentioned before, all new email will come into your Inbox unless you have a rule that has certain types of email going straight to other folders. I also mentioned that new email will show as bold, and email that you have read will not show as bold.

One thing I like to configure right way is the Outlook Reading Pane, which will show you the contents of an email just by clicking once on it without having to open it in a different window. The Reading Pane settings are located on the *View* tab under the *Layout* group. You can have the Reading Pane show on the bottom or on the right side of Outlook. As you can see in figure 8.50, the Reading Pane is on the bottom, and when the email about the Microsoft Outlook Test Message is highlighted the content of the email is displayed in the Reading Pane. Also notice that there are two bold emails, indicating that they are unread.

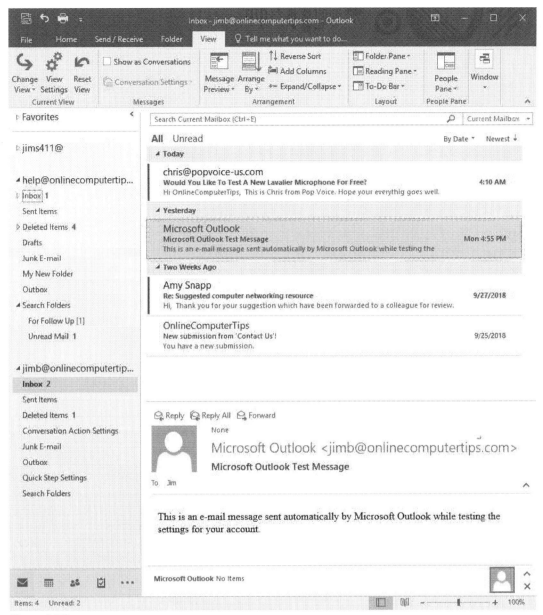

Figure 8.50

When I double click the email, it opens in a new window (as shown in figure 8.51). Notice how I get a bunch of options and groups in the Ribbon that I can use with this email. Next I will go over some of these groups so you have a better idea of what kind of things you can do with the emails you read.

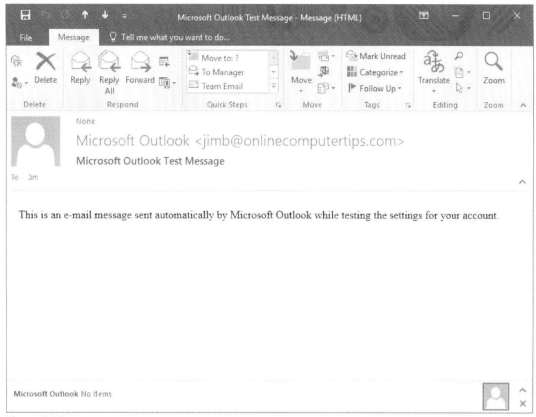

Figure 8.51

Delete

Obviously the *Delete* button will delete the email and send it to your trash, but you also have the option to mark the email as junk so next time you get one from this address it will go directly to your junk folder. The *Ignore Conversation* button will take this current conversation and future messages regarding this conversation and move them directly to the trash.

Respond

I have covered the Reply, Reply All, and Forward features, but wanted to mention the *Reply With Meeting* button. What this will do is request a new meeting right from this email. When you click the button, it will open a meeting request addressed to the sender of the email with today's date. Then, all you need to do is adjust the date and fill in the details and you can send the meeting request out via email.

Quick Steps
I want to go into a little more detail about the default *Quick Steps,* even though I covered them a little bit already. Quick Steps are used to perform an action or series of actions quickly to save you some time. You can even set up keyboard shortcuts for each Quick Step.

- **Move to** – When you choose this option, Outlook will move the email to a selected folder and mark it read at the same time. This comes in handy if you get a lot of emails that you want to keep, but really don't need to have sitting in your Inbox because you don't need to read them or give them too much attention.

- **To Manager** – If you have a manager with an email address, then clicking on *To Manager* will forward the email to that particular manager with one click. (You will first need to tell Outlook the email address of your manager before using this feature.)

- **Team Email** – This is similar to the To Manager choice, but instead will send the selected email to a group of people rather than just one. (Again, you will need to specify the team email addresses or email group before using this.)

- **Done** – Clicking the Done button will mark the email as complete, move it to a folder of your choosing, and then mark it as read.

- **Reply & Delete** – This option will send a reply to the sender of the email and then delete the original email.

Clicking on *Manage Quick Steps* will allow you to create your own Quick Step that you can use with email messages, giving you additional time saving tools.

Move
There is more than one way to move an email in Outlook. For example, you can simply drag an email from one folder to another to get the job done. But on the *Move* group within an email you have some additional options to fine tune your move.

If you click on the Move button it will bring up some suggestions based on folders you have recently been working with (figure 8.52), as well as some other choices.

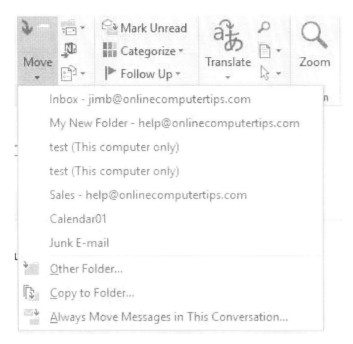

Figure 8.52

The *Other Folder* option will let you select another folder from your email account or a different email account if you have more than one configured in Outlook. *Copy to Folder* will just create a copy of the email in a different folder rather than move it. Finally, the *Always Move Messages in This Conversation* will automatically move future messages from the same conversation to a folder of your choosing.

Right Click Options
If you are a Microsoft Windows user, then you probably know that Windows, as well as most Windows-based software, will have additional options to choose from when you right click on an item. The same goes for Outlook and right clicking on emails. As you can see in figure 8.53, you get many of the options that you see in the Ribbon when right clicking on an email, plus a *Copy* and *Quick Print* option.

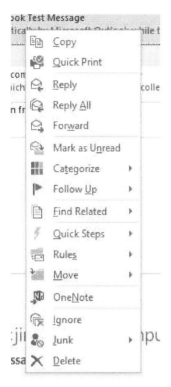

Figure 8.53

The *Copy* option will let you copy the email and then paste it in a Windows folder or on your desktop (etc.) as an email file. Then you can do things like copy it to a USB flash drive to take it elsewhere, or back it up for future reference and even email it to someone as an attachment.

The *Quick Print* option will print the email with one click to your default printer with the default settings without you having to do anything else.

Using the Outlook Calendar
Besides all the cool email features that Outlook offers, it also has some nice calendar features as well, and works great as a standalone calendar or as a shared calendar on a corporate network.

For the average home user, you will most likely only have or need one calendar, but you can create additional calendars in Outlook if you need them. For example, you might want one for your personal affairs and then another for your home business so you can keep things separated. If you are an iPhone user, you might even have your iCloud calendar imported into Outlook so you can sync it with your phone.

The first thing I would do when using the calendar is select the view that works best for you. From the Home tab and the Arrange group you can choose to view your calendar by day, work week (Mon-Fri), week, month, or according to your schedule. I prefer to see the month view and then double click on any events that I might want to get details on. To navigate around the calendar you can either use the scroll bar on the right, or the left and right arrows on the top to go from month to month or day to day etc. depending on what view you use.

Creating Appointments

The Outlook calendar is a great place to keep track of upcoming appointments and can even send you reminders so you don't miss them. To create an appointment, you can either click the *New Appointment* button on the Home tab, or what I like to do is right click the day of the appointment and select New Appointment.

Once you get the new appointment window you can start filling in the details, such as the subject, location, start time, and end time. In the Options group (figure 8.54), there is the *Reminder* area where you can have Outlook pop up a reminder on your screen at the designated time you specify.

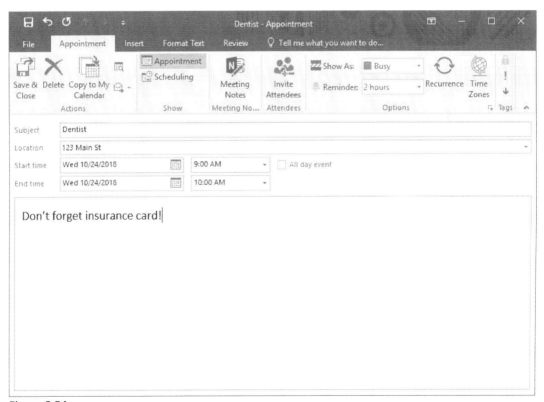

Figure 8.54

If this is a recurring appointment, then clicking on the *Recurrence* button will allow you to set up the appointment to be repeated on your calendar at whatever interval you choose (figure 8.55).

Appointment Recurrence ✕

Appointment time

Start: 9:00 AM

End: 10:00 AM

Duration: 1 hour

Recurrence pattern

○ Daily   Recur every 1   week(s) on:

● Weekly   ☐ Sunday   ☐ Monday   ☐ Tuesday   ☑ Wednesday

○ Monthly   ☐ Thursday   ☐ Friday   ☐ Saturday

○ Yearly

Range of recurrence

Start: Wed 10/24/2018   ● No end date

○ End after: 10   occurrences

○ End by: Wed 12/26/2018

OK   Cancel   Remove Recurrence

Figure 8.55

When you are finished setting all of you options click on Save & Close and the appointment will be shown on your calendar (as you can see in figure 8.56). To edit the appointment simply double click on it to bring up the appointment window once again.

A good thing to use the recurrence option for is to remind you of birthdays. You can put in the persons birthday one time and set the recurrence for every year at the same time and never ending so you will always get your yearly reminder and won't forget to buy a gift!

Figure 8.56

Creating Meetings

Setting up a meeting is similar to setting up an appointment, but with a few differences. To start the process either click the *New Meeting* button on the Home tab in the *New* group, or right click the day of the meeting and choose New Meeting.

As you can see from figure 8.57, that the meeting window looks similar to the appointment window, but has an option to send the meeting as an email.

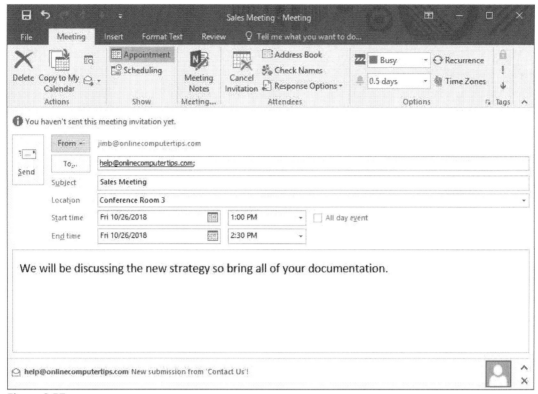

Figure 8.57

Once you get all the information entered and add the email addresses of the people you want to attend the meeting, you can click on Send and it will send the meeting invitation out to the recipients for them to accept or reject. If you are in a corporate setting with an Exchange email server, then you will be notified when they accept or reject your meeting. If they do accept, it will be added to their Outlook calendar for them.

Figure 8.58 shows the received meeting invitation in the inbox of the person who it was sent to. They can then open it and accept or decline the meeting invitation, and also reply as tentative or propose a new time.

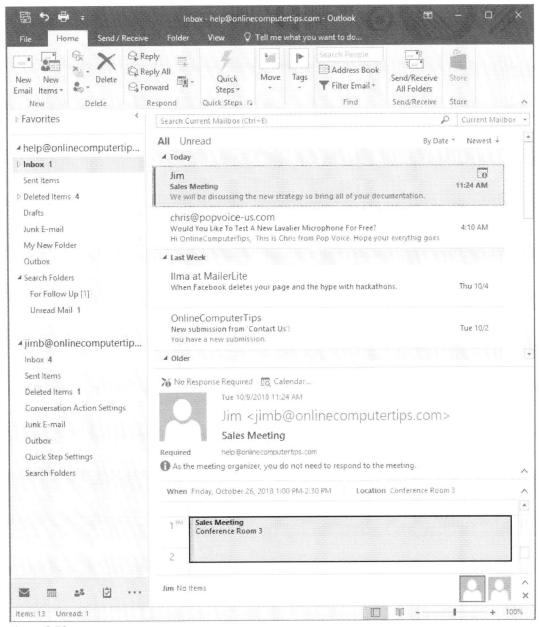

Figure 8.58

And once again, if you right click on a particular day in the calendar (figure 8.59), you will have some additional items you can choose from, such as making a new all-day event or recurring event, as well as going to a specific date on the calendar or even the current date.

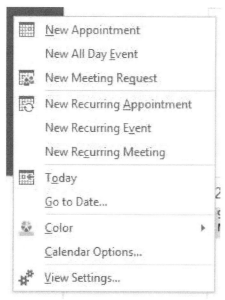

Figure 8.59

Creating Tasks and Notes

One last topic I want to go over regarding the Outlook calendar is the use of Tasks and Notes. Using these items can help you keep yourself organized, and might even get you out of the habit of using sticky notes for everything!

Tasks

Tasks are used to assign yourself (or even someone else) a specific task to complete. Think of it as a to-do or chore list. Once you have some tasks in place, you can edit them as needed, as well as mark them as a percentage of completion or even completed. To create a new task click on the Tasks icon down by the email and calendar choices in the lower left of Outlook (like shown in figure 8.60).

Figure 8.60

Once you are in the Task view you will see any tasks that you have assigned to yourself in this area (figure 8.61). Notice under the Arrangement group that you can view your tasks by things such as categories, start date, due date, folder, type, and importance. And if you want to view a task in progress simply double click on it to see the details or make any changes.

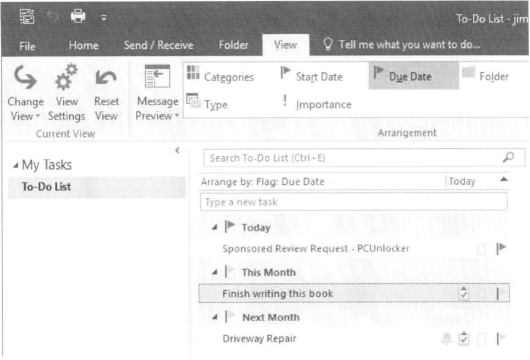

Figure 8.61

To create a new task click on the *New Task* button on the Home tab and then fill in the details for your new task (figure 8.62). I created a task to learn how to use Outlook and set it to start on October 17th and to be completed by November 16th.

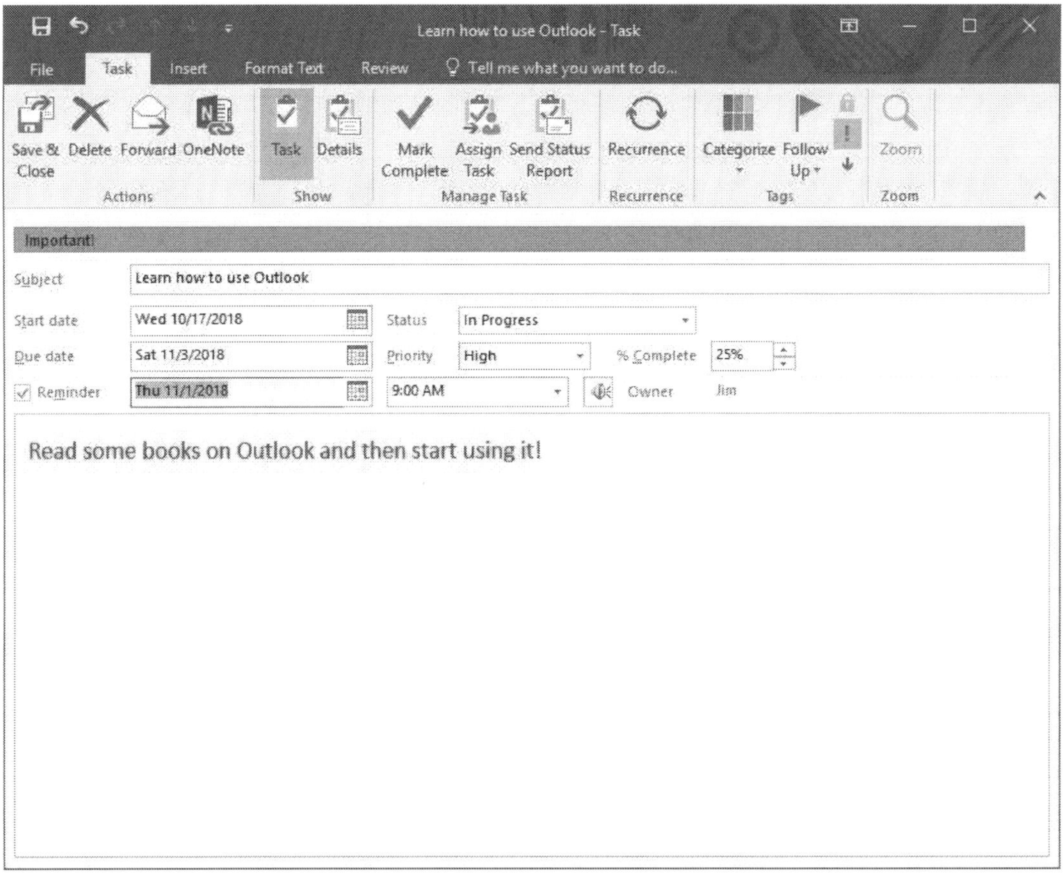

Figure 8.62

For the Status I set it to *In Progress*, the priority as high, and determined that I was already 25% complete. I then clicked on the Categorized button and chose the *Important!* category which we created earlier in this chapter. Finally, I set a reminder for 11/1 in case I forgot about this task. Once you have everything looking the way you want, you would click on *Save & Close* to have the task added to your list.

When you have finished a task you can click the *Mark Complete* button from the Manage Task group, or you can also click the *Remove from List* button. There is also an option to forward a task via email to someone else so they can add it to their task list in Outlook. Right clicking the task and choosing *Assign Task* will do the same thing.

As you are working on an assigned task, it might be required that you send updates to the person who assigned the task to you. If that's the case, then all you need to do is open the task, click on the *Send Status Report* button, and enter the email address of the person you need to report to.

Notes

Outlook has a *Notes* feature that lets you jot down things you need to remember, yet aren't important enough to create a document for. I'm sure you have posted sticky notes on your monitor with things like your passwords (bad idea!) or the number for a business you call often.

To get to the Outlook sticky note feature go back down where you opened Tasks, click the three dots, and then choose Notes. It will then bring up the Notes interface and show you any notes that you have already made (figure 8.63).

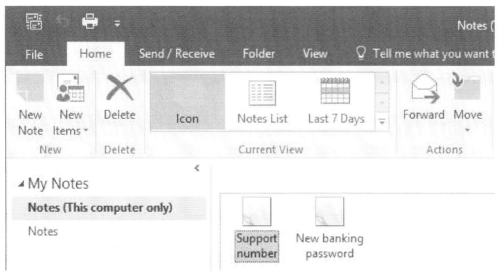

Figure 8.63

If you have never used Notes, this section will be blank, and all you need to do to create a new note is click the *New Note* button. Then type in the information you want to have on the note (figure 8.64) and press enter on your keyboard.

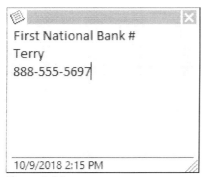

Figure 8.64

Then your new note will be added to your list of existing notes. Right clicking a note in the list will give you the option to copy, print, forward, or delete the note. Clicking on the top left of the note itself when it's open will give you some additional options, such as save as and cut, copy, and paste options for the text.

Contacts

The final Outlook subject I want to discuss will be that of Contacts. Think of the Contacts area of Outlook as an address book (or even a Rolodex if you are old enough to remember those!). It's a place where you can save information about people you contract frequently, or even those you don't.

To open your contacts, once again go to the lower left corner of Outlook and click on the Contacts icon. If you already have contacts entered in Outlook, they will be shown here. If not, then we will be adding some in a bit.

Figure 8.65 shows an Outlook contact list in card format. You can also view your contacts as a list or as business cards (etc.) by going to the Home tab and the *Current View* group.

Figure 8.65

Once you click on a contact you can use one of the many options from the Ribbon to do things such as email or setup a meeting request for that person, and even assign a task to that person. Double clicking on a contact will bring up that person's or company's information for you to view or edit.

So, let's create a new contact for our new fictitious associate Bob Smith. I will first click the *New Contact* button on the Home tab in the *New* group. Then I will add in the information for Bob as well as a picture (seen in figure 8.66), then click on *Save & Close*.

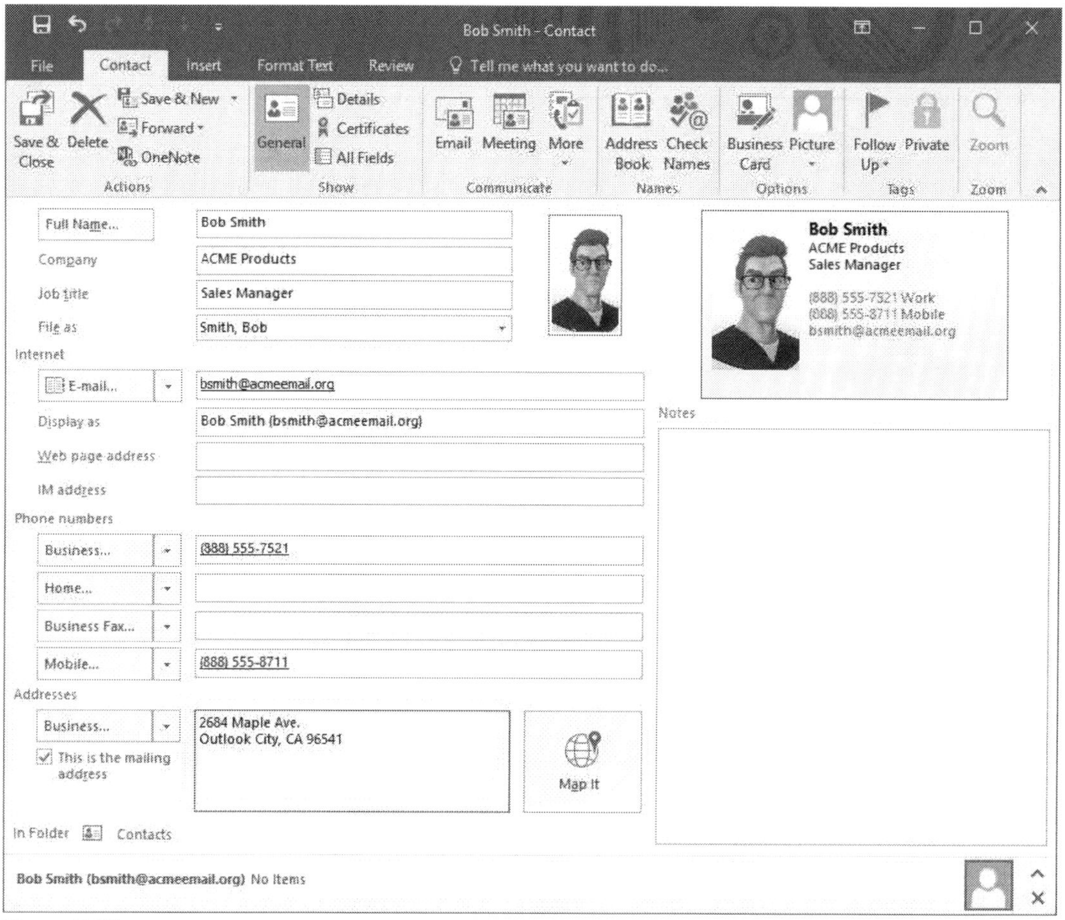

Figure 8.66

Now Bob Smith is in our contacts and will appear with the other contacts we have in Outlook, and when we go to compose a new email and click the To button to search our contacts, Bob should show up in there as well.

One other thing I want to mention is the *Details* button in the *Show* group (figure 8.67). Here you can add additional details to your contact such as their department, manager's name, and birthday. By doing this, it also gives you more information to search on in case you have a lot of contacts and want to find one who has a manager named Cindy Peters.

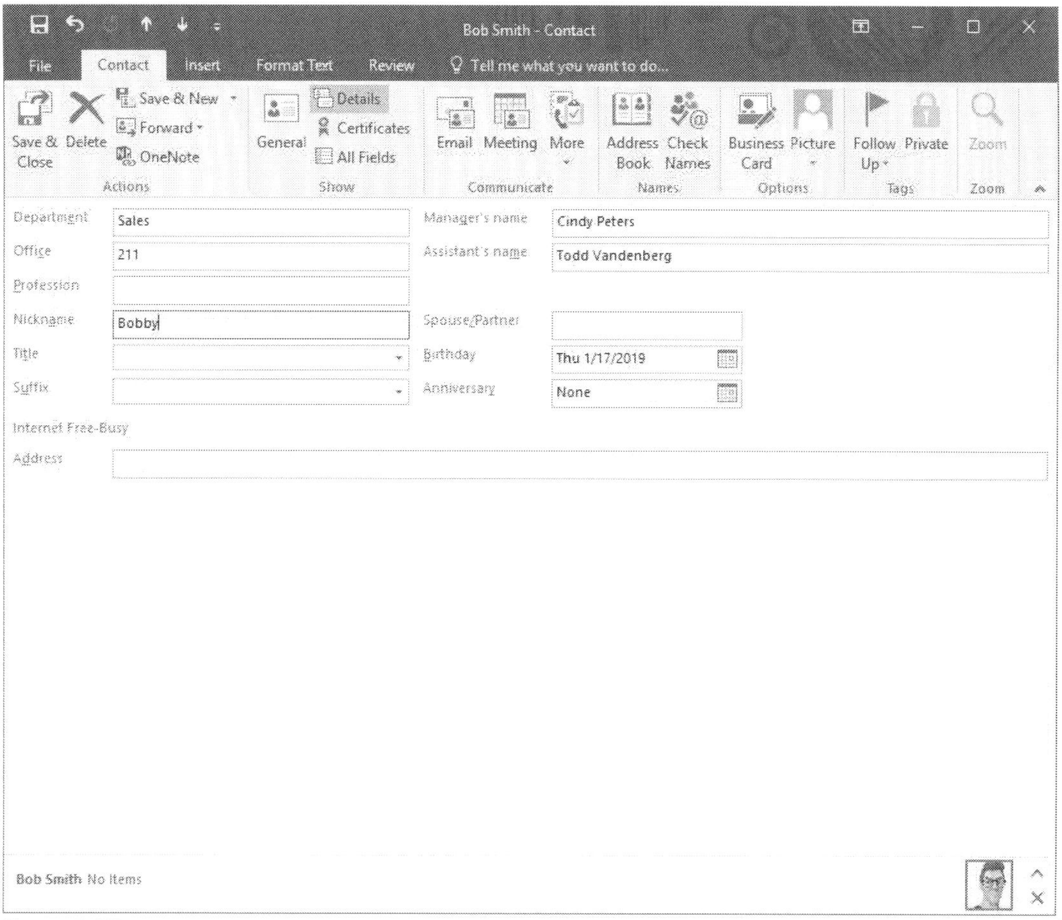
Bob Smith - Contact
File
Contact
Insert
Format Text
Review
Tell me what you want to do...
Save & Close
Delete
Save & New
Forward
OneNote
Actions
General
Details
Certificates
All Fields
Show
Email
Meeting
More
Communicate
Address Book
Check Names
Names
Business Card
Picture
Options
Follow Up
Private
Tags
Zoom
Zoom
Department
Sales
Office
211
Profession
Nickname
Bobby
Title
Suffix
Manager's name
Cindy Peters
Assistant's name
Todd Vandenberg
Spouse/Partner
Birthday
Thu 1/17/2019
Anniversary
None
Internet Free-Busy
Address
Bob Smith No Items

Figure 8.67

Chapter 9 –Microsoft OneNote

Microsoft OneNote has been around since 2003, and the first version was actually included in Office 2003. OneNote is an information gathering and collaboration program that allows you to organize your information in tabs and pages, making it easy to find the stuff you need when you need it. It's a great tool to use when working on a project to keep information organized in a structured manner that can be shared with other people on the project. One thing I want to mention which is really important regarding OneNote is that it saves your information automatically as you go along, meaning there is no save option, so be careful when deleting and changing things.

OneNote Specific Tabs and Groups
Just like you are used to seeing, I will begin this chapter with a discussion of OneNote specific tabs and groups so you have a better idea of how you can work with the program. There will be many similarities between the OneNote tabs and the other tabs you have seen, so I will just be going over the new stuff.

Home Tab
There are only two groups that I want to discuss from the Home tab (figure 9.1), and the first on is the *Tags* group.

Figure 9.1

When you have a lot of information in your notebook you might want to tag something to make it stand out. To add a tag, simply select the item or text you want to tag and choose the appropriate tag from the list of available tags. Figure 9.2 shows the available OneNote tags.

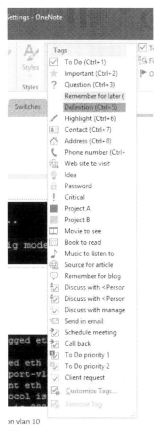

Figure 9.2

Clicking on the bottom entry called *Customize Tags* will let you edit the existing tags to make them work the way you like.

The *Outlook Tasks* button will create a task associated with the item you have selected, and then you can open that task in Outlook to view its details, edit the task, or even mark it as completed.

The other group I wanted to discuss from the Home tab is the *Meetings* group. Here you can insert details from a meeting that you have scheduled in your Outlook calendar (figure 9.3). Then you can view the details in OneNote, and it will even give you a link to open the meeting in Outlook.

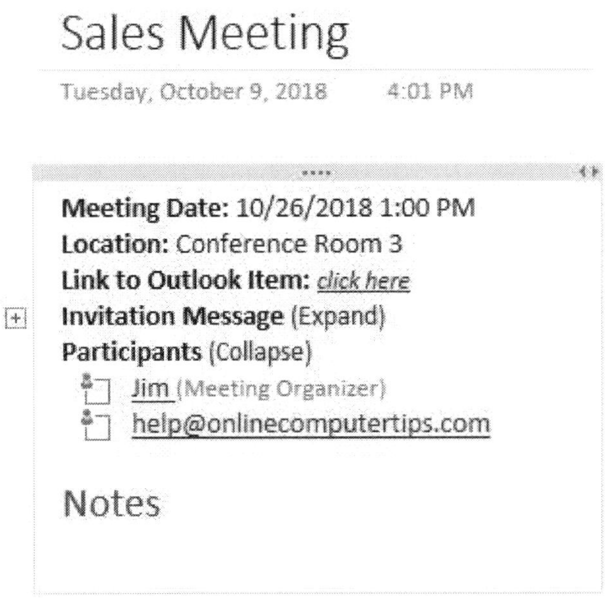
Sales Meeting
Tuesday, October 9, 2018 4:01 PM
Meeting Date: 10/26/2018 1:00 PM
Location: Conference Room 3
Link to Outlook Item: click here
Invitation Message (Expand)
Participants (Collapse)
Jim (Meeting Organizer)
help@onlinecomputertips.com
Notes

Figure 9.3

Insert Tab

OneNote has a couple of groups that I want to discuss on the Insert tab that you might find useful. As you can see in figure 9.4, there are many of the familiar tools we saw in other Office programs.

Sales Meeting - OneNote
File
Home
Insert
Draw
History
Review
View
Jim Bernstein
Insert Space
Table
File Printout
File Attachment
Spreadsheet
Screen Clipping
Pictures
Online Pictures
Link
Record Audio
Record Video
Date
Time
Date & Time
Page Templates
Equation
Symbol
Insert
Tables
Files
Images
Links
Recording
Time Stamp
Pages
Symbols

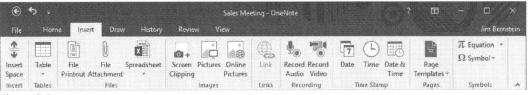

Figure 9.4

The *File Printout* button in the *Files* group will let you copy the content of a file into your notebook. So, if you have document that has information you want to place into your OneNote file, you can do that from here. One thing I noticed is that it seems to work better with things like Word documents compared to PDFs, and the smaller the document the better.

Also in the Files group is the *File Attachment* button. This will actually attach\embed the file into your notebook and allow you to open it directly from the page. (Just keep in mind that attaching files will increase the size of your OneNote file.)

One thing I want to mention from the Images group is the *Screen Clipping* tool. When you click this button, OneNote will let you draw a box around any part of your screen and then turn that into a screenshot that you can place within your notebook.

Finally, in the Pages group there is the *Page Templates* button. You can use this to add some excitement to your file while at the same time adding some functionality. Figure 9.5 shows a OneNote page with a business template applied. There are many built-in templates to choose from.

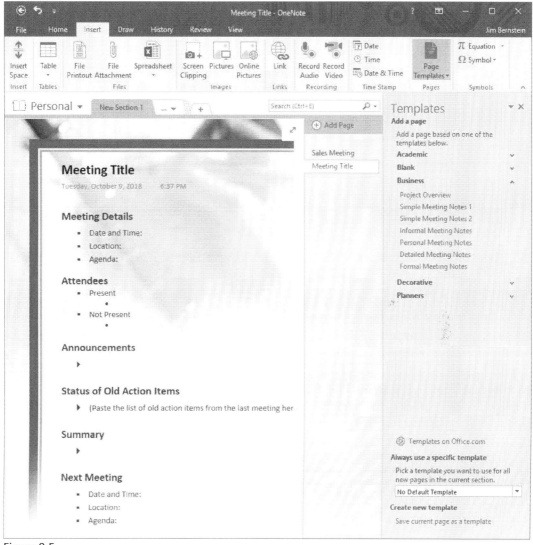

Figure 9.5

Draw Tab

When taking notes, you might also want to have a way to scribble things down or insert some shapes, such as an arrow, to point to something in particular. The Draw tab (figure 9.6) has a lot of tools you can use to make this happen.

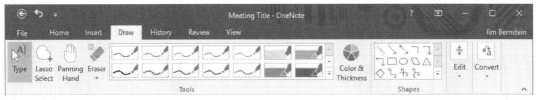

Figure 9.6

The *Tools* group consists of the following tools.

- **Type Tool** – Lets you insert anywhere on the page and start typing text.

- **Lasso Select** – If you have a bunch of items on the page that you want to select all at once, you can draw around them and then they will all be selected.

- **Panning Hand** – This allows you to click and drag on the page to move it around. Think of it as a scroll bar that you can move in any direction with your mouse.

- **Eraser** – If you add some type of shape or drawing and want it gone, then you can erase it with the Eraser tool.

- **Pens** – Here you can select colors and pen types for drawing and highlighting freehand style.

- **Color & Thickness** – Allows you to choose your pen and highlighter colors as well as their line thickness.

Shapes

Here you have the capability to insert the same type of shapes that the other Office programs offer with a few additional types (such as graphs).

If you choose a pen type before choosing a shape, then the shape will take on the characteristics of that pen in regards to color and thickness.

I wanted to mention the Convert tool just in case you try to use it and don't get the results you want. What it does is takes letters that you draw and tries to convert it to actual text. It also will try to convert numbers you draw into math equations. I have not had the best luck with either of these tools being able to correctly recognize what I'm drawing, so maybe you will have better luck than me if your drawing skills are better than mine!

History Tab
The History tab (figure 9.7) is useful when you have multiple people working on one notebook in a shared situation.

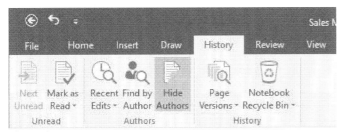

Figure 9.7

Unread
This group has two options for looking at changes in your notebook. The *Next Unread* button can be used to find pages with unread notes in your notebook. So, if it's a shared notebook and you want to see what's new, then this is the button for you. The *Mark as Read* button can make the notebook show as read and also as unread.

Authors
This group can be used to find changes made by other authors that are working on your notebook. The *Recent Edits* button will let you search for changes within a specified time range and then list them all so you can review each one as needed. In figure 9.8, I chose to have all the changes that were made today be listed.

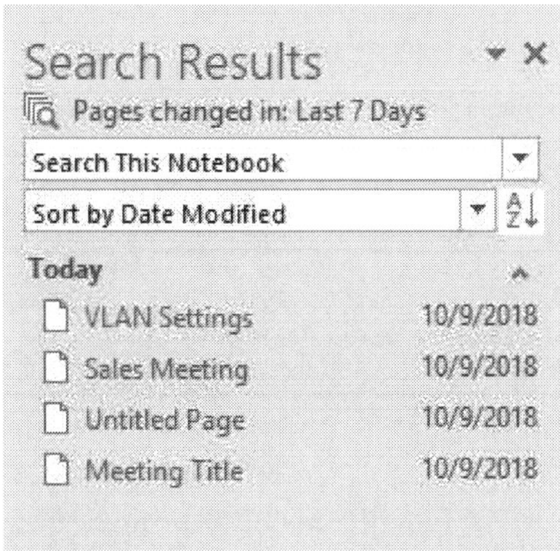

Figure 9.8

Find by Author will do a search for changes made by a particular person so you can see what they have been up to. You can also tell OneNote what parts of your file you want it to search such as the entire notebook or just a section.

If you don't want to see the initials of the author next to their changes, then click on the Hide Authors button. If it's just you working on the notebook then you don't need to worry about this.

History

OneNote will keep previous versions of pages that you have changed in case you need to go back and look at the way the page was prior to how it is currently. To do this, go to the page you want to view, click the *Page Versions* button, and select *Page Versions*. OneNote will display all the older versions on the sidebar with the page title, dates, and author names (figure 9.9). Then you can click on the one you want to view and see the older version.

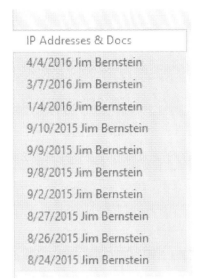

Figure 9.9

When you delete a page it will go into a trash holding area for sixty days before it's permanently deleted. So, if you want to get something back, click on *Notebook Recycle Bin,* then right click the page and select *Move* or *Copy* and tell OneNote where to restore the page to within your notebook.

Review Tab

The only really new thing on the Review tab is the Password button in the Section group (figure 9.10), so let's take a minute and go over this feature.

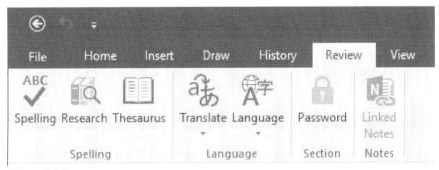

Figure 9.10

Just like with other Office programs, you have the option to password protect your work so only people who know that password can edit those sections. To set this up, go to the section you want to password protect, click on the Password button, and then click on Set Password (figure 9.11).

Figure 9.11

Then, when someone goes to that section in your notebook (or even when you go there), they will see the message shown in figure 9.12.

Figure 9.12

View Tab

The View tab is where you will go to change things such as how the sections are displayed on the screen and how your page is set up for viewing and printing. Figure 9.13 shows the View tab with all of its included groups.

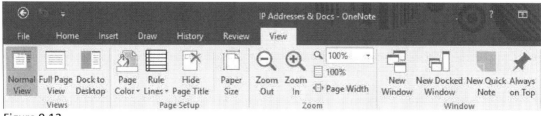
Figure 9.13

Views

There are three different views you can use for your OneNote notebook:

- **Normal View** – This is the default view and will show the Ribbon, your section tabs, and the page bar on the right.

- **Full Page View** – Choosing this view will make the section full screen and hide the Ribbon and page bar.

- **Dock to Desktop** – If you want your notes to always be visible, then you can try this view, which will anchor OneNote to the side of your desktop and keep it on top of all other programs.

Page Setup

Here you can change the way your notebook looks by adding a background color using the Page Color button. You can also add various types of lines to your section, including gridlines (like shown in figure 9.14). This can be used to help align images and other objects.

Figure 9.14

When you create a new page, OneNote will add a title to that page that matches the name you gave the actual page. In figure 9.15 I underlined the Sales Meeting title on the left, as well as the Sales Meeting page name on the right. If you click the *Hide Title Page* button, it will remove the title that is showing on the left.

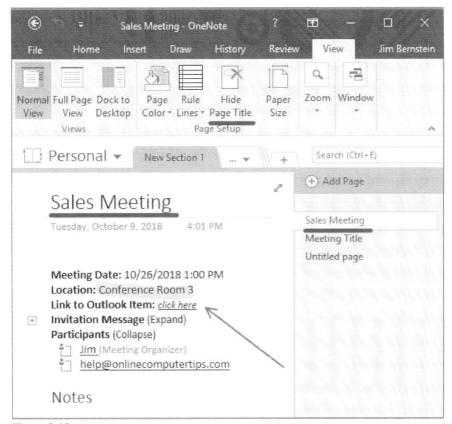

Figure 9.15

The *Paper Size* button will let you choose what paper size your notebook will use. This comes in handy for printing purposes.

Window

This group allows you to do things such as open a section in a new window, as well as open a section as a docked window, which will do something similar to what the Dock to Desktop button does, but only for that section.

OneNote has a sticky note feature similar to Outlook, and if you click on the *New Quick Note* button, it will bring up a new note where you can type in whatever you like and also add things like pictures, tables, links, and so on (figure 9.16).

Figure 9.16

To get to your notes, click on the dropdown arrow next to your notebook name and choose Quick Notes (figure 9.17) and they will all be listed there.

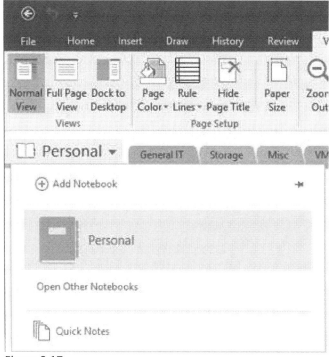

Figure 9.17

Creating a OneNote Notebook

It's that time again where we will take what we've learned about the OneNote tabs and groups and put it into practice by creating a new OneNote notebook that we can use to take notes and collaborate with other people if we choose to do so.

When you go to the File tab and go to New, you will have several options when it comes to creating your new notebook (figure 9.18). If you have a OneDrive cloud storage account, you can create it there, and this will allow you to share it with other people who have access to your OneDrive files.

We want to use the Browse option because we are going to create our notebook on the local hard drive, so click on *Browse*, navigate to where you want to save the notebook, give it a name, and click on *Create*.

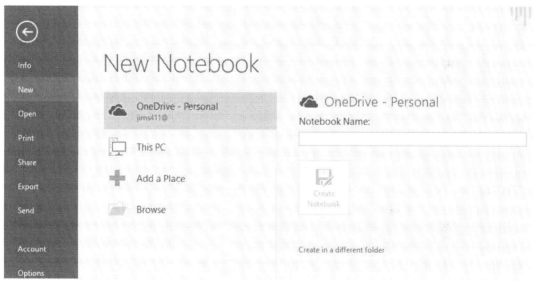

Figure 9.18

OneNote will create a new blank notebook with the name of the file you've chosen. For my example (in figure 9.19) I named my file *Important Stuff* and OneNote gave the notebook the same name. Notice how there's a section called New Section with a page called Untitled page? These are there to help get you going creating your notebook.

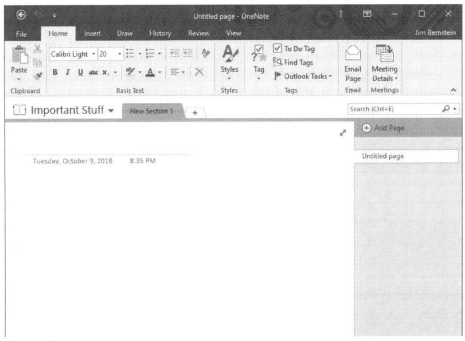

Figure 9.19

From here we can rename *New Section 1* by right clicking on it and choosing *Rename,* or simply by double clicking it. I am going to name my tab *Finances*. Next I will right click the Untitled page and rename it *Bank Accounts*. Then I will type in some bank names with their account numbers (figure 9.20 shows the results).

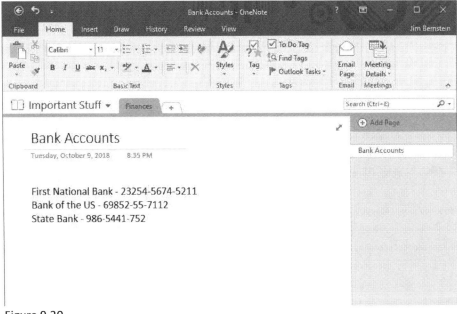

Figure 9.20

Now I want to add a new page to my Bank Accounts tab, and I will do that by clicking on the Add Page + sign, then entering in a name for my page. This time I will call it *Retirement Accounts*. Next I will add some information there (including a table) and attach a Word document to the page. Both of these steps were done from the Insert tab under the Tables and Files groups.

Next I will add a new tab for my bills and call it *Bills*. From there I will right click the new *Bills* tab and change the color to green by clicking on Section Color. The results of all these actions are shown in figure 9.21.

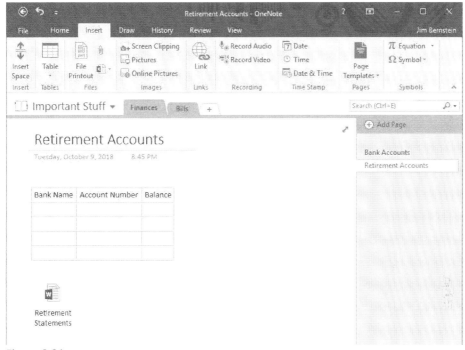

Figure 9.21

Now that we have a basic notebook created, it's time to go over some of the things we can do with our notebook.

Sharing Your Notebook

I have mentioned that you can share your OneNote notebook with other users, so let's give that a try now and see how it works. Keep in mind that you will need to have a OneDrive or Office 365 account to do so. I will be discussing both later on in this book, but for now we will use a OneDrive account to share our new notebook.

To begin, we will go to the File tab and then click on *Share*. Next we will select the OneDrive option and give the shared file a name (figure 9.22). Then click on the Move Notebook button to send the notebook to your OneDrive account.

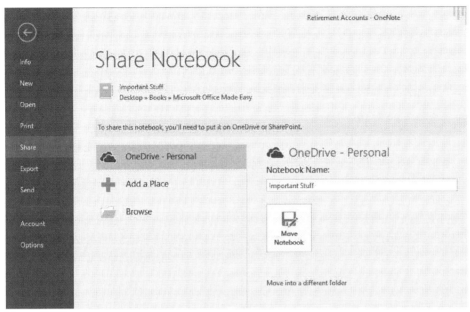

Figure 9.22

While it's being uploaded, you will see a message (as shown in figure 9.23).

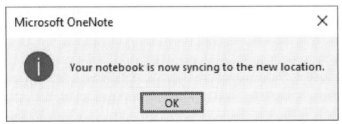

Figure 9.23

When the upload is complete, you will be able to share the notebook with others by adding their names or email addresses in the list and determining what level or permissions you will give them (figure 9.24). The choices you have to assign them are to view or to edit. Finally, you can type in a message in the box that they will see when they open your workbook. When everything is looking the way you like, then click on the Share button.

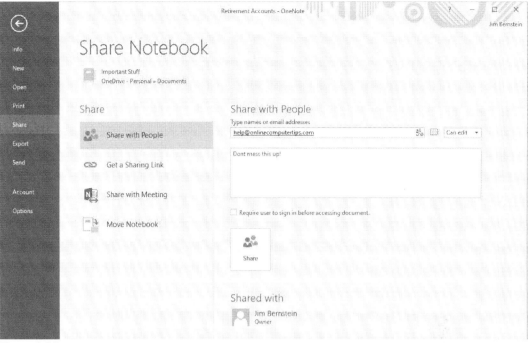

Figure 9.24

Notice in figure 9.25 that the new users email address is listed under *Shared with*.

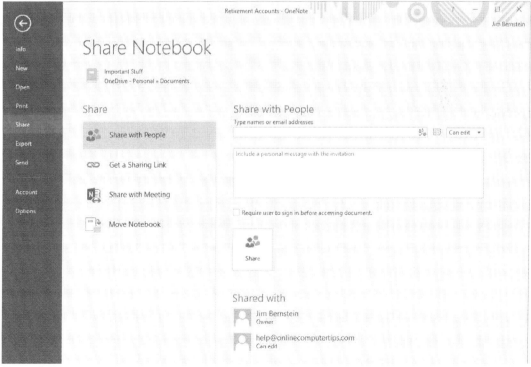

Figure 9.25

Figure 9.26 shows what the person who was invited to access your notebook will see in their email when the invitation arrives. Then they just need to click on *View in OneDrive* to have the notebook open in their web browser (figure 9.27). From there they can make changes that you will be able to see on your end.

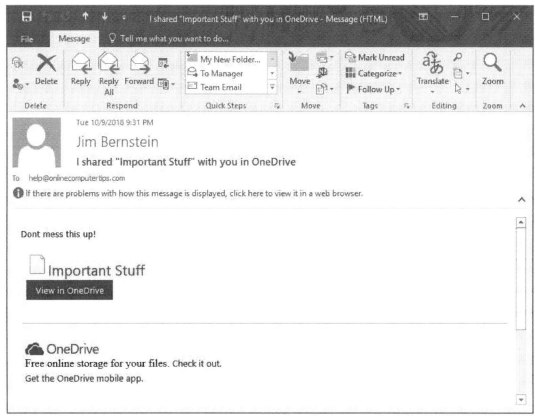

Figure 9.26

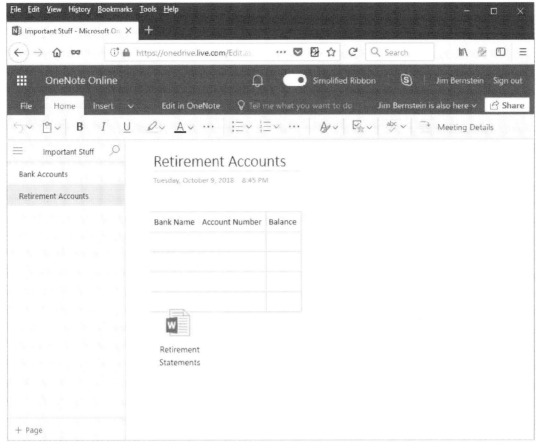

Figure 9.27

Printing Your Notebook

Printing OneNote notebooks is not as common as printing Word documents (or even Publisher publications), but sometimes there is a need to do so. If you have a large notebook with many sections and pages, you most likely won't want to print all of them, so knowing how to print just what you want is important.

Just like with the other Office programs, you will need to go to the File tab to print (unless you have a print shortcut in the QuickAccess Toolbar). If you take a look at figure 9.28, you will see that the print options for OneNote are quite different than the other Office programs that we have been looking at.

Figure 9.28

There are only two options to choose from, and if you click on the Print icon then it will just bring up the usual print dialog box (figure 9.29) where you can select your printer and what pages you want to print (etc.).

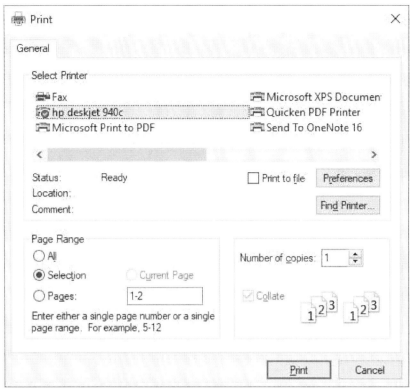

Figure 9.29

If you click on the Print Preview button you will get some additional options (figure 9.30) that will allow you to print exactly what you need.

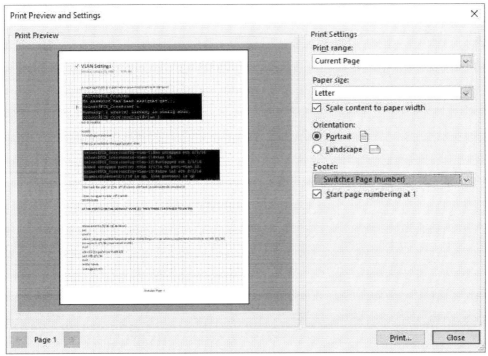

Figure 9.30

- **Print range** – Here you can choose from Current Page, Page Group, or Current Selection.

- **Paper size** – This will allow you to change the paper to match whatever size paper you have in your printer.

- **Scale content to paper** – Checking this box will shrink or enlarge the printing to fit the selected paper size.

- **Orientation** – Just like with the other Office programs, you can set your print jobs to be either portrait or landscape (tall or wide).

- **Footer** – OneNote can print a footer at the bottom of the page showing some details about what part of the notebook the printout came from, or simply just add page numbers for you.

- **Start page numbering at 1** – If you choose to use page numbers, checking this box will begin the numbering sequence with 1.

Chapter 10 – Office 365 and Office Online

Having Office installed locally on your computer is not the only option you have if you want to use the software at home or at the office. Microsoft has a couple of other offerings (called Office 365 and Office Online) which are available to you if you choose to go that route. In this chapter I will be discussing what those are, and how they work so you can decide which way you want to go.

Cloud Storage & Applications

Just like every other software company, Microsoft is pushing for its users to start using "the cloud" for things like storage and running applications. By "cloud" I mean that you store your files on servers located at some other location and you access them via the Internet. For cloud-based applications, you would run them in a web browser connected to their application servers over the Internet.

Many companies use cloud-based storage and applications to save money because they don't need to buy the hardware to support them and hire the IT people to maintain them. The main downside is that if you lose your Internet connection, then you lose access to your storage and programs. But for big corporations, it's rare that they have much or any downtime.

For us home users we have the same types of choices, but on a smaller scale. We also don't have as reliable Internet connections. Plus, you are leaving the safety of all your personal files in the hands of strangers who store them on servers who knows where. Then again, most people I know don't backup their computer anyways, so maybe it's better to leave it up to someone else!

Microsoft's offering for home user cloud storage is called OneDrive (and that will be the topic of the next chapter). There are many cloud storage providers that offer low cost and even free storage that you can use for things like pictures, music, documents, and so on. Many people use these services for purposes like having a place to back up their files, a way to share their files, or even a way to be able to access their files from wherever they are. Figure 10.1 shows how a basic cloud storage setup would work. You have all your Internet connected devices (such as your computer, smartphone, and tablet) uploading their data to servers via the Internet that have large quantities of storage they can use to store your files.

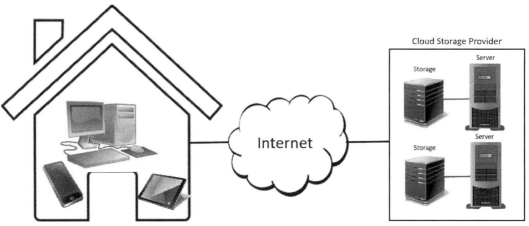

Figure 10.1

To upload and download your files you typically use a web browser that connects to the cloud storage service. Some of these services have client software that you can install on your computer to keep both of them synchronized with each other, and for many of them it's possible to share specific files or folders with other people.

What is Office 365?

Office 365 is Microsoft's cloud-based subscription to its suite of office productivity programs identical to the desktop version of Office, but with some extra features. It is a subscription-based service with various levels of plans to choose from. The plan you choose will determine what programs (or applications) you will have access to, so it's important to base your choice on what you *need* and how much you can *afford*.

There are home subscription plans as well as business subscription plans. Here is a list the plans with their pricing, as well as what you get with each one as of the writing of this book:

Home Users

Office 365 Home - $99.99 per year or $9.99 per month for up to 6 users.
- Word
- Excel
- PowerPoint
- Outlook
- Publisher (PC only)
- Access (PC only)
- OneDrive

- Skype
- OneNote
- 1TB (terabyte) of OneDrive cloud storage per person (for up to 6 people)
- Phone and chat support

Office 365 Home - $69.99 per year or $6.99 per month for 1 user
- Word
- Excel
- PowerPoint
- Outlook
- Publisher (PC only)
- Access (PC only)
- OneDrive
- Skype
- OneNote
- 1TB (terabyte) of OneDrive cloud storage per person (for 1 person)
- Phone and chat support

Business Users

Office 365 Business - $8.25 per month for up to 5 devices per user
- Word
- Excel
- PowerPoint
- Outlook
- Access (PC only)
- OneDrive
- 1TB (terabyte) of OneDrive cloud storage
- Desktop versions of Office programs
- 24/7 phone and web support

Office 365 Business Premium - $12.50 per month for up to 5 devices per user
- Word
- Excel
- PowerPoint
- Outlook
- Access (PC only)
- OneDrive
- Exchange

- SharePoint
- Microsoft Teams
- 1TB (terabyte) of OneDrive cloud storage
- Desktop versions of Office programs
- Online meetings and video conferencing for up to 250 people
- Outlook Customer Manager
- Microsoft Invoicing, Microsoft Bookings, MileIQ, and Business center
- Microsoft Planner
- 24/7 phone and web support

Office 365 Business Essentials - $5.00 per month for 5 phones and 5 tablets only
- Word
- Excel
- PowerPoint
- Outlook
- Access (PC only)
- OneDrive
- Exchange
- SharePoint
- Microsoft Teams
- 1TB (terabyte) of OneDrive cloud storage
- Online meetings and video conferencing for up to 250 people
- Microsoft Planner
- 24/7 phone and web support

Since Office 365 is web-based you can easily access your applications on devices (such as smartphones and tablets) where you normally couldn't install Windows-based programs. You can even use it on your Mac if you are an Apple person. And, if you keep your documents online in the cloud, you pretty much have access to your information anywhere you are. One very important thing to keep in mind is that if you're a teacher or student and have a school email address, you can get yourself a copy of Office 365 for free.

Using Office 365
If you are comfortable using Office programs on your computer, then you should be okay using them online as well. Microsoft did a pretty good job making the interface between the two work the same way, so you don't have to learn how to use Office all over again if you switch to Office 365.

When you log into your account you will see all of your available apps (figure 10.2). These will vary based on your subscription, so not everyone will have the same apps available to them.

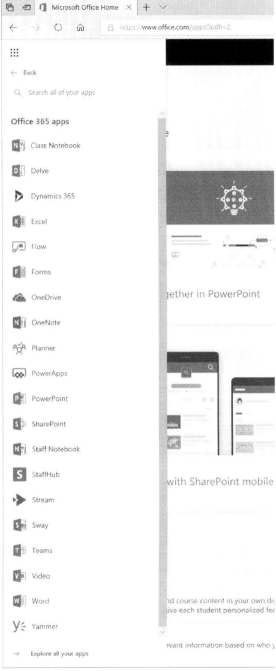

Figure 10.2

To begin, I have opened Word Online and then opened a resume template. As you can see in figure 10.3, there is a very similar Ribbon with the same tabs and groups that we saw in the locally installed version of Word that we were working with before.

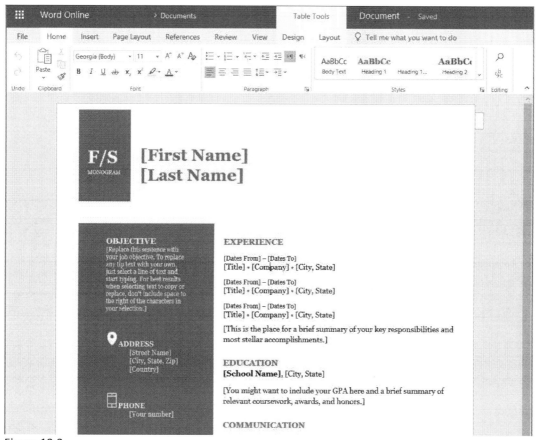

Figure 10.3

File Tab

Just like in the desktop version of the Office programs, there is the File tab, but with the online version the choices will be a little different. I will now take a little time to go over some of the key differences. Keep in mind that some of the choices will vary depending on what Office program you are using, but for now I will go over the choices for Word.

- **Info** – This section is where you can go if you want to open the online document you are working on in the desktop version of the program (figure 10.4).

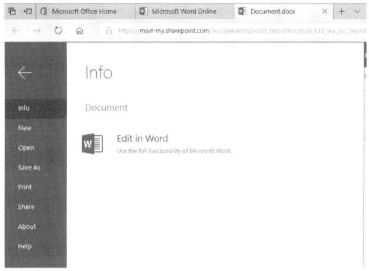

Figure 10.4

- **New** – Here you will find similar choices to create a new blank document or use one of the preconfigured templates that are available.

- **Open** – Clicking here will show you your recently accessed documents as well as give you a link to open additional documents stored on your OneDrive cloud storage (discussed in Chapter 11).

- **Save As** – There are many options to choose from here, as you can see in figure 10.5. You can do things like *Save As* to save a copy in a different location with a different name or rename the file to something else. There are several download options to choose from as well, such as downloading a copy to your computer or downloading a PDF or ODT version of the file. One thing to note is how it says the file is being automatically saved. Word Online will save your files for you as you go so you don't need to do it manually.

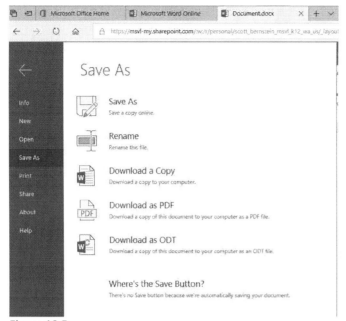

Figure 10.5

- **Print** – When it's time to print your document, you will be prompted with the typical print dialog box that you are used to seeing, but it will just look a little different because it will be web-based. You will still have the same choices as to paper size, number of copies, etc.

- **Share** – Since you will be working with your documents online, it makes sense to be able to share them with others online as well. From the *Share* section you can click on *Share with People* or *Embed* (figure 10.6).

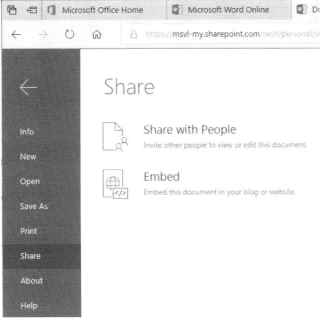

Figure 10.6

When you choose the *Share with People* option all you need to do is enter a name or email address of the person you want to share with (figure 10.7). It will most likely be an email address for home users, and then you can click on the *Anyone with this link can edit* button to fine-tune how you want to share your document (figure 10.8).

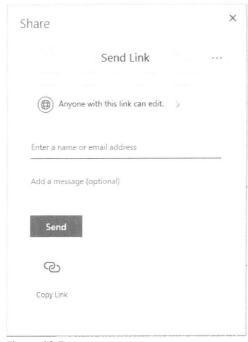

Figure 10.7

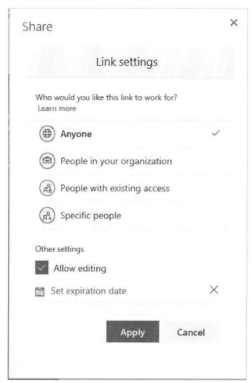

Figure 10.8

- **About** - This section simply shows you legal information, and you most likely won't ever need to go here.

- **Help** – If you need any assistance using Office 365, you can go to the *Help* section and do a search for the thing you would like help with.

Other Office 365 Apps
Besides the standard Word, Excel, PowerPoint, and so on, Office 365 comes with a variety of different apps that can help you stay productive. I will now go over the ones I think are most useful for the home and small business user.

Delve – Delve is used to show you information that it thinks is most important to you. It allows you to do things such as click on someone's name to see what they are working on, or add documents as favorites and so on. It's most useful when collaborating with other users and sharing documents.

Flow – This allows you to tie your Microsoft applications and other apps together, allowing one app to talk to another app, such as when you get an email with an attachment. You can have it save that attachment and send them a reply without having to do it manually. This is done by creating workflows that work with various apps to get the job done.

Planner – If you are working on a team project, you can use Planner to assign tasks and perform status checks on team members to keep things organized.

Staffhub – This app will help you track what your employees are doing and allow you to take control of schedules and the shared information that they use.

Stream – You and your colleges can share videos with each other all in one place. You can add descriptions and notes to the videos as well as tags to help them get to the part of the video they want/need to watch.

Sway – Sway is used to create interactive reports and presentations using text, images, and video (similar to PowerPoint).

Teams – This is a collaboration app that can be used to organize your team members and allow you to have meetings, conversations, and share files.

Yammer – Yammer is used as a social networking communication app for your business. It helps you to communicate with associates and keep on top of what everyone is doing and the latest trends.

Office Online vs. Office 365
Not everyone can justify the cost of an Office 365 subscription, especially if you only need to create a Word document every once in a while. This is where Office Online can help you out, because it lets you access many of the Office 365 features without costing you anything.

Of course, this free version doesn't offer as many of the bells and whistles as the subscription based Office 365 version, but for many people it will give you enough functionality to do what you would normally do with Office software at home or even in the office.

The main programs included with Office Online include Word, Excel, PowerPoint, and OneNote. There are other apps you can use with Office Online as well, such as Mail, Calendar, and OneDrive. To use Office Online, all you need to do is sign in with your Microsoft account or create one for free if you don't have one.

Office Online doesn't have all the functionality of the desktop version of Office or Office 365 would have, but you might not even notice. Some of the things missing from the free version include other apps like Access and Publisher. However, there are other things you can do, like run a macros in Excel, edit files offline, add custom animations to PowerPoint, or open password protected Word documents. But, for the most part, you can get the job done with this free version of Office.

To access Office Online simply go to their website at **https://www.office.com/** and sign in with your Microsoft account. Then you will be presented with the apps that you are allowed to use and any recent documents you have worked on (figure 10.9).

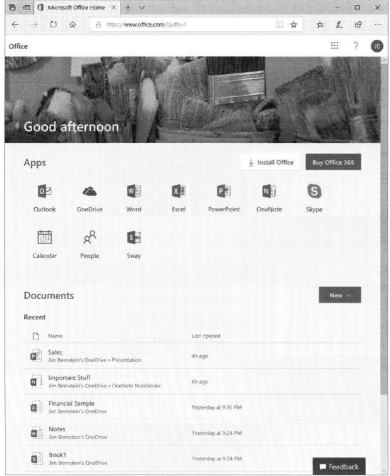

Figure 10.9

Of course, you will be encouraged to buy Office 365 so Microsoft can make some money off you. If you have a Microsoft email account (such as one from outlook.com) then you can access your email, calendar, and contacts from here as well. When you open an app (such as Word, for example) it will show you your recent files and allow you to create a new blank document or choose from a template just like you are used to seeing (figure 10.10).

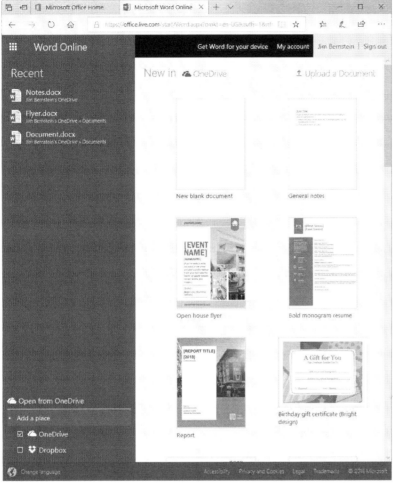

Figure 10.10

Notice on the bottom of figure 10.10 there is an option to add another place where you can open files from (such as DropBox), giving you additional online storage options.

So, if you are thinking of going the Office 365 route, then I would recommend you give Office Online a try first to see if it's right for you. You might not like it, and would prefer to have the locally installed version of Office on your computer, but keep in mind that it won't be free like Office Online is.

Chapter 11 – Microsoft OneDrive

I had mentioned Microsoft OneDrive earlier in this book, and if you remember, it is Microsoft's free cloud-based storage service. Of course, they also have pay-for plans with more storage space and other options, which I will get to shortly. If you plan on using Office 365 or Office Online, you should probably take advantage of the free space you get with OneDrive so you can be fully cloud integrated.

What is Microsoft OneDrive?

Just like with Office 365, there are personal subscription plans as well as business subscription plans. Once again, I will list the plans with their pricing, as well as what you get with each one as of the writing of this book. I won't go over the OneDrive plans that come with Office 365 since I did that in the last chapter. If you don't know what some of the features mean, then you are officially tasked with looking them up online to find out!

Personal

OneDrive Basic 5 GB - Free
- 5 GB of storage only

OneDrive Basic 50 GB - $1.99 per month
- 50 GB of storage only

Business

OneDrive for Business Plan 1 - $60/year per user
- 1 TB of storage
- 15 GB file upload limit
- Advanced sync technology
- Mobile apps
- Web-based access
- Enterprise-grade security
- Secure sharing
- Microsoft phone & email support
- Search & discover
- Photos
- Edit & annotate files

- Rich previewers
- Workflow
- Auditing and reporting
- API access

OneDrive for Business Plan 2 - $120/year per user
- 15 GB file upload limit
- Advanced sync technology
- Mobile apps
- Web-based access
- Enterprise-grade security
- Secure sharing
- Microsoft phone & email support
- Search & discover
- Photos
- Edit & annotate files
- Rich previewers
- Workflow
- PowerApps
- Auditing and reporting
- eDiscovery
- Data loss prevention
- In-place hold
- API access

Using OneDrive

To sign up for a OneDrive account all you need to do is sign up for a Microsoft account. There is a good chance you already have one, especially if you are using Windows 10. Once you have your account configured, simply go to the OneDrive login page and sign in to access your OneDrive at **https://onedrive.live.com.**

If you have been using OneDrive, then you will see the files and folders that you have saved in your storage (like shown in figure 11.1). If you are completely new to OneDrive, then you won't have anything there except maybe a file called Getting Started With OneDrive or something similar that you can open to read up on using OneDrive.

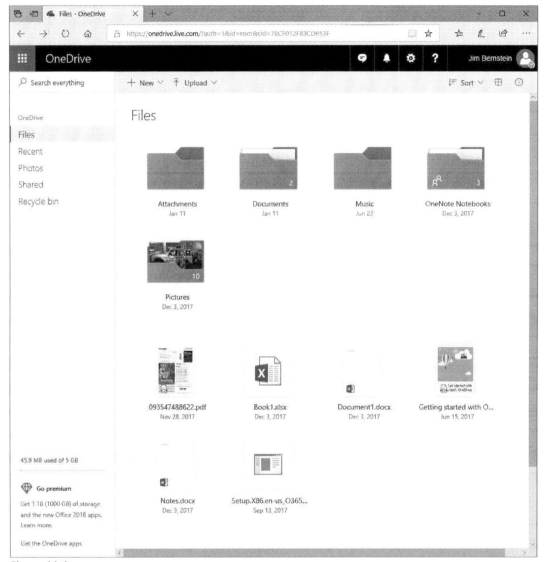

Figure 11.1

As you can see in my example, in the *Files* area I have files and folders for different types of items such as documents and pictures, and even the shared OneNote notebook we worked on in Chapter 9.

The *Recent* section on the right will show you files and folders that have recently been added to OneDrive. So, if you have a lot of files and are looking for something you just uploaded, then the Recent section is a quick way to find it.

If you keep your pictures in the *Photos* area then when you go into them they will be displayed by date and in a thumbnail view so you can see them without having to open each one individually. You can also create photo albums to categorize your pictures as well as add tags to images so you can search or view images by the tags later on. Right clicking on a picture will give you some options such as adding it to an album, downloading the picture, renaming the picture, and so on (figure 11.2).

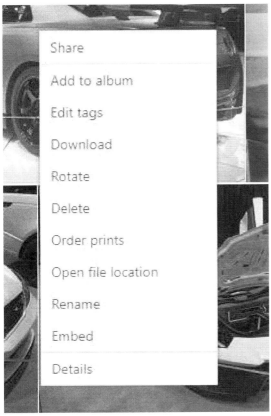

Figure 11.2

For files you want to share with other people (such as our OneNote notebook), you can find them in the *Shared* section. However, just because it's here doesn't mean that that's where it's stored. OneDrive just lists shared files and folders here as shortcuts to the actual file or folder.

When you delete items they go into the *Recycle Bin,* just like they do in Windows. If you need to get them back, you can go to the Recycle Bin section, select them, and choose *Restore* to have them go back to their original location.

 I have accessed my OneDrive account using the Edge web browser that comes with Windows 10 and noticed it was a little buggy, so you might want to try something else like Chrome or Firefox. Good job Microsoft!

When you click on an Office file (such as a Word document or Excel spreadsheet), OneDrive will attempt to open it in your web browser using an online version of the program like shown with an Excel file in figure 11.3. It will even do so for things like PDF files or pictures that can be opened within a web browser.

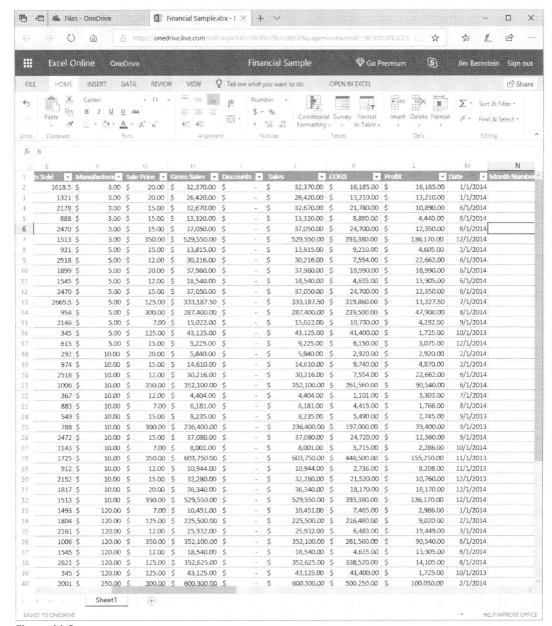

Figure 11.3

If you click on a file that OneDrive can't preview in a browser, then you will get a message like the one shown in figure 11.4, and you will have the option to download the file and try to open it directly from your computer.

MTB-4K.prel

Hmm... looks like this file doesn't have a preview we can show you.

Download

Figure 11.4

When you select a file or folder, you will have some options as to what you can do with that file or folder. To select a file or folder, click in the circle on the top right of the file to put a check mark in it (like shown in figure 11.5). If you are viewing your files in a list view, then the circle will be to the left of the file.

Figure 11.5

Once you have a file or folder checked, there will be some options that appear at the top of the page that you can use with that file or folder (figure 11.6). Most of them should be obvious, but I will go over the ones that might not be.

Figure 11.6

Move to and *Copy to* will allow you to move or copy the file to a different folder within your OneDrive account. When you click on one of these choices, you will be given a choice as to where you want to move or copy the file to based on your available folders (figure 11.7).

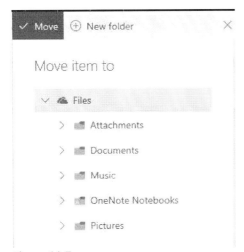

Figure 11.7

The *Embed* option is used to insert your file into a web page so it's integrated with the page itself (figure 11.8). OneDrive will convert the file into HTML code that you can copy and paste into your web page editor and then upload to your website.

Figure 11.8

If you have files that have been in your OneDrive account for some time, then you might have some older versions that you can restore or download to your computer. You can find out by selecting a file and then clicking on *Version history*. If you *do* have some older versions, you can view them by clicking on the specific date you want to look at (figure 11.9) before deciding if you want to restore or download them.

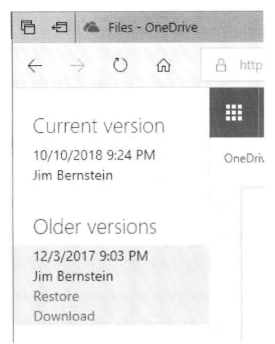

Figure 11.9

Creating Folders and Uploading Files
Cloud storage is no good to anyone unless you know how to upload files and create folders to put those files in, so now I want to discuss how to do exactly that. While in the Files area of OneDrive, on the top of the window there should be an option called *New* and another one called *Upload*. Next to *New* and *Upload* should be a drop down arrow giving your more choices as to what types of items you want to work with (figure 11.10). You can also right click a blank area and choose *New* or *Upload* from the menu that pops up.

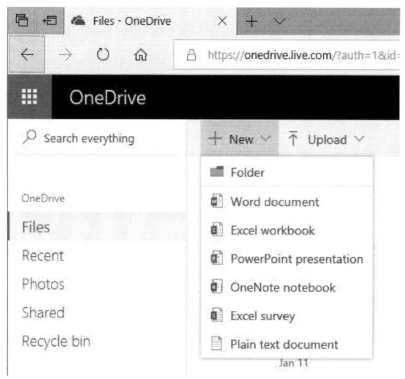

Figure 11.10

Since OneDrive is a Microsoft product, of course they will have choices such as Word document and Excel workbook under the New section. That way you can create a new Office file and work on it online directly from OneDrive. In our case though, we want to create a new folder, so I will click on the Folder option, enter the name *Presentation*, and click the *Create* button. Then this new folder will appear with the other files and folders in the Files section. Next, I will click on the folder to open it and will see that there is nothing inside of the folder since it's new (figure 11.11).

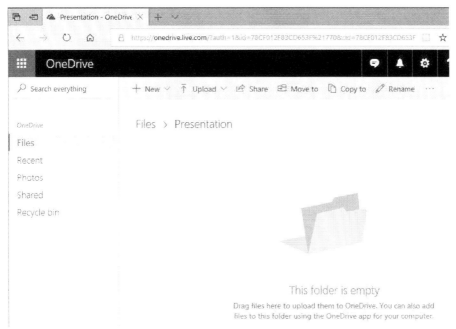

Figure 11.11

One important thing to note in figure 11.11 is the path to the folder indicated by *Files > Presentation*. This shows us that the Presentation folder is within the File section. If I create another folder within the Presentation folder called *Sales* then the path would read as *Files > Presentation > Sales*.

Now it's time to add a file to the new Presentation folder. To do so, click on *Upload* and choose *Files,* since we want to upload a file rather than a folder. Then browse to the location of the file and click on *Open* to have it uploaded to your OneDrive folder. You will see it appear when the upload is complete (figure 11.12).

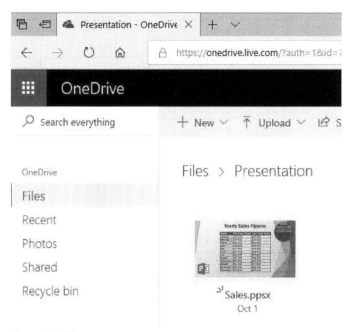

Figure 11.12

If you want to preview the file in your browser, all you need to do is click on it and it will open with the online version of the program the file is using (which is PowerPoint in this example because it's a PowerPoint presentation that was uploaded).

OneDrive will also let you drag files to folders if you don't want to go through the process of using the *Move to* option from the toolbar. It's the same process as dragging and dropping a file in Windows. However, if you want to move a file from a folder to another folder, then you will have to use the *Move to* option because you won't be able to see both folders at the same time to drag the file from one to the other.

To search for files and folders within OneDrive, all you need to do is type in your search term in the search box at the upper left hand side of the window and it will show you all the results that match your search criteria.

One thing to keep in mind when using OneDrive is how much space you are using and how much space you have left. Just like with your computer, it's always a good idea to do periodic cleanups to remove files that you don't need to keep things clean and organized. If you look at the bottom left corner of the OneDrive window, it will tell you how much space you have used and how much space you have left (figure 11.13), and, of course, give you a link to upgrade to a higher level plan at a higher cost!

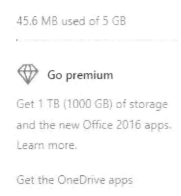

Figure 11.13

Installing the OneDrive App

If you decide to use OneDrive on a regular basis, it's a good idea to install the OneDrive application on your local computer so you don't have to do everything from your web browser. Starting with Windows 8, Microsoft introduced Windows Apps which work a little differently than Windows programs and are more like apps you would install on your smartphone.

To get the OneDrive app for Windows, you need to go to the Microsoft Store and search for it, or click on the link shown at the bottom of figure 11.13. To use the Microsoft Store method, open the Microsoft Store on your computer, do a search for OneDrive (as shown in figure 11.14), follow the prompts to install it on your computer, and then open it from your Apps.

Figure 11.14

If you are running Windows 8 or Windows 10, there's a very good chance that the OneDrive app is already installed on your computer, so if you go to the Microsoft Store and search for OneDrive and it says Launch rather than Install, that means you already have it on your computer.

As you can see from figure 11.15, it looks very similar to the web browser version that we were working with previously, and has similar categories on the left side of the window. There are a few differences between the app and the web version, and I will discuss those next.

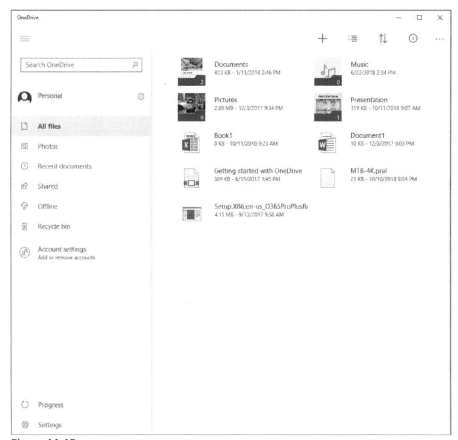

Figure 11.15

The *Offline* section is used to keep files on your computer so you can access them if you are somewhere that doesn't have an Internet connection. Then, when you reconnect to the Internet, your changes will sync up with the online version of your OneDrive folder.

When you create your OneDrive account, *you* are the only one that has access to your files unless you decide to add additional users to your account. Clicking on *Account settings* will bring up a listing showing everyone who has access to your OneDrive app, and will let you add or remove users as you see fit. To add an account, the user must have a Microsoft account or a work or school account that has been configured by your organization. You will use their email address to add them to your account.

The *Progress* area will show you the status of any files or folders that are currently downloading or uploading so you can see whether or not the transfer has been completed. This comes in handy for larger files that might take a long time to transfer.

One thing I want to point out when using the OneDrive app is that when you click on a file, it will automatically try to open it for you, which might not always be what you're looking to do. To select a file all you need to do is right click on it. Doing so will also bring up additional options, such as download, rename, delete, and so on. If you look at the choices in figure 11.16, you will notice there is one called *Copy link*. This can be used to send a link to that file to someone that you don't want to give access to your account, but only want them to have access to that file.

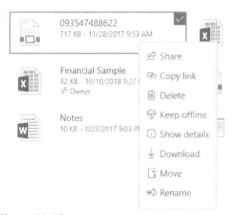

Figure 11.16

Sharing Files and Folders

One great things about OneDrive is the ability to share your files so you don't have to email files back and forth. Plus, a lot of the time the files you want to share will be too large to email.

When you choose the *Copy link* option I was just talking about, it will ask you if you want to allow *view only* or *view and edit* rights to whoever has this link. Then it will copy the link to your clipboard and all you need to do is paste it into an email and send it off to whoever you want to view the file. Then, when that person clicks on the link, they will be able to view or edit the file based on what permissions you gave them. An example of one of these links looks like this.

https://1drv.ms/b/s!Aj8lzYMvAc93d2jtUANxO3ZcJlg

Another choice from the right click menu is the *Share* option. When choosing *Share,* you will be asked how you want to share the file, and there are many options to choose from (as seen in figure 11.17).

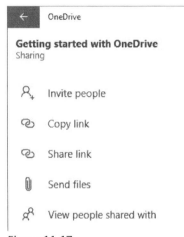

Figure 11.17

Here is a quick overview of what each choice does.

- **Invite people** – This will allow you to send out an email to one or more people, giving them access to that file. You can also check the box to allow editing if that's what you want them to be able to do.

- **Copy link** – I just went over this, so it's the same procedure as described above.

- **Share link** – This is similar to the *Copy link* option, but OneDrive will want to know how you will be sharing the link and ask you to make a choice from the list as shown in figure 11.18.

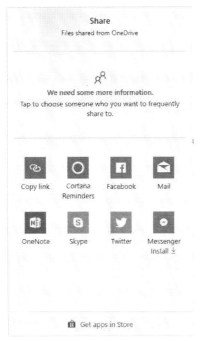

Figure 11.18

- **Send files** – This option is similar to the *Share link* option, but will give you different choices similar to figure 11.18.

- **View people shared with** – If you already have a file shared, then clicking on this option will show you who you have shared it with and what their permissions are.

Now that you know how to create various types of Office files, as well as being able to manipulate them to your liking and share them in the cloud, it's time to get busy being productive!

What's Next?

Now that you have read through this book and taken your Office skills to the next level, you might be wondering what you should do next. Well, that depends on where you want to go. Are you happy with what you have learned, or do you want to further your knowledge and learn about one or more specific Office programs in more detail?

If you do want to expand your knowledge on specific Office programs or the entire Office Suite itself the you can look into more advanced books on the subject. Just be sure to find out as much as you can before buying a book to make sure it covers what you need. Focus on one subject at a time, then apply what you have learned to the next subject.

There are many great video resources as well, such as Pluralsight or CBT Nuggets, which offer online subscriptions to training videos of every type imaginable. YouTube is also a great source for training videos if you know what to search for. Sometimes it helps to see the software in action, especially if you don't have a copy of your own yet.

Thanks for reading *Office Made Easy*. If you like this title, please leave a review. Reviews help authors build exposure. Plus, I love hearing from my readers! You can also check out the other books in the Made Easy series for additional computer related information and training.

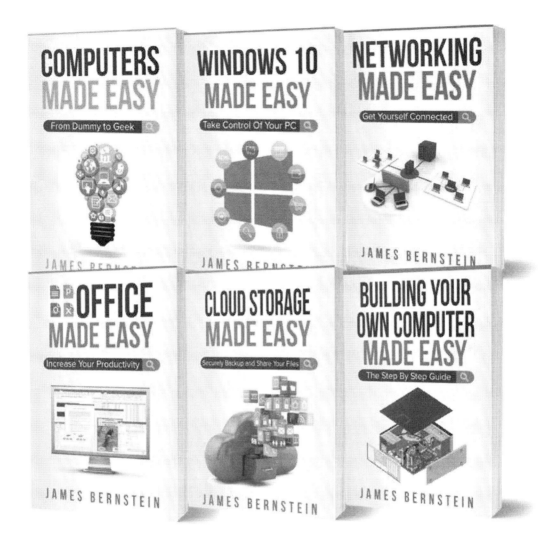

You should also check out my website at www.onlinecomputertips.com, as well as follow it on Facebook at https://www.facebook.com/OnlineComputerTips/ to find more information on all kinds of computer topics.

About the Author

James Bernstein has been working with various companies in the IT field since 2000, managing technologies such as SAN and NAS storage, VMware, backups, Windows Servers, Active Directory, DNS, DHCP, Networking, Microsoft Office, Exchange, and more.

He has obtained certifications from Microsoft, VMware, CompTIA, ShoreTel, and SNIA, and continues to strive to learn new technologies to further his knowledge on a variety of subjects.

He is also the founder of the website onlinecomputertips.com, which offers its readers valuable information on topics such as Windows, networking, hardware, software, and troubleshooting. James writes much of the content himself, and adds new content on a regular basis. The site was started in 2005 and is still going strong today.

34731808R00175

Made in the USA
San Bernardino, CA
04 May 2019